ONLY THE END OF THE WORLD AGAIN™

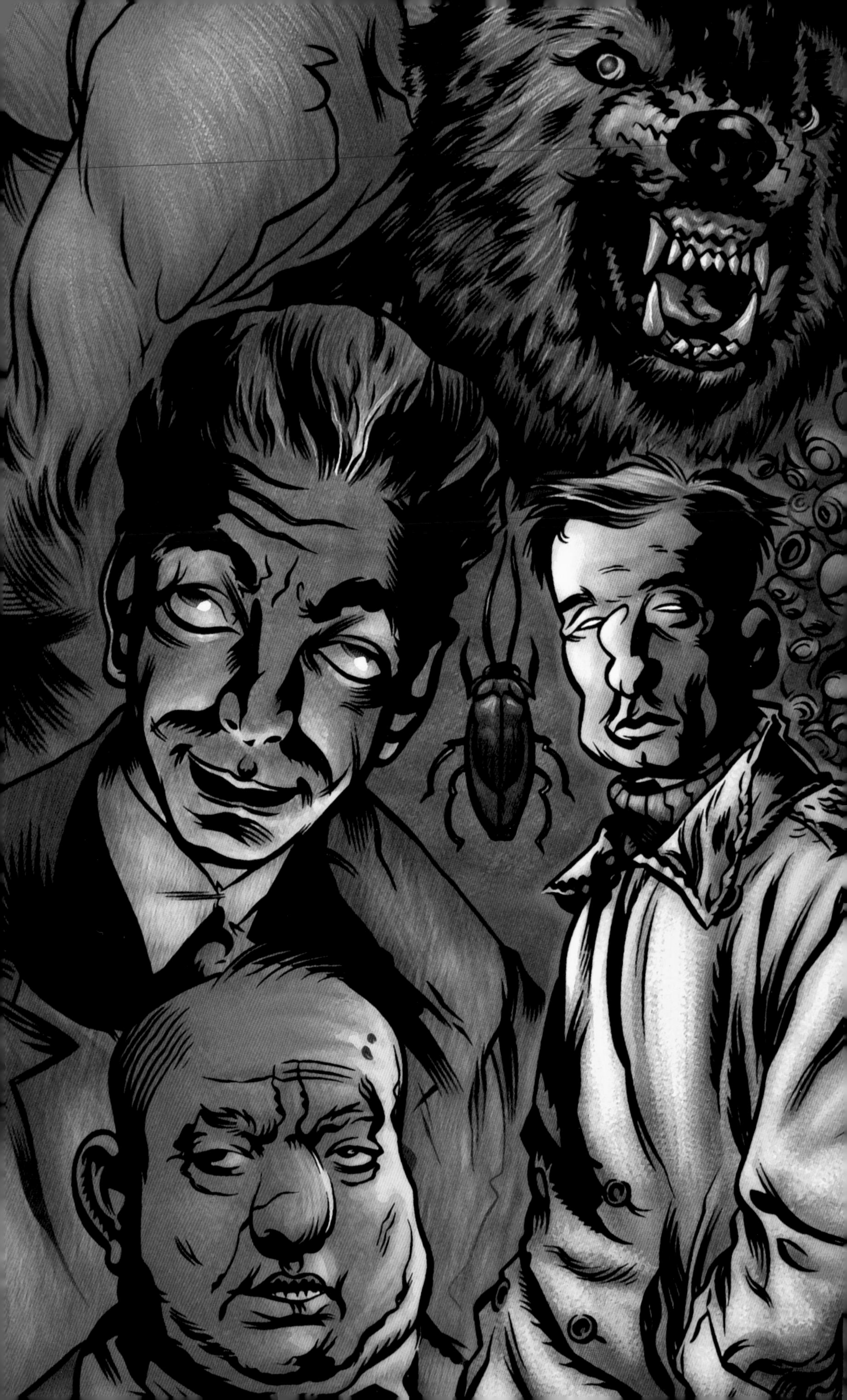

ONLY THE END OF THE WORLD AGAIN™

STORY AND WORDS
NEIL GAIMAN

ADAPTATION AND LAYOUTS
P. CRAIG RUSSELL

ART
TROY NIXEY

COLORS
MATTHEW HOLLINGSWORTH

LETTERING
SEAN KONOT

DARK HORSE BOOKS

PRESIDENT AND PUBLISHER **MIKE RICHARDSON**   EDITOR **DANIEL CHABON**   ORIGINAL SERIES EDITOR **BOB SCHRECK**

ASSISTANT EDITOR **RACHEL ROBERTS**   DESIGNER **ETHAN KIMBERLING**   DIGITAL ART TECHNICIAN **ADAM PRUETT**

SPECIAL THANKS TO **WALT PARRISH**

Published by Dark Horse Books
A division of Dark Horse Comics, Inc.
10956 SE Main Street
Milwaukie, OR 97222

DarkHorse.com

To find a comics shop in your area, visit comicshoplocator.com
International Licensing: (503) 905-2377

First Edition: January 2018
ISBN 978-1-50670-612-2

10 9 8 7 6 5 4 3 2 1
Printed in China

This volume collects *Only the End of the World Again*, originally
published by Oni Press, Inc.

Library of Congress Cataloging-in-Publication Data

Names: Gaiman, Neil, author. I Russell, P. Craig, illustrator. I Nixey, Troy,
   artist. I Hollingsworth, Matt, colourist. I Konot, Sean, letterer.
Title: Only the end of the world again / story and words, Neil Gaiman ;
   adaptation and layouts, P. Craig Russell ; art, Troy Nixey ; colors,
   Matthew Hollingsworth ; lettering, Sean Konot.
Description: First edition. I Milwaukie, OR : Dark Horse Books, 2018.
Identifiers: LCCN 2017037805 I ISBN 9781506706122 (hardback)
Subjects: LCSH: Graphic novels. I BISAC: COMICS & GRAPHIC NOVELS / Fantasy. I
   COMICS & GRAPHIC NOVELS / Horror.
Classification: LCC PN6737.G3 O55 2018 I DDC 741.5/942--dc23
LC record available at https://lccn.loc.gov/2017037805

It was a bad day.

I woke up naked in the bed,
with a cramp in my stomach,
feeling more or less like hell.
Something about the quality
of the light, stretched and
metallic, like the color of
a migraine, told me it was
afternoon.

The room was freezing...
literally: there was a thin
crust of ice on the inside of
the windows. The sheets on the
bed around me were ripped
and clawed, and there was
animal hair in the bed.

It itched.

ONLY THE END of the WORLD AGAIN™

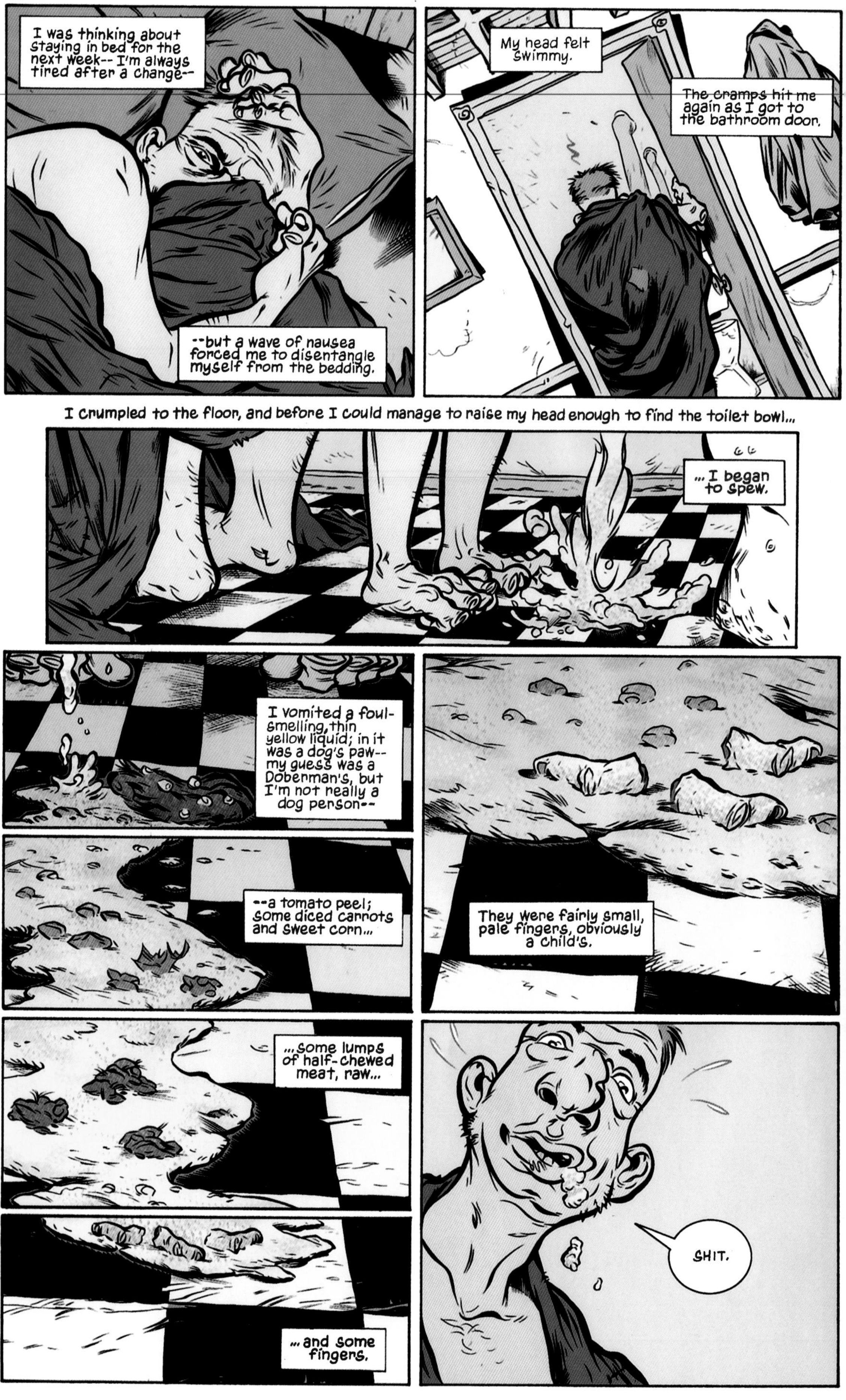
I was thinking about staying in bed for the next week-- I'm always tired after a change--
--but a wave of nausea forced me to disentangle myself from the bedding.
My head felt swimmy.
The cramps hit me again as I got to the bathroom door.
I crumpled to the floor, and before I could manage to raise my head enough to find the toilet bowl...
...I began to spew.
I vomited a foul-smelling, thin yellow liquid; in it was a dog's paw-- my guess was a Doberman's, but I'm not really a dog person--
--a tomato peel; some diced carrots and sweet corn...
...some lumps of half-chewed meat, raw...
...and some fingers.
They were fairly small, pale fingers, obviously a child's.
SHIT.

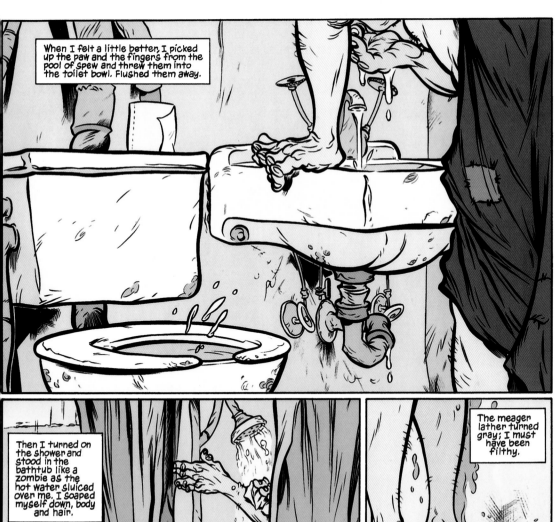

When I felt a little better, I picked up the paw and the fingers from the pool of spew and threw them into the toilet bowl. Flushed them away.

Then I turned on the shower and stood in the bathtub like a zombie as the hot water sluiced over me. I soaped myself down, body and hair.

The meager lather turned gray; I must have been filthy.

My hair was matted with something that felt like dried blood, and I worked at it with the bar of soap until it was gone.

Then I stood under the shower until the water turned icy.

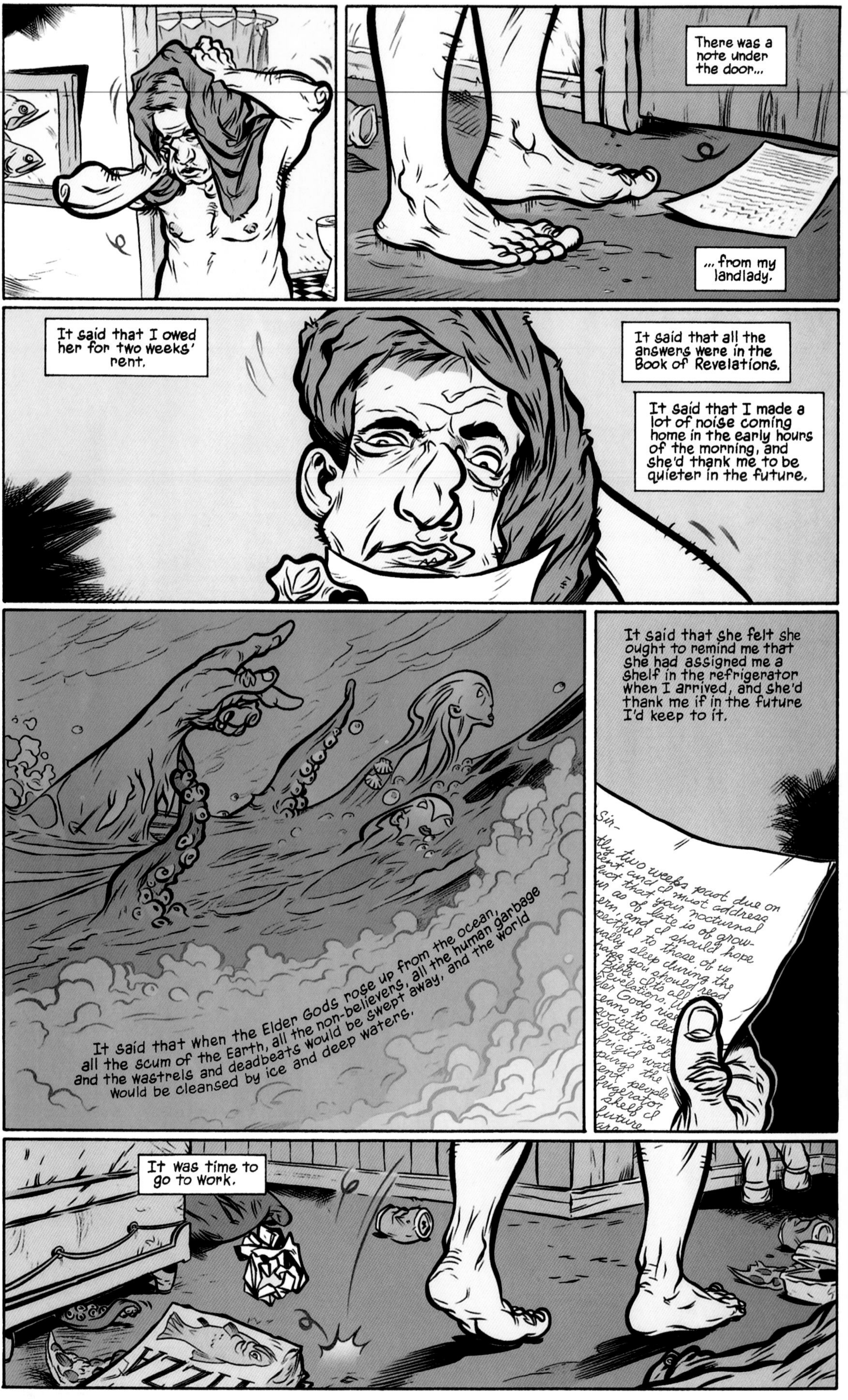

There was a note under the door...
...from my landlady.
It said that I owed her for two weeks' rent.
It said that all the answers were in the Book of Revelations.
It said that I made a lot of noise coming home in the early hours of the morning, and she'd thank me to be quieter in the future.
It said that when the Elder Gods rose up from the ocean, all the scum of the Earth, all the non-believers, all the human garbage and the wastrels and deadbeats would be swept away, and the world would be cleansed by ice and deep waters.
It said that she felt she ought to remind me that she had assigned me a shelf in the refrigerator when I arrived, and she'd thank me if in the future I'd keep to it.
It was time to go to work.

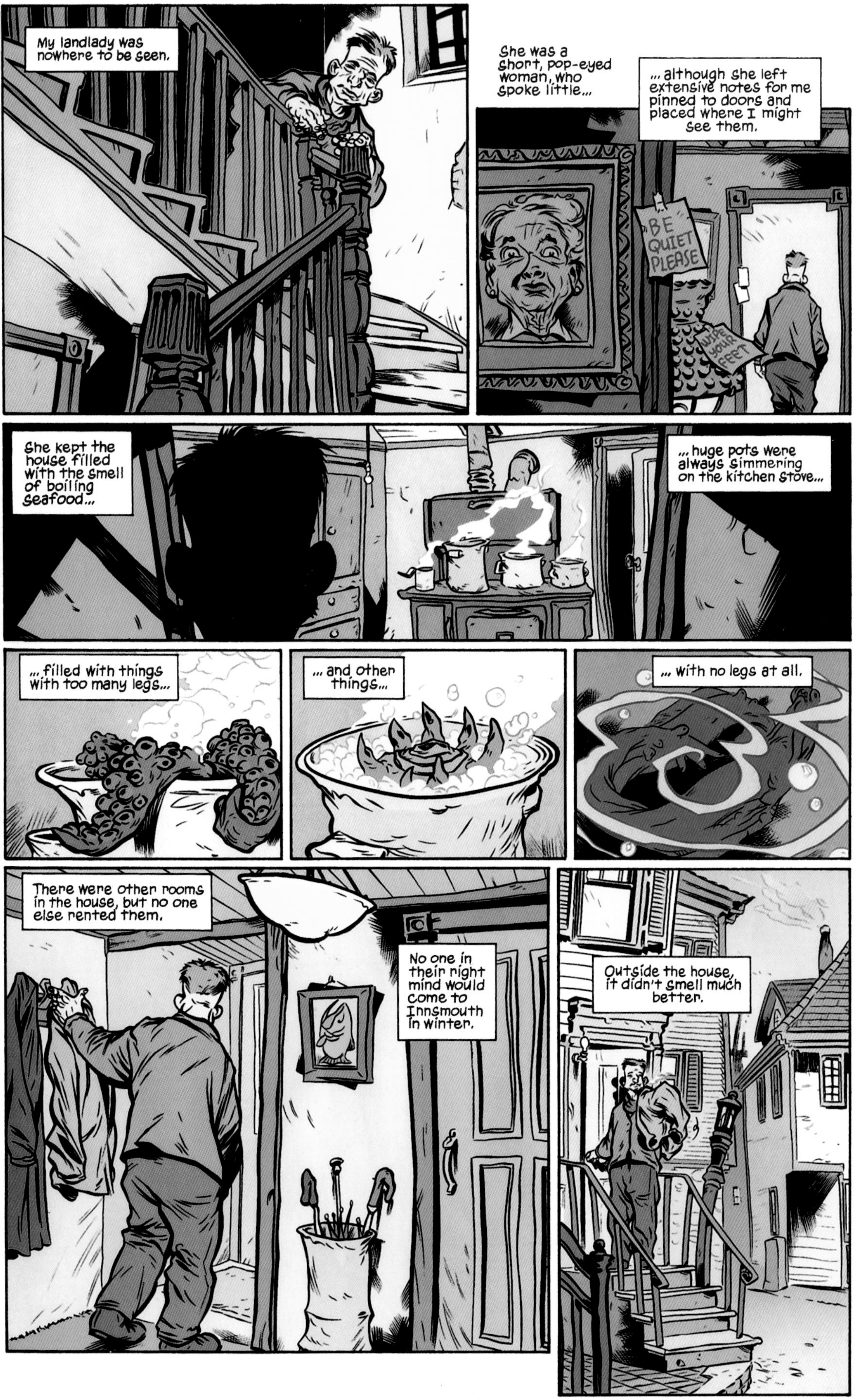
My landlady was nowhere to be seen.
She was a short, pop-eyed woman, who spoke little...
...although she left extensive notes for me pinned to doors and placed where I might see them.
BE QUIET PLEASE
WIPE YOUR FEET
She kept the house filled with the smell of boiling seafood...
...huge pots were always simmering on the kitchen stove...
...filled with things with too many legs...
...and other things...
...with no legs at all.
There were other rooms in the house, but no one else rented them.
No one in their right mind would come to Innsmouth in winter.
Outside the house, it didn't smell much better.

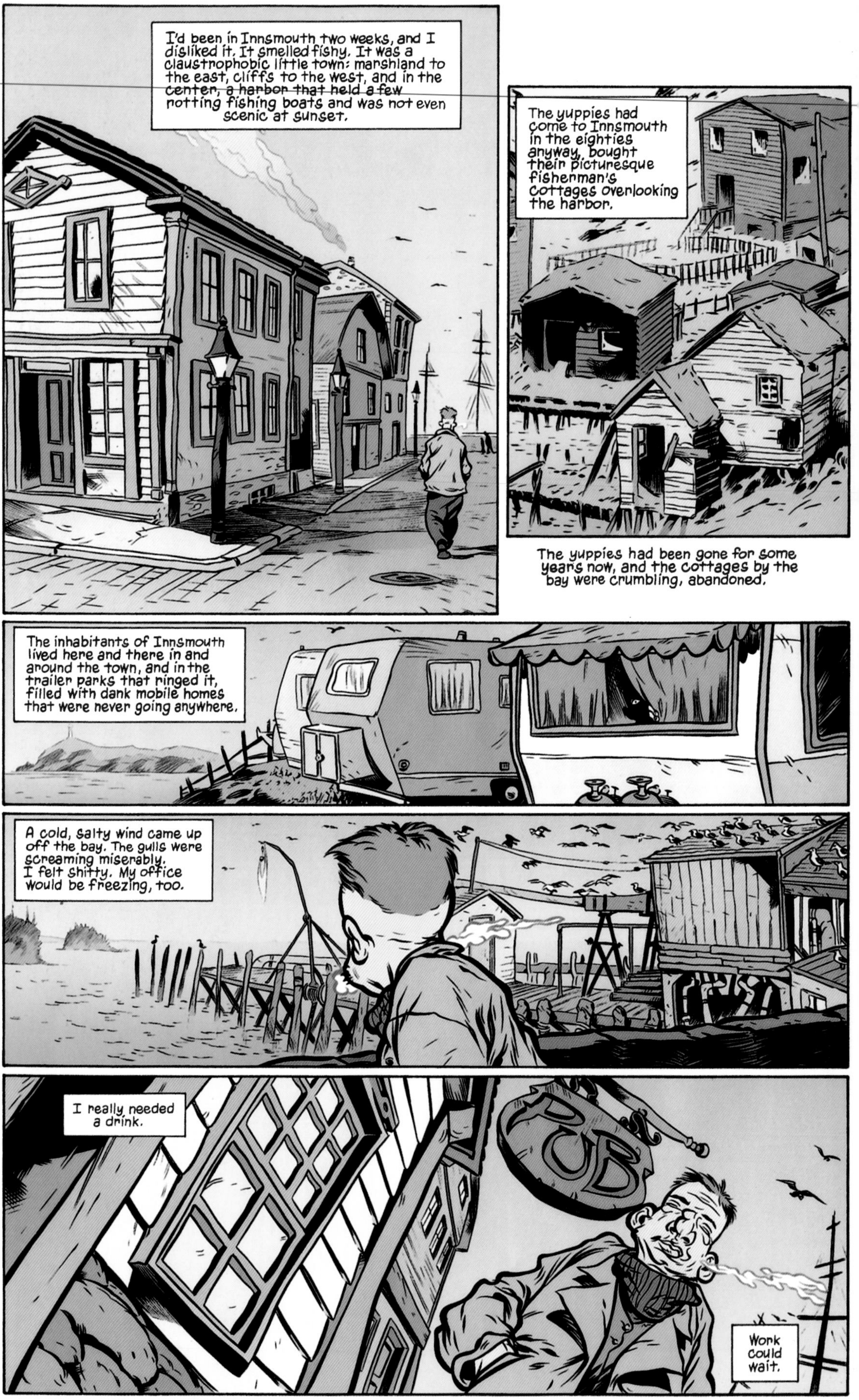
I'd been in Innsmouth two weeks, and I disliked it. It smelled fishy. It was a claustrophobic little town: marshland to the east, cliffs to the west, and in the center, a harbor that held a few rotting fishing boats and was not even scenic at sunset.
The yuppies had come to Innsmouth in the eighties anyway, bought their picturesque fisherman's cottages overlooking the harbor.
The yuppies had been gone for some years now, and the cottages by the bay were crumbling, abandoned.
The inhabitants of Innsmouth lived here and there in and around the town, and in the trailer parks that ringed it, filled with dank mobile homes that were never going anywhere.
A cold, salty wind came up off the bay. The gulls were screaming miserably. I felt shitty. My office would be freezing, too.
I really needed a drink.
PUB
Work could wait.

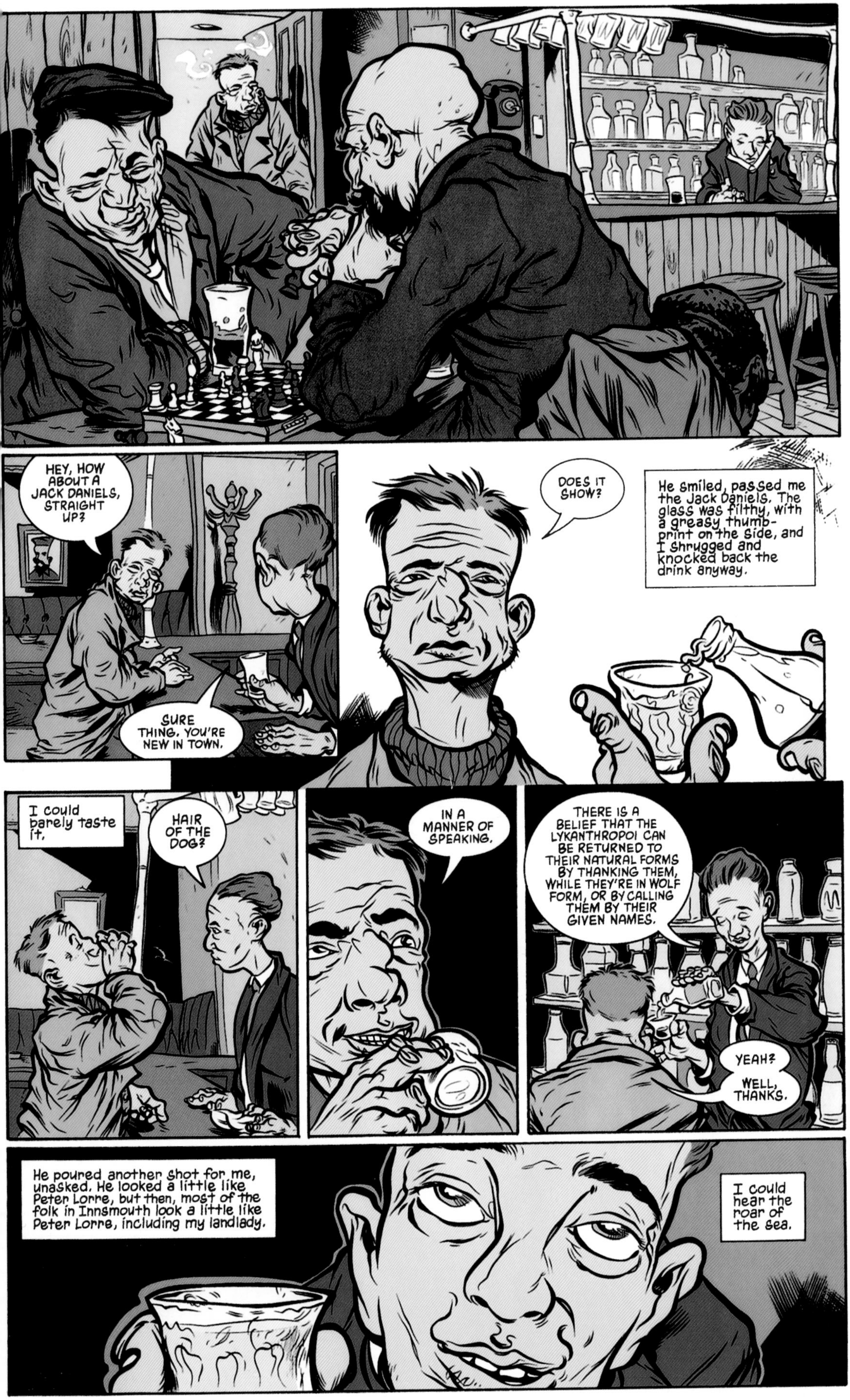
HEY, HOW ABOUT A JACK DANIELS, STRAIGHT UP?
SURE THING. YOU'RE NEW IN TOWN.
DOES IT SHOW?
He smiled, passed me the Jack Daniels. The glass was filthy, with a greasy thumb-print on the side, and I shrugged and knocked back the drink anyway.
I could barely taste it.
HAIR OF THE DOG?
IN A MANNER OF SPEAKING.
THERE IS A BELIEF THAT THE LYKANTHROPOI CAN BE RETURNED TO THEIR NATURAL FORMS BY THANKING THEM, WHILE THEY'RE IN WOLF FORM, OR BY CALLING THEM BY THEIR GIVEN NAMES.
YEAH?
WELL, THANKS.
He poured another shot for me, unasked. He looked a little like Peter Lorre, but then, most of the folk in Innsmouth look a little like Peter Lorre, including my landlady.
I could hear the roar of the sea.

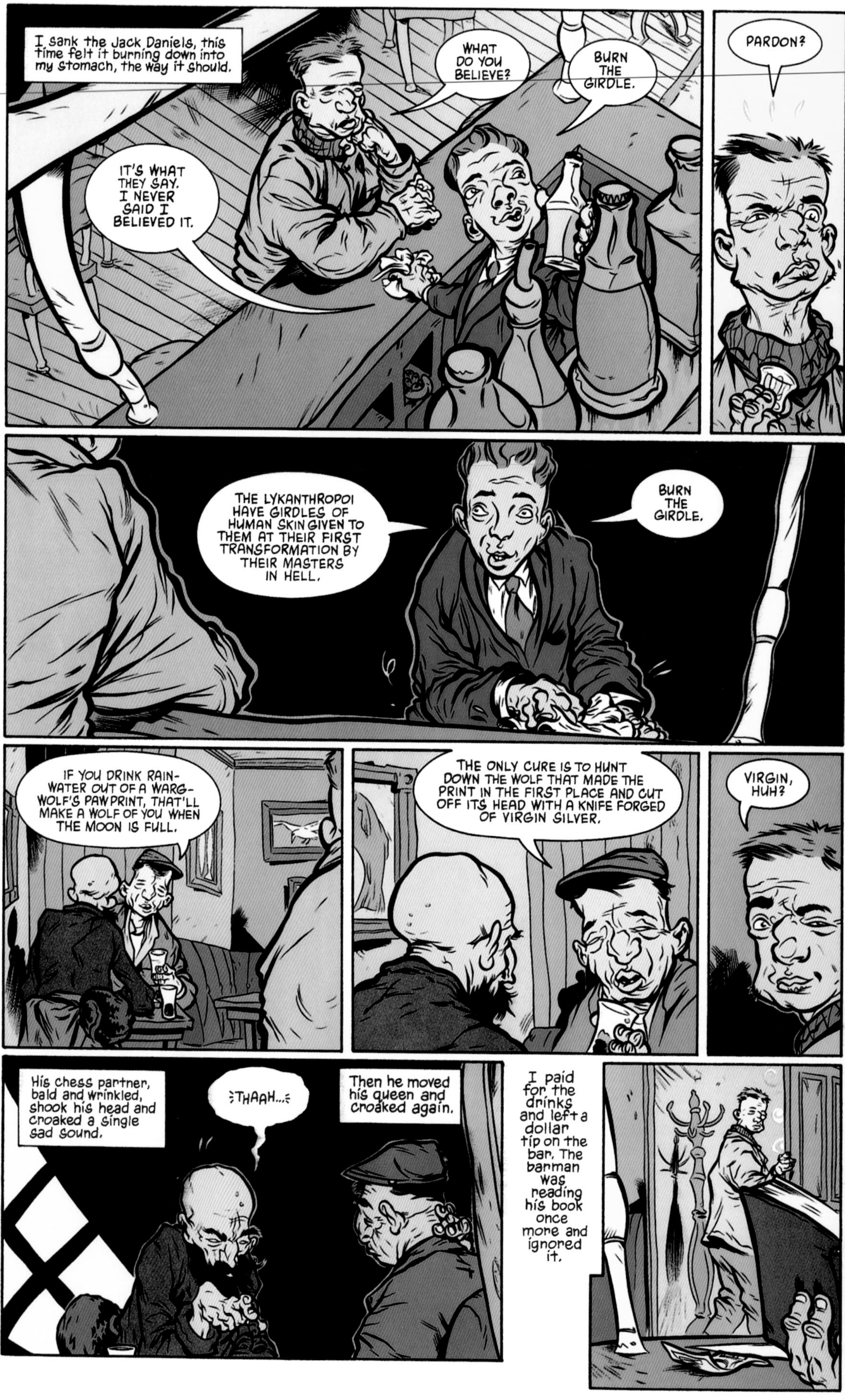
I sank the Jack Daniels, this time felt it burning down into my stomach, the way it should.
WHAT DO YOU BELIEVE?
BURN THE GIRDLE.
IT'S WHAT THEY SAY. I NEVER SAID I BELIEVED IT.
PARDON?
THE LYKANTHROPOI HAVE GIRDLES OF HUMAN SKIN GIVEN TO THEM AT THEIR FIRST TRANSFORMATION BY THEIR MASTERS IN HELL.
BURN THE GIRDLE.
IF YOU DRINK RAIN-WATER OUT OF A WARG-WOLF'S PAWPRINT, THAT'LL MAKE A WOLF OF YOU WHEN THE MOON IS FULL.
THE ONLY CURE IS TO HUNT DOWN THE WOLF THAT MADE THE PRINT IN THE FIRST PLACE AND CUT OFF ITS HEAD WITH A KNIFE FORGED OF VIRGIN SILVER.
VIRGIN, HUH?
His chess partner, bald and wrinkled, shook his head and croaked a single sad sound.
THAAH...
Then he moved his queen and croaked again.
I paid for the drinks and left a dollar tip on the bar. The barman was reading his book once more and ignored it.

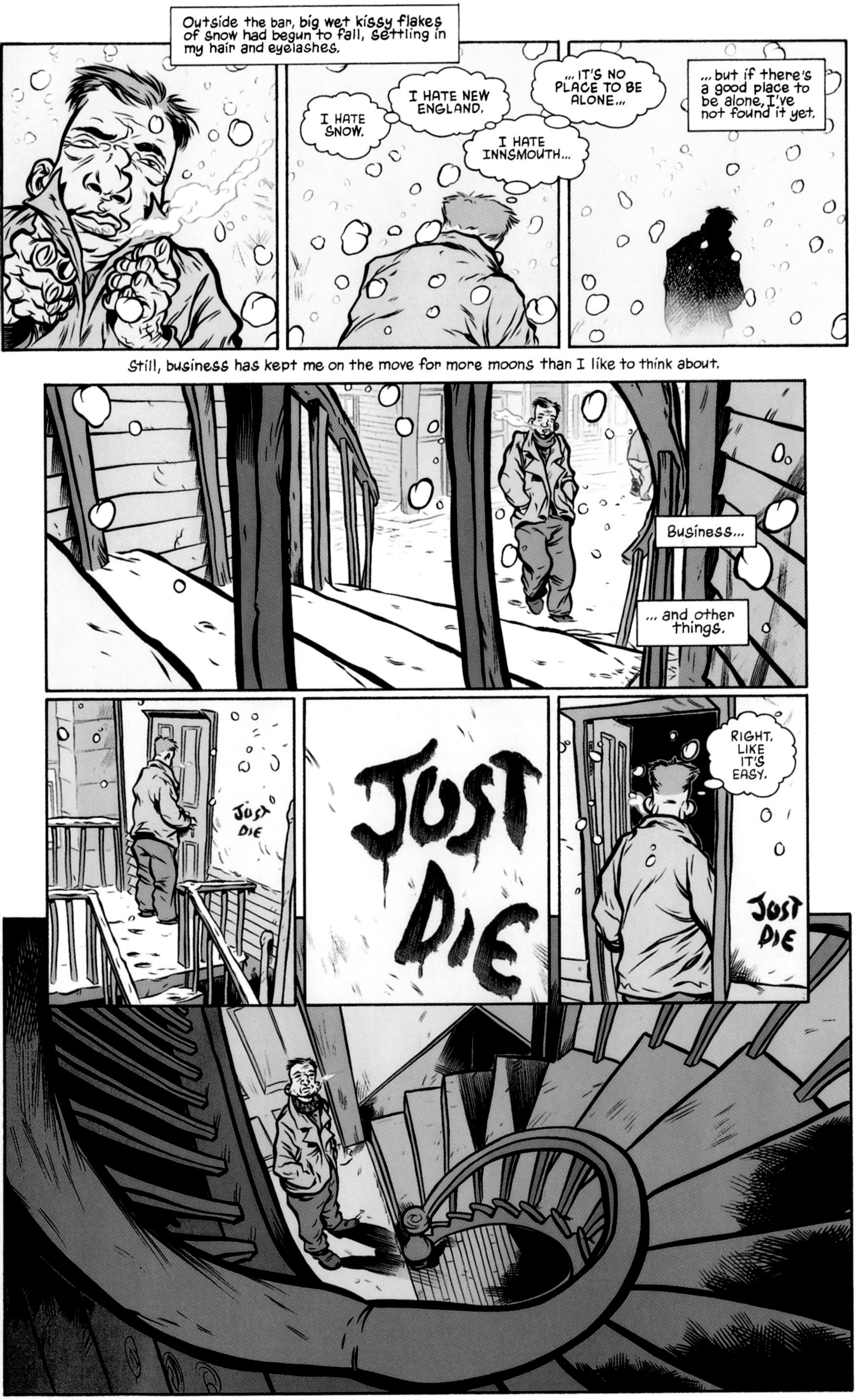
Outside the bar, big wet kissy flakes of snow had begun to fall, settling in my hair and eyelashes.
I HATE SNOW.
I HATE NEW ENGLAND.
I HATE INNSMOUTH...
...IT'S NO PLACE TO BE ALONE...
...but if there's a good place to be alone, I've not found it yet.
Still, business has kept me on the move for more moons than I like to think about.
Business...
...and other things.
JUST DIE
JUST DIE
RIGHT. LIKE IT'S EASY.
JUST DIE

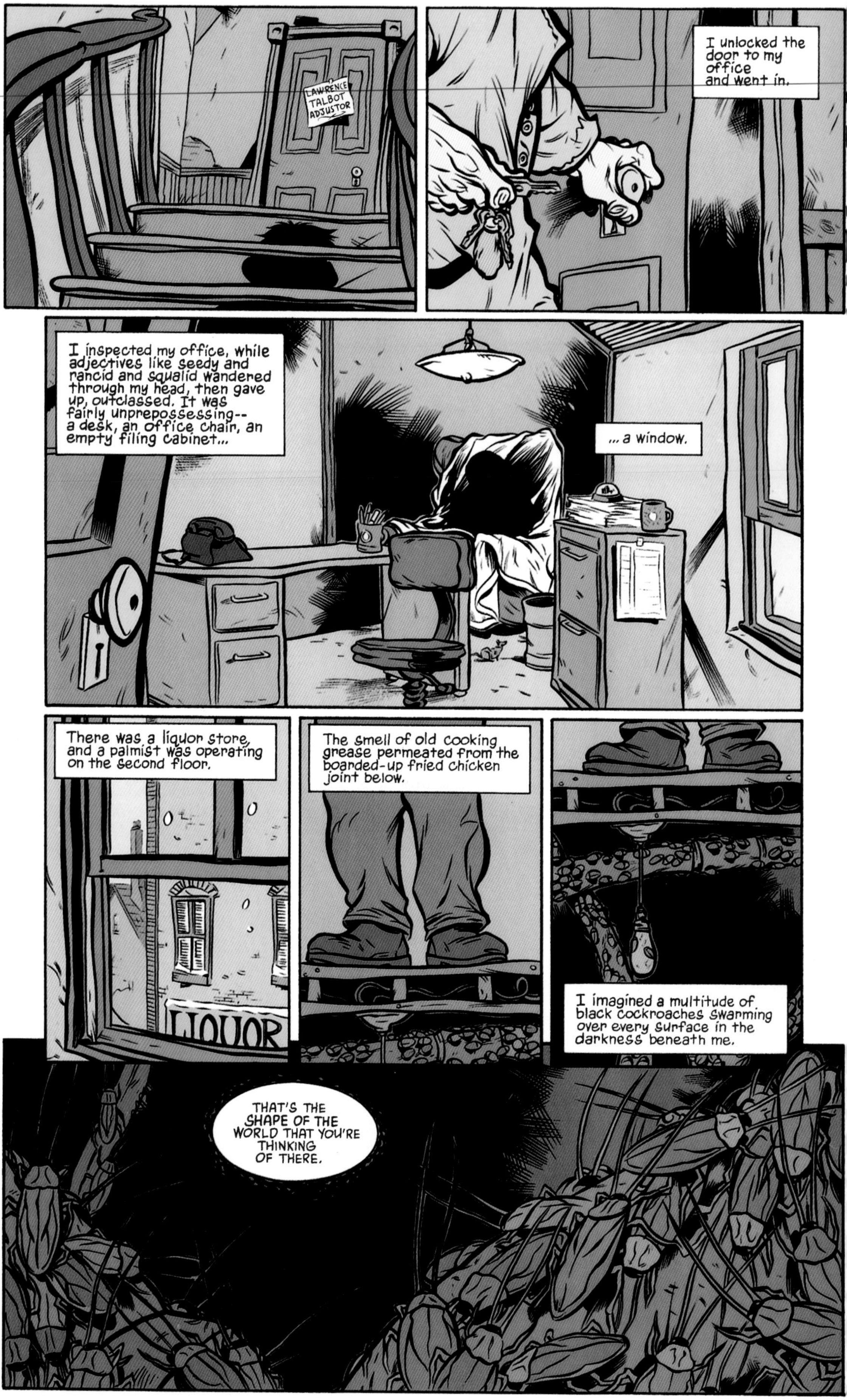
LAWRENCE TALBOT ADJUSTOR
I unlocked the door to my office and went in.
I inspected my office, while adjectives like seedy and rancid and squalid wandered through my head, then gave up, outclassed. It was fairly unprepossessing-- a desk, an office chair, an empty filing cabinet...
... a window.
There was a liquor store, and a palmist was operating on the second floor.
LIQUOR
The smell of old cooking grease permeated from the boarded-up fried chicken joint below.
I imagined a multitude of black cockroaches swarming over every surface in the darkness beneath me.
THAT'S THE SHAPE OF THE WORLD THAT YOU'RE THINKING OF THERE.

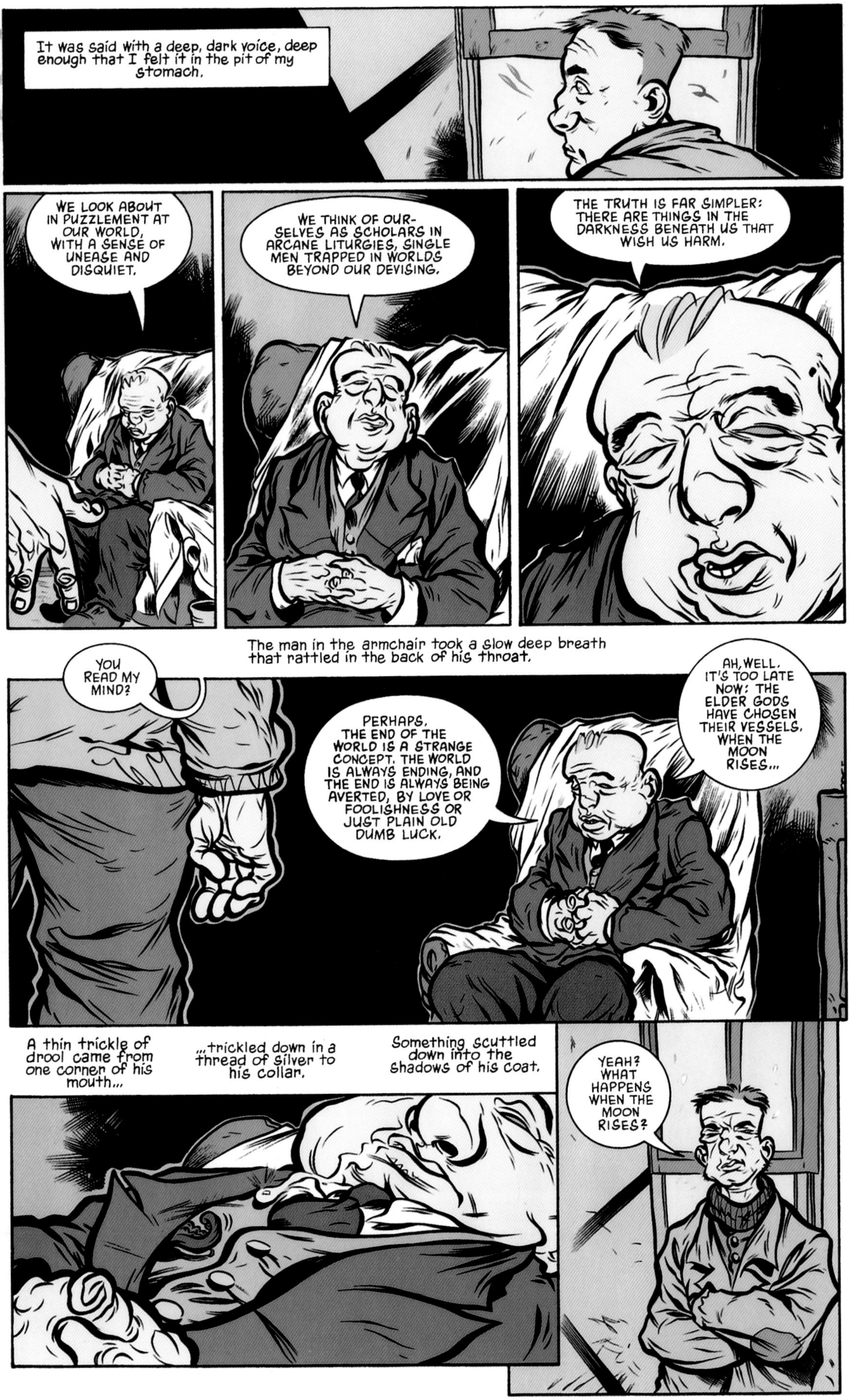

It was said with a deep, dark voice, deep enough that I felt it in the pit of my stomach.
WE LOOK ABOUT IN PUZZLEMENT AT OUR WORLD, WITH A SENSE OF UNEASE AND DISQUIET.
WE THINK OF OURSELVES AS SCHOLARS IN ARCANE LITURGIES, SINGLE MEN TRAPPED IN WORLDS BEYOND OUR DEVISING.
THE TRUTH IS FAR SIMPLER: THERE ARE THINGS IN THE DARKNESS BENEATH US THAT WISH US HARM.
The man in the armchair took a slow deep breath that rattled in the back of his throat.
YOU READ MY MIND?
PERHAPS. THE END OF THE WORLD IS A STRANGE CONCEPT. THE WORLD IS ALWAYS ENDING, AND THE END IS ALWAYS BEING AVERTED, BY LOVE OR FOOLISHNESS OR JUST PLAIN OLD DUMB LUCK.
AH, WELL. IT'S TOO LATE NOW: THE ELDER GODS HAVE CHOSEN THEIR VESSELS. WHEN THE MOON RISES...
A thin trickle of drool came from one corner of his mouth...
...trickled down in a thread of silver to his collar.
Something scuttled down into the shadows of his coat.
YEAH? WHAT HAPPENS WHEN THE MOON RISES?

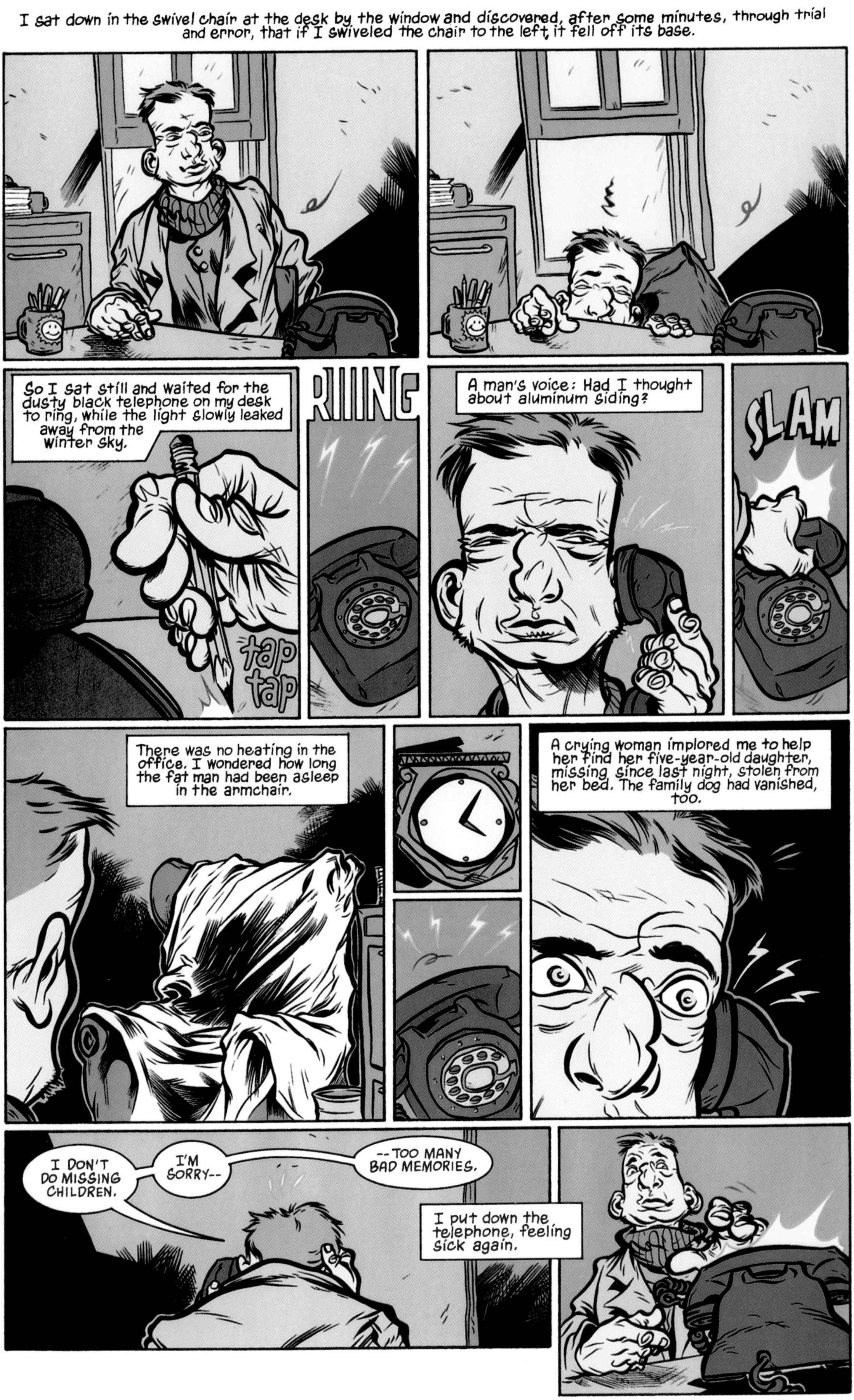
I sat down in the swivel chair at the desk by the window and discovered, after some minutes, through trial and error, that if I swiveled the chair to the left, it fell off its base.
So I sat still and waited for the dusty black telephone on my desk to ring, while the light slowly leaked away from the winter sky.
tap tap
RIIING
A man's voice: Had I thought about aluminum siding?
SLAM
There was no heating in the office. I wondered how long the fat man had been asleep in the armchair.
A crying woman implored me to help her find her five-year-old daughter, missing since last night, stolen from her bed. The family dog had vanished, too.
I DON'T DO MISSING CHILDREN.
I'M SORRY--
--TOO MANY BAD MEMORIES.
I put down the telephone, feeling sick again.

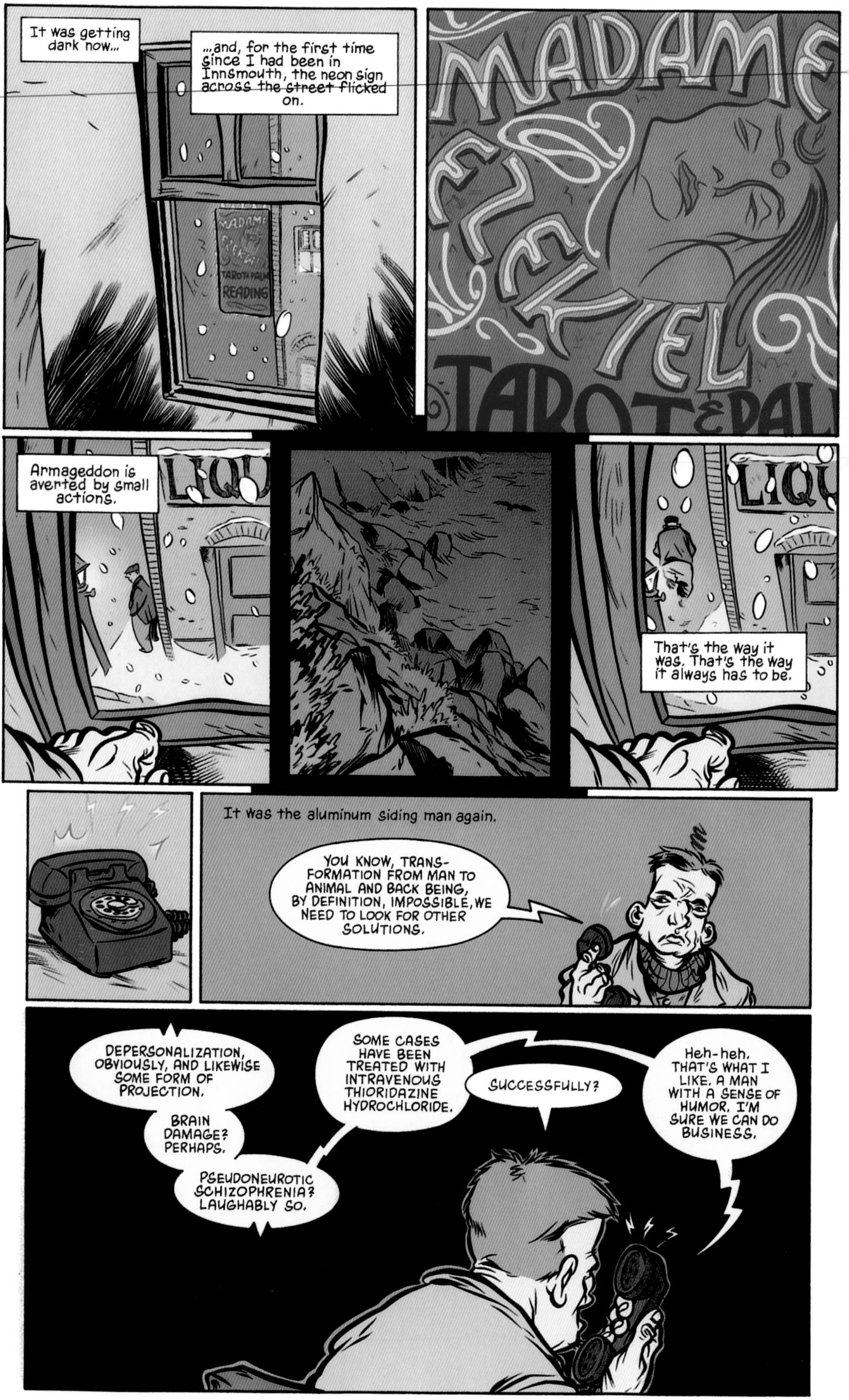
It was getting dark now...
...and, for the first time since I had been in Innsmouth, the neon sign across the street flicked on.
MADAME
READING
MADAME
TAROT & PAL
Armageddon is averted by small actions.
LIQU
LIQU
That's the way it was. That's the way it always has to be.
It was the aluminum siding man again.
YOU KNOW, TRANS-FORMATION FROM MAN TO ANIMAL AND BACK BEING, BY DEFINITION, IMPOSSIBLE, WE NEED TO LOOK FOR OTHER SOLUTIONS.
DEPERSONALIZATION, OBVIOUSLY, AND LIKEWISE SOME FORM OF PROJECTION.
BRAIN DAMAGE? PERHAPS.
PSEUDONEUROTIC SCHIZOPHRENIA? LAUGHABLY SO.
SOME CASES HAVE BEEN TREATED WITH INTRAVENOUS THIORIDAZINE HYDROCHLORIDE.
SUCCESSFULLY?
Heh-heh. THAT'S WHAT I LIKE. A MAN WITH A SENSE OF HUMOR. I'M SURE WE CAN DO BUSINESS.

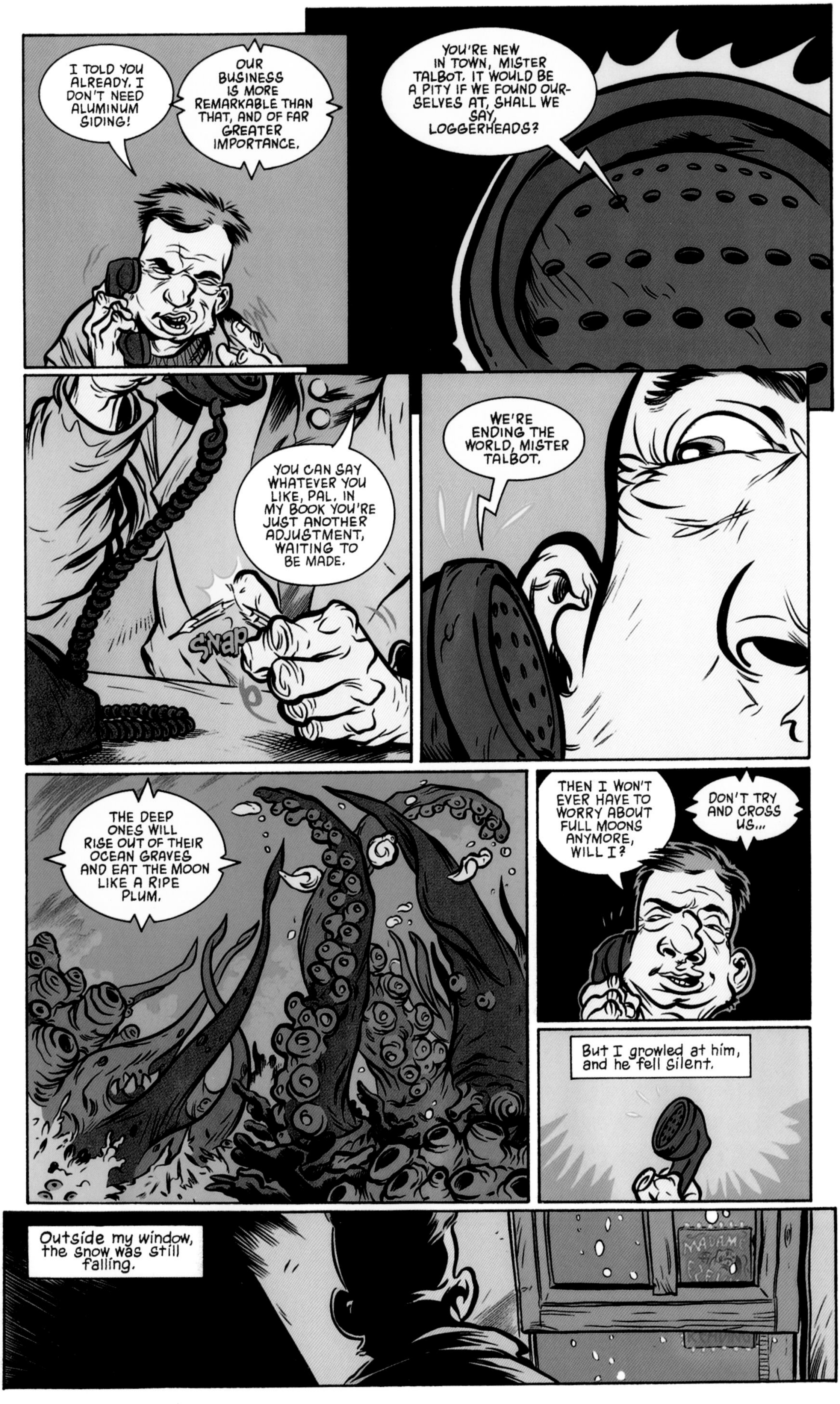
I TOLD YOU ALREADY. I DON'T NEED ALUMINUM SIDING!
OUR BUSINESS IS MORE REMARKABLE THAN THAT, AND OF FAR GREATER IMPORTANCE.
YOU'RE NEW IN TOWN, MISTER TALBOT. IT WOULD BE A PITY IF WE FOUND OURSELVES AT, SHALL WE SAY, LOGGERHEADS?
YOU CAN SAY WHATEVER YOU LIKE, PAL. IN MY BOOK YOU'RE JUST ANOTHER ADJUSTMENT, WAITING TO BE MADE.
SNAP
WE'RE ENDING THE WORLD, MISTER TALBOT.
THE DEEP ONES WILL RISE OUT OF THEIR OCEAN GRAVES AND EAT THE MOON LIKE A RIPE PLUM.
THEN I WON'T EVER HAVE TO WORRY ABOUT FULL MOONS ANYMORE, WILL I?
DON'T TRY AND CROSS US...
But I growled at him, and he fell silent.
Outside my window, the snow was still falling.

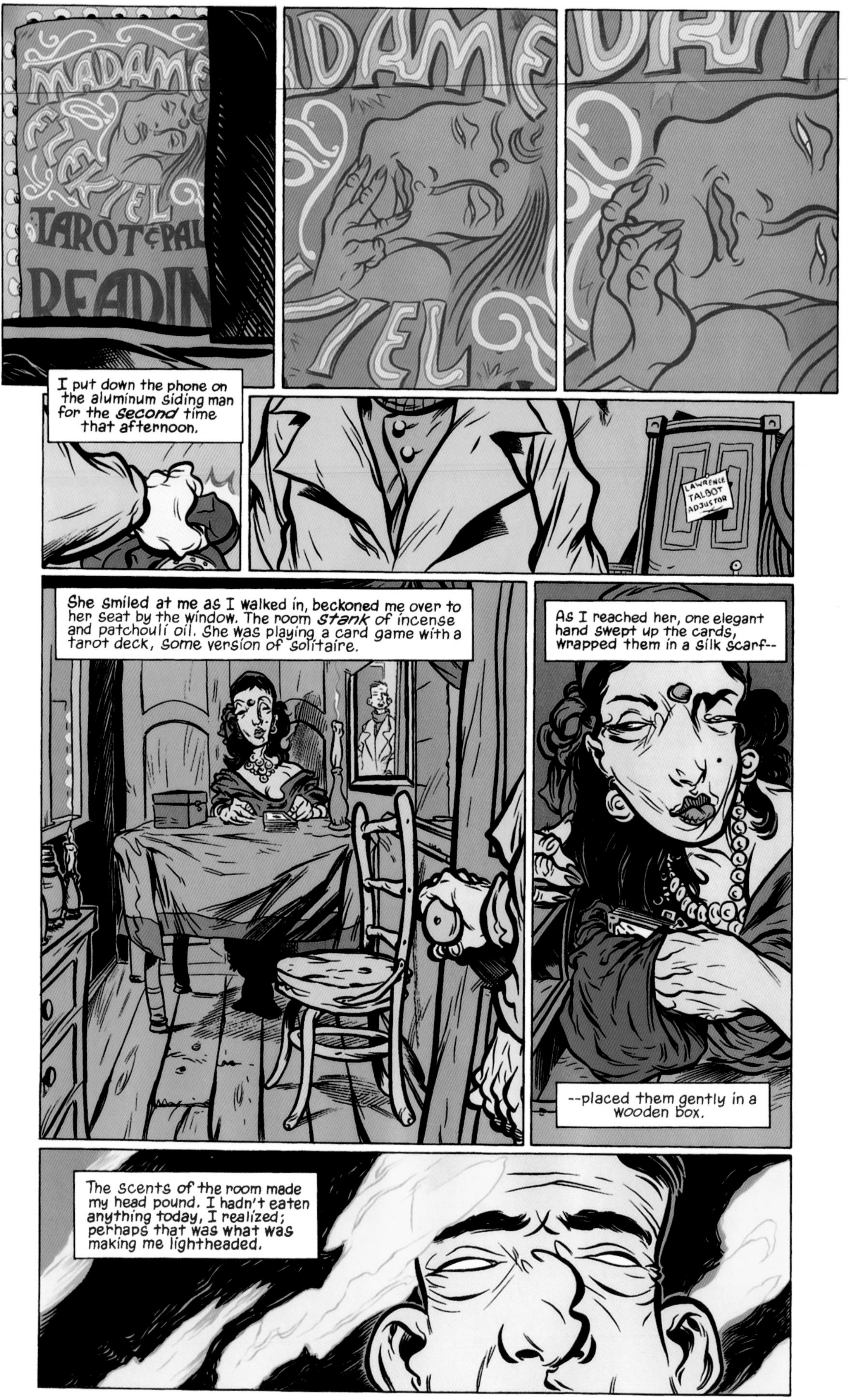
MADAME
TAROT & PAL
READIN
I put down the phone on the aluminum siding man for the *second* time that afternoon.
LAWRENCE TALBOT ADJUSTOR
She smiled at me as I walked in, beckoned me over to her seat by the window. The room *stank* of incense and patchouli oil. She was playing a card game with a tarot deck, some version of solitaire.
As I reached her, one elegant hand swept up the cards, wrapped them in a silk scarf--
--placed them gently in a wooden box.
The scents of the room made my head pound. I hadn't eaten anything today, I realized; perhaps that was what was making me lightheaded.

I sat down, across the table from her, in the candlelight. She extended her hand, and took my hand in hers.

HAIR?

YEAH, WELL, I'M ON MY OWN A LOT.

I grinned.

I hoped it was a friendly grin.

WHEN I LOOK AT YOU, THIS IS WHAT I SEE.

I SEE THE EYE OF A MAN.

ALSO, I SEE THE EYE OF A WOLF.

IN THE EYE OF A MAN, I SEE HONESTY, DECENCY, INNOCENCE.

I SEE AN UPRIGHT MAN WHO WALKS ON A SQUARE.

"AND IN THE EYE OF A WOLF, I SEE A GROANING AND A GROWLING, NIGHT HOWLS AND CRIES, I SEE A MONSTER RUNNING WITH BLOOD-FLECKED SPITTLE IN THE DARKNESS OF THE BORDERS OF THE TOWN."

HOW CAN YOU SEE A GROWL OR A CRY?

Her accent was not American. It was Russian, or Maltese, or Egyptian, perhaps.

IT IS NOT HARD. IN THE EYE OF THE MIND, WE SEE MANY THINGS.

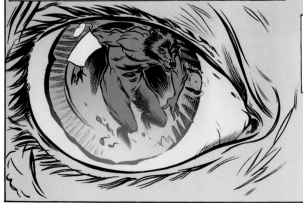

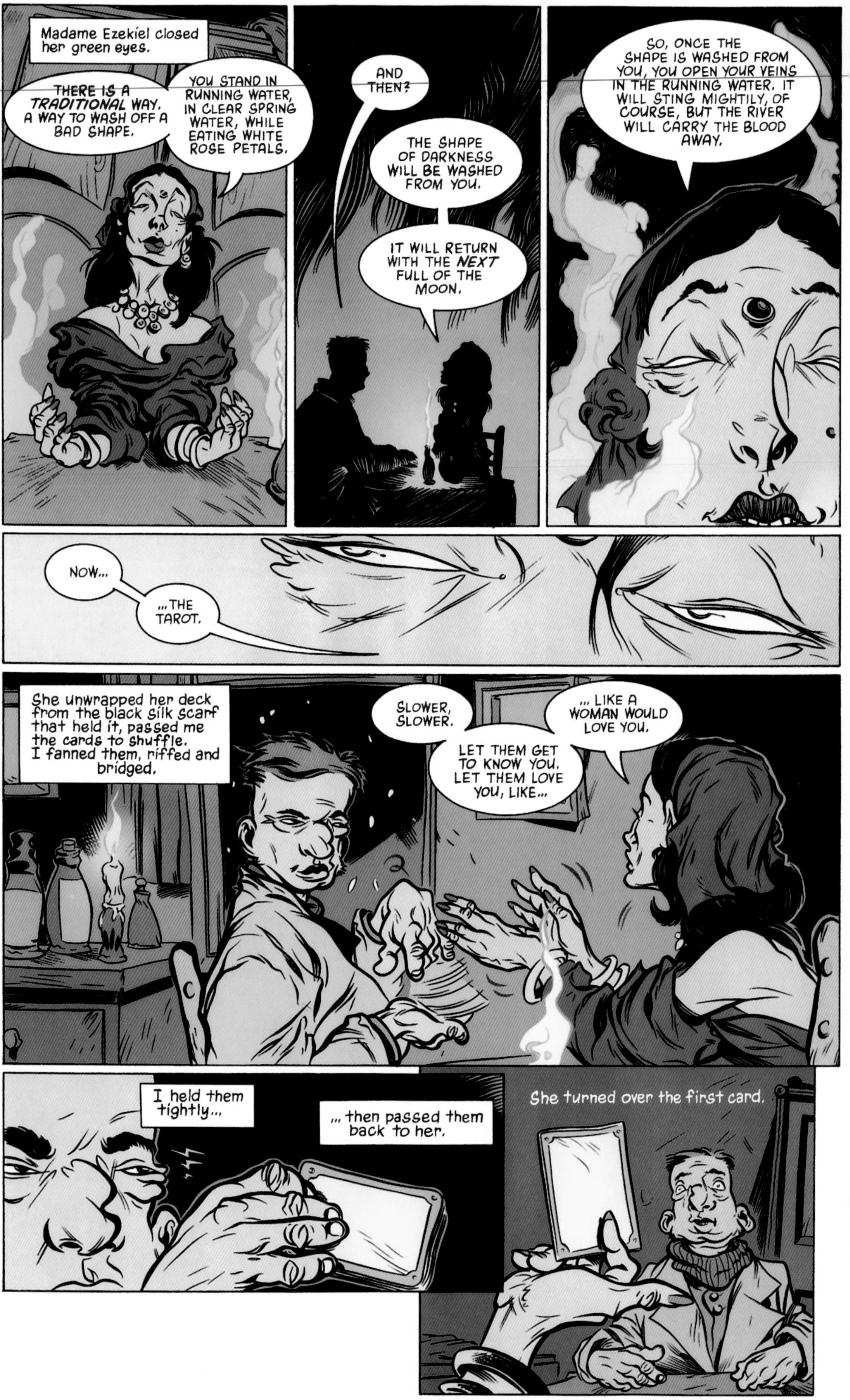

Madame Ezekiel closed her green eyes.
THERE IS A *TRADITIONAL* WAY. A WAY TO WASH OFF A BAD SHAPE.
YOU STAND IN RUNNING WATER, IN CLEAR SPRING WATER, WHILE EATING WHITE ROSE PETALS.
AND THEN?
THE SHAPE OF DARKNESS WILL BE WASHED FROM YOU.
IT WILL RETURN WITH THE *NEXT* FULL OF THE MOON.
SO, ONCE THE SHAPE IS WASHED FROM YOU, YOU OPEN YOUR VEINS IN THE RUNNING WATER. IT WILL STING MIGHTILY, OF COURSE, BUT THE RIVER WILL CARRY THE BLOOD AWAY.
NOW...
...THE TAROT.
She unwrapped her deck from the black silk scarf that held it, passed me the cards to shuffle. I fanned them, riffed and bridged.
SLOWER, SLOWER.
LET THEM GET TO KNOW YOU. LET THEM LOVE YOU, LIKE...
... LIKE A WOMAN WOULD LOVE YOU.
I held them tightly...
... then passed them back to her.
She turned over the first card.

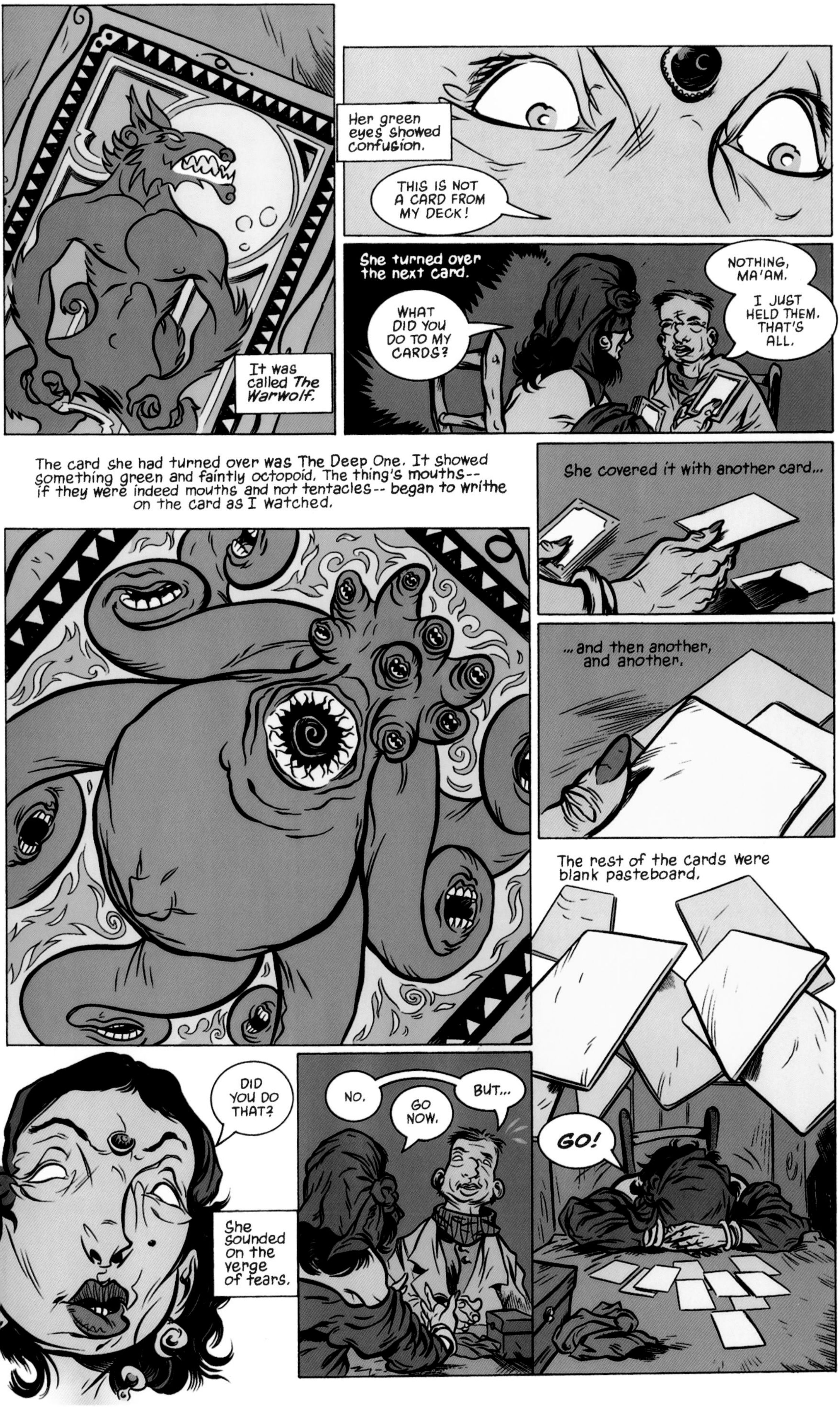
It was called *The Warwolf.*
Her green eyes showed confusion.
THIS IS NOT A CARD FROM MY DECK!
She turned over the next card.
WHAT DID YOU DO TO MY CARDS?
NOTHING, MA'AM.
I JUST HELD THEM. THAT'S ALL.
The card she had turned over was The Deep One. It showed something green and faintly octopoid. The thing's mouths-- if they were indeed mouths and not tentacles-- began to writhe on the card as I watched.
She covered it with another card...
...and then another, and another.
The rest of the cards were blank pasteboard.
DID YOU DO THAT?
She sounded on the verge of tears.
NO.
BUT...
GO NOW.
GO!

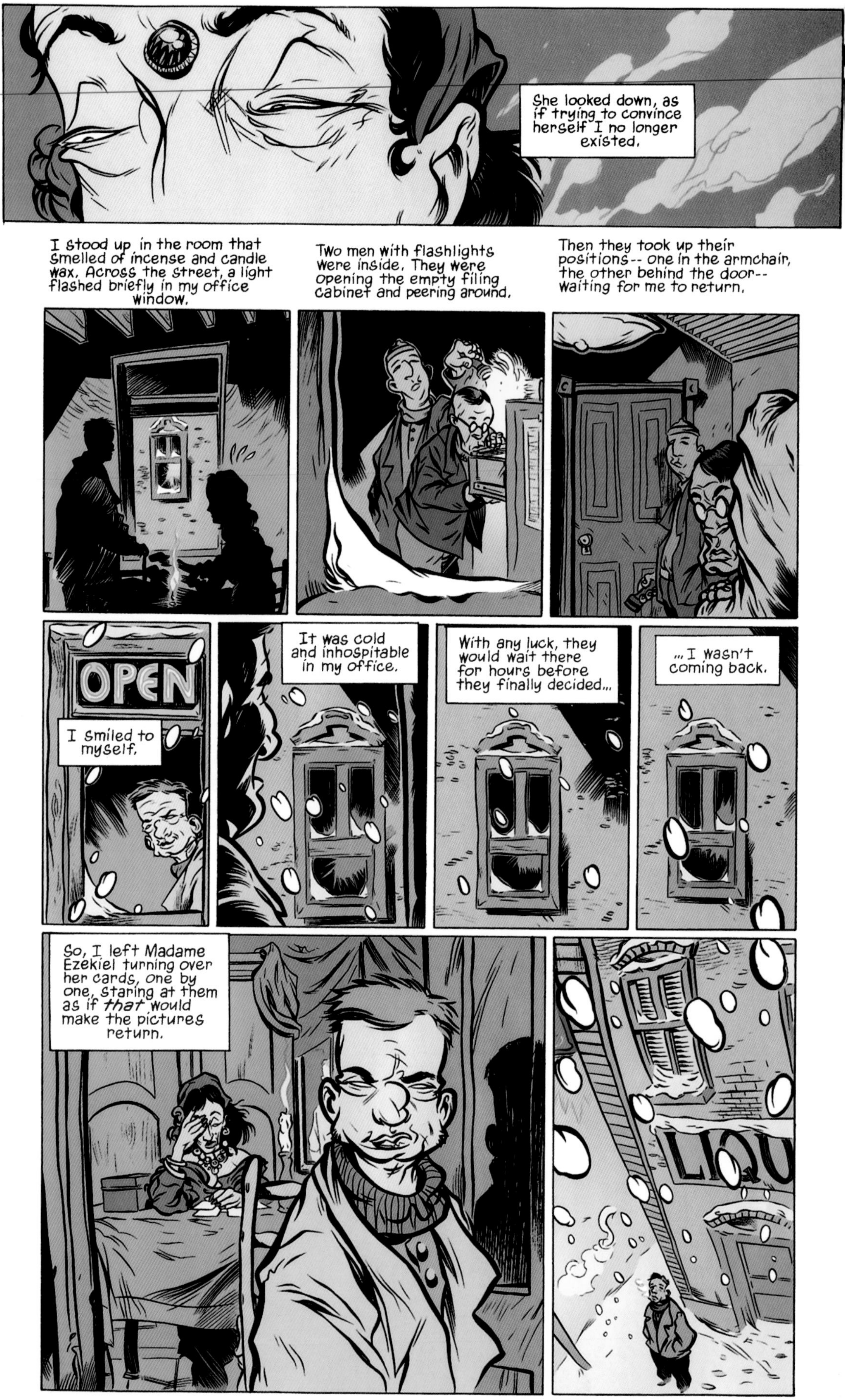
She looked down, as if trying to convince herself I no longer existed.
I stood up in the room that smelled of incense and candle wax. Across the street, a light flashed briefly in my office window.
Two men with flashlights were inside. They were opening the empty filing cabinet and peering around.
Then they took up their positions-- one in the armchair, the other behind the door-- waiting for me to return.
OPEN
I smiled to myself.
It was cold and inhospitable in my office.
With any luck, they would wait there for hours before they finally decided...
...I wasn't coming back.
So, I left Madame Ezekiel turning over her cards, one by one, staring at them as if *that* would make the pictures return.
LIQU

WHERE ARE THE CHESS FIENDS?

IT'S A BIG NIGHT FOR THEM TONIGHT. THEY'LL BE DOWN AT THE BAY. LET'S SEE... YOU'RE A JACK DANIELS, RIGHT?

SOUNDS GOOD.

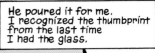

He poured it for me. I recognized the thumbprint from the last time I had the glass.

GOOD BOOK.

He took his book from me...

SO? WHAT'S YOUR POINT?

...and read:

"BELOW THE THUNDERS OF THE UPPER DEEP; FAR, FAR BENEATH IN THE ABYSMAL SEA, HIS ANCIENT, DREAMLESS, UNINVADED SLEEP... THE KRAKEN SLEEPETH..."

COME OVER HERE.

SEE? OUT THERE?

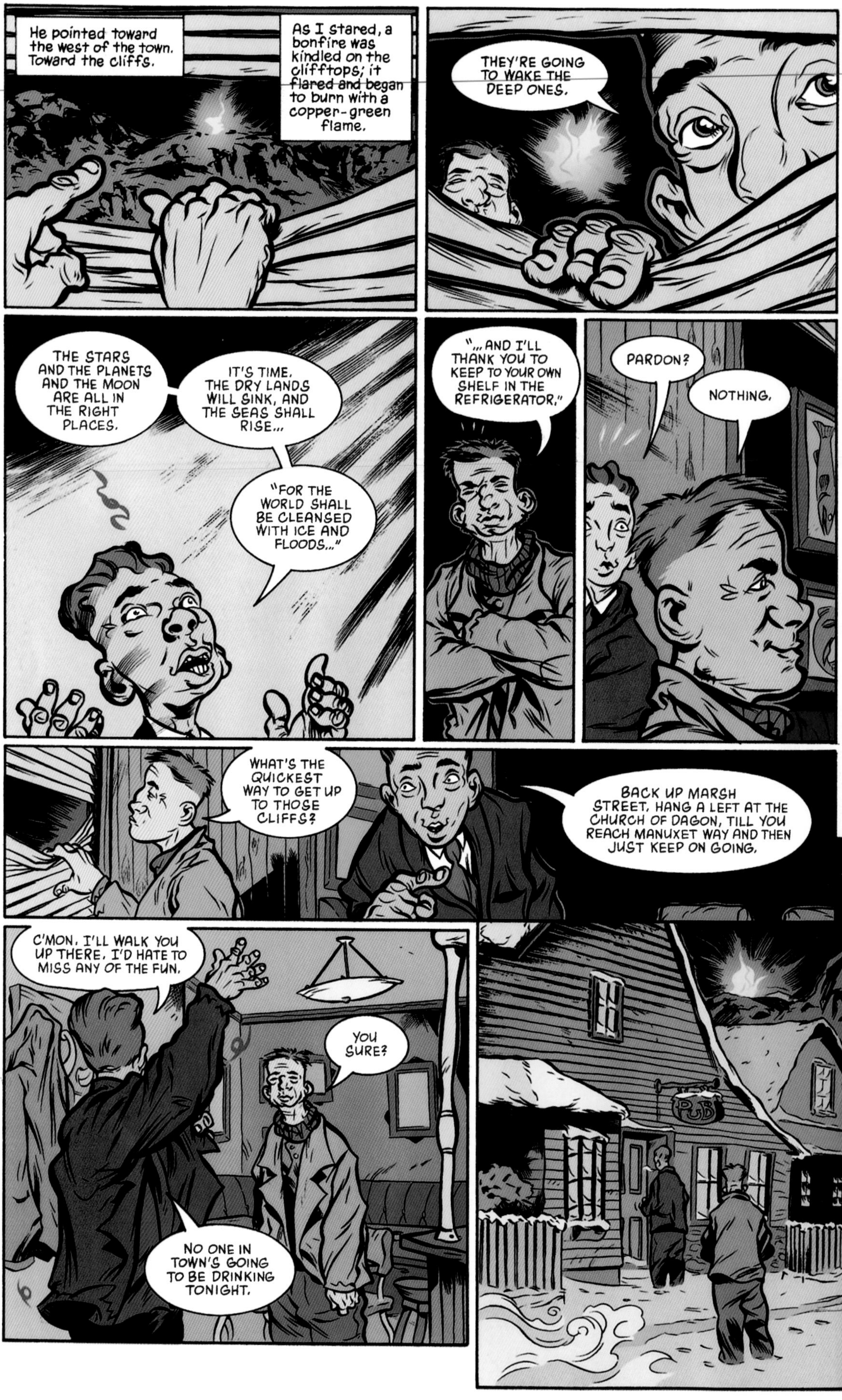
He pointed toward the west of the town. Toward the cliffs.
As I stared, a bonfire was kindled on the clifftops; it flared and began to burn with a copper-green flame.
THEY'RE GOING TO WAKE THE DEEP ONES.
THE STARS AND THE PLANETS AND THE MOON ARE ALL IN THE RIGHT PLACES.
IT'S TIME. THE DRY LANDS WILL SINK, AND THE SEAS SHALL RISE...
"FOR THE WORLD SHALL BE CLEANSED WITH ICE AND FLOODS..."
"...AND I'LL THANK YOU TO KEEP TO YOUR OWN SHELF IN THE REFRIGERATOR."
PARDON?
NOTHING.
WHAT'S THE QUICKEST WAY TO GET UP TO THOSE CLIFFS?
BACK UP MARSH STREET. HANG A LEFT AT THE CHURCH OF DAGON, TILL YOU REACH MANUXET WAY AND THEN JUST KEEP ON GOING.
C'MON. I'LL WALK YOU UP THERE. I'D HATE TO MISS ANY OF THE FUN.
YOU SURE?
NO ONE IN TOWN'S GOING TO BE DRINKING TONIGHT.
PUB

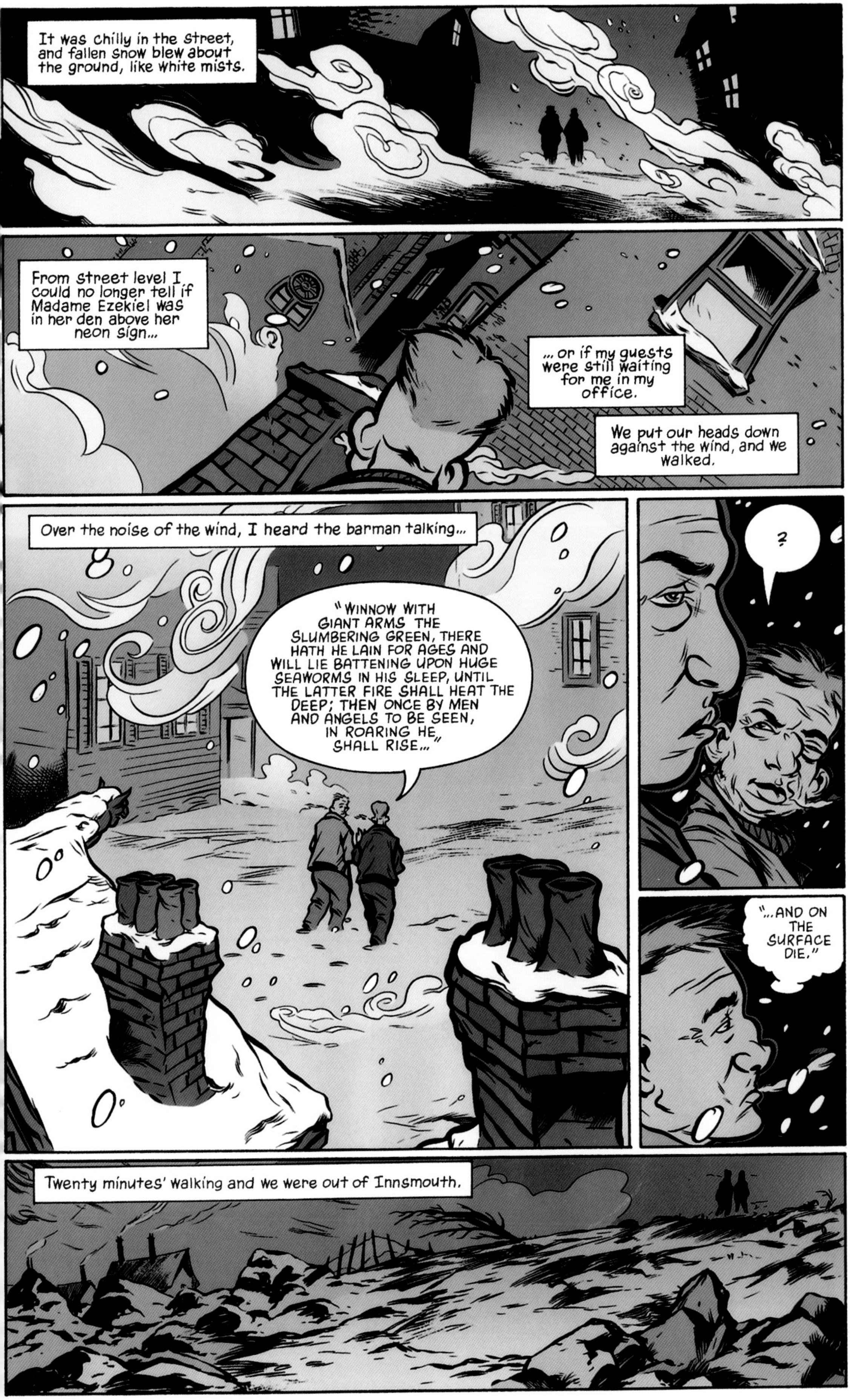
It was chilly in the street, and fallen snow blew about the ground, like white mists.
From street level I could no longer tell if Madame Ezekiel was in her den above her neon sign...
...or if my guests were still waiting for me in my office.
We put our heads down against the wind, and we walked.
Over the noise of the wind, I heard the barman talking...
"WINNOW WITH GIANT ARMS THE SLUMBERING GREEN, THERE HATH HE LAIN FOR AGES AND WILL LIE BATTENING UPON HUGE SEAWORMS IN HIS SLEEP, UNTIL THE LATTER FIRE SHALL HEAT THE DEEP; THEN ONCE BY MEN AND ANGELS TO BE SEEN, IN ROARING HE SHALL RISE..."
?
"...AND ON THE SURFACE DIE."
Twenty minutes' walking and we were out of Innsmouth.

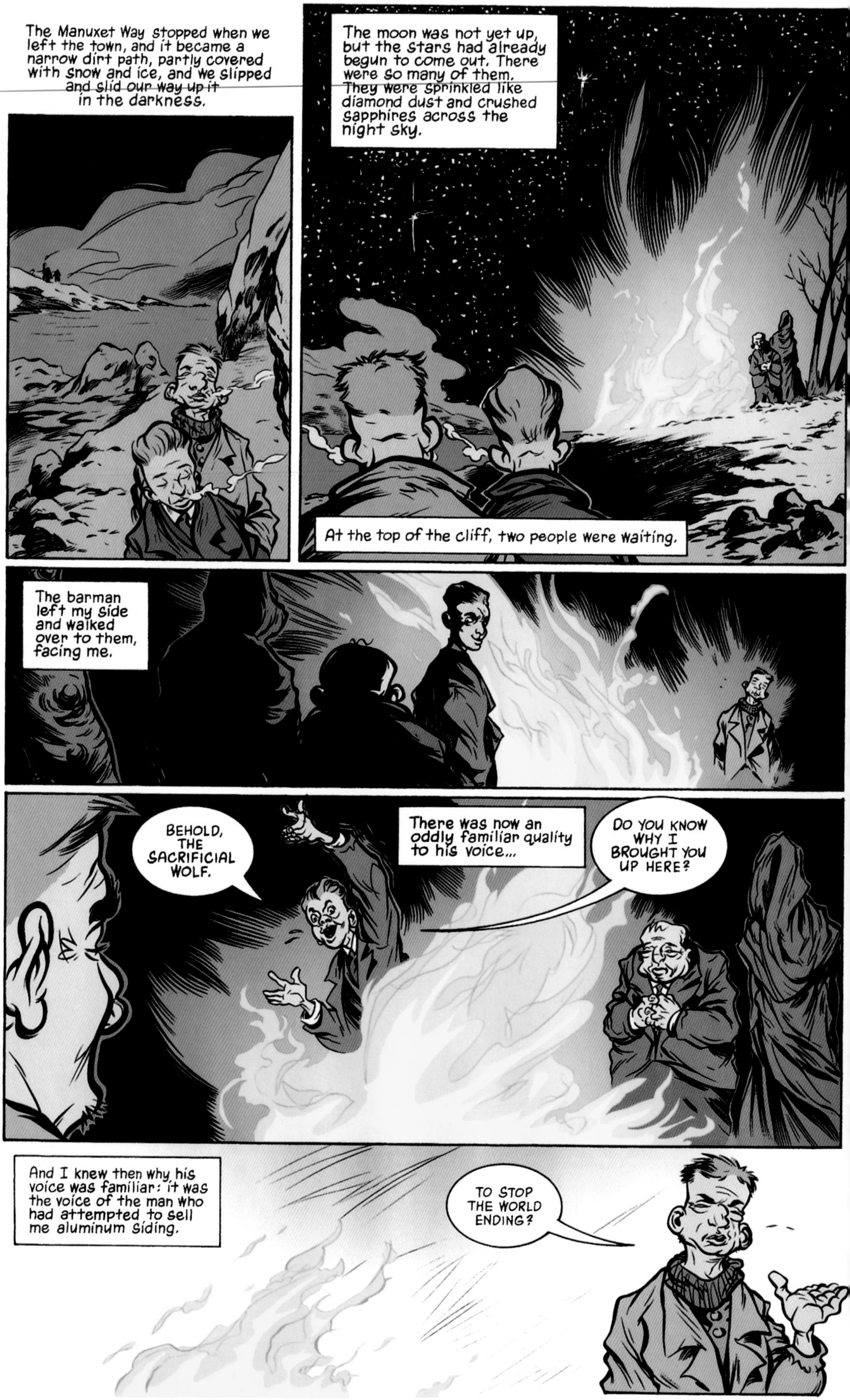
The Manuxet Way stopped when we left the town, and it became a narrow dirt path, partly covered with snow and ice, and we slipped and slid our way up it in the darkness.
The moon was not yet up, but the stars had already begun to come out. There were so many of them. They were sprinkled like diamond dust and crushed sapphires across the night sky.
At the top of the cliff, two people were waiting.
The barman left my side and walked over to them, facing me.
BEHOLD, THE SACRIFICIAL WOLF.
There was now an oddly familiar quality to his voice...
DO YOU KNOW WHY I BROUGHT YOU UP HERE?
And I knew then why his voice was familiar: it was the voice of the man who had attempted to sell me aluminum siding.
TO STOP THE WORLD ENDING?

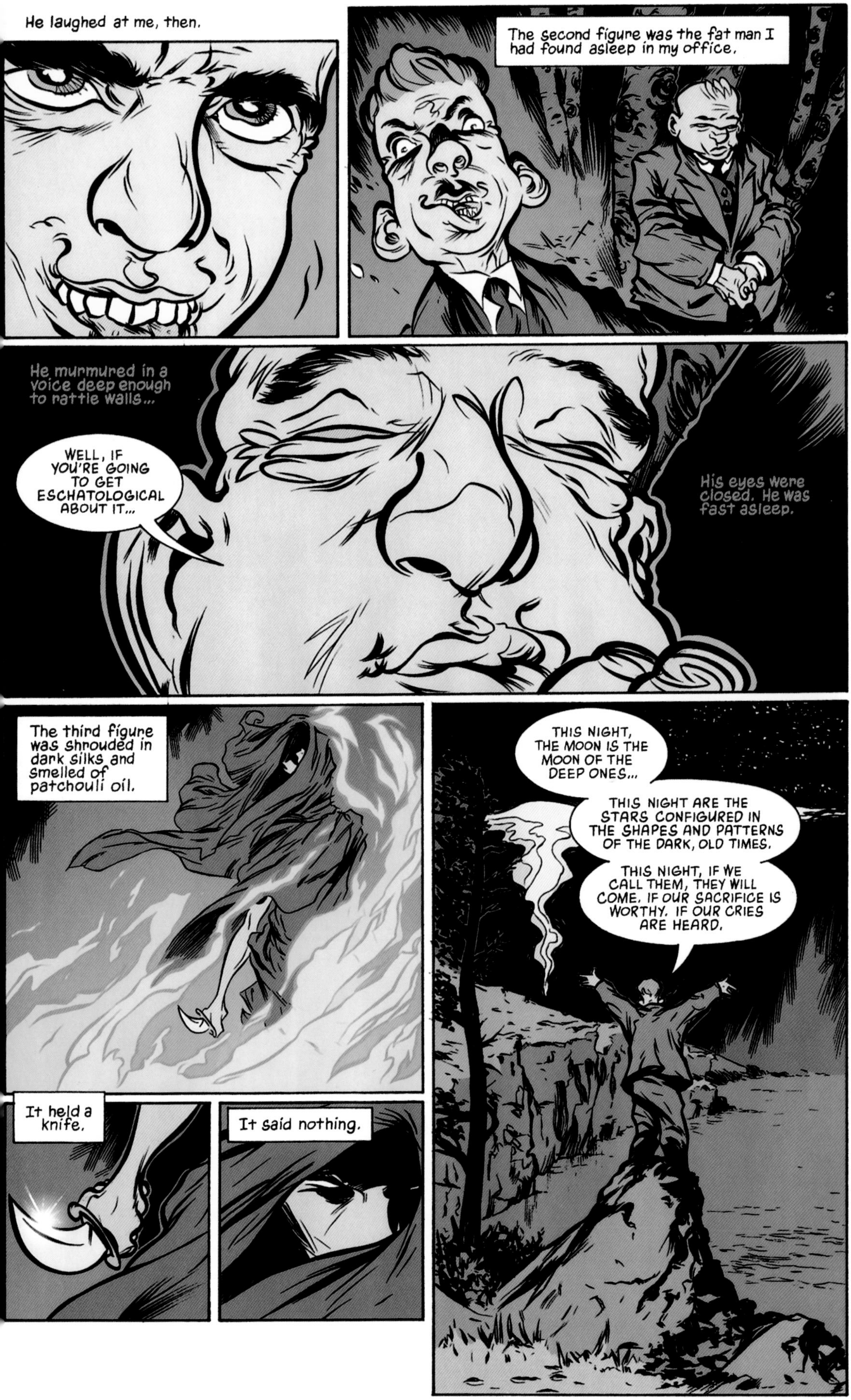
He laughed at me, then.
The second figure was the fat man I had found asleep in my office.
He murmured in a voice deep enough to rattle walls...
WELL, IF YOU'RE GOING TO GET ESCHATOLOGICAL ABOUT IT...
His eyes were closed. He was fast asleep.
The third figure was shrouded in dark silks and smelled of patchouli oil.
It held a knife.
It said nothing.
THIS NIGHT, THE MOON IS THE MOON OF THE DEEP ONES...
THIS NIGHT ARE THE STARS CONFIGURED IN THE SHAPES AND PATTERNS OF THE DARK, OLD TIMES.
THIS NIGHT, IF WE CALL THEM, THEY WILL COME. IF OUR SACRIFICE IS WORTHY. IF OUR CRIES ARE HEARD.

The moon rose, huge and amber and heavy, on the other side of the bay.

And a chorus of low croaking rose with it from the ocean far beneath us.

Moonlight on snow and ice is not day-light...

...but it will do.

And my eyes were getting sharper with the moon.

In the cold waters, men like frogs were surfacing and submerging in a slow waterdance. Men like frogs, and women, too: it seemed to me that I could see my landlady down there, writhing and croaking in the bay with the rest of them.

It was too soon for another change-- I was still exhausted from the night before-- but I felt strange under that amber moon.

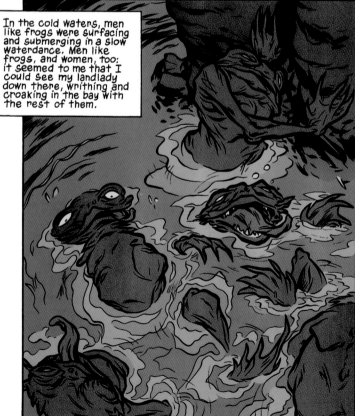

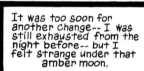

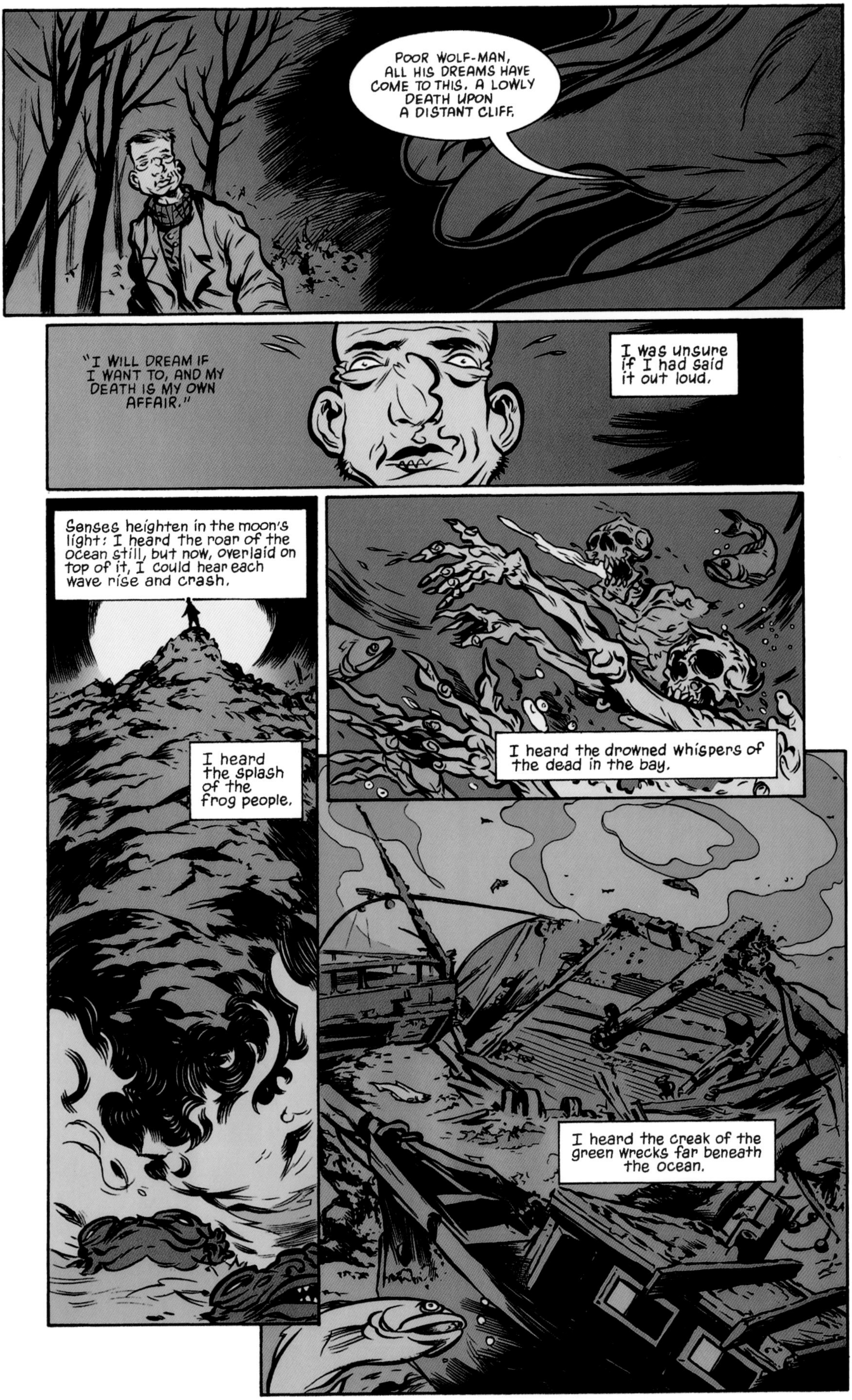
POOR WOLF-MAN, ALL HIS DREAMS HAVE COME TO THIS. A LOWLY DEATH UPON A DISTANT CLIFF.
"I WILL DREAM IF I WANT TO, AND MY DEATH IS MY OWN AFFAIR."
I was unsure if I had said it out loud.
Senses heighten in the moon's light: I heard the roar of the ocean still, but now, overlaid on top of it, I could hear each wave rise and crash.
I heard the splash of the frog people.
I heard the drowned whispers of the dead in the bay.
I heard the creak of the green wrecks far beneath the ocean.

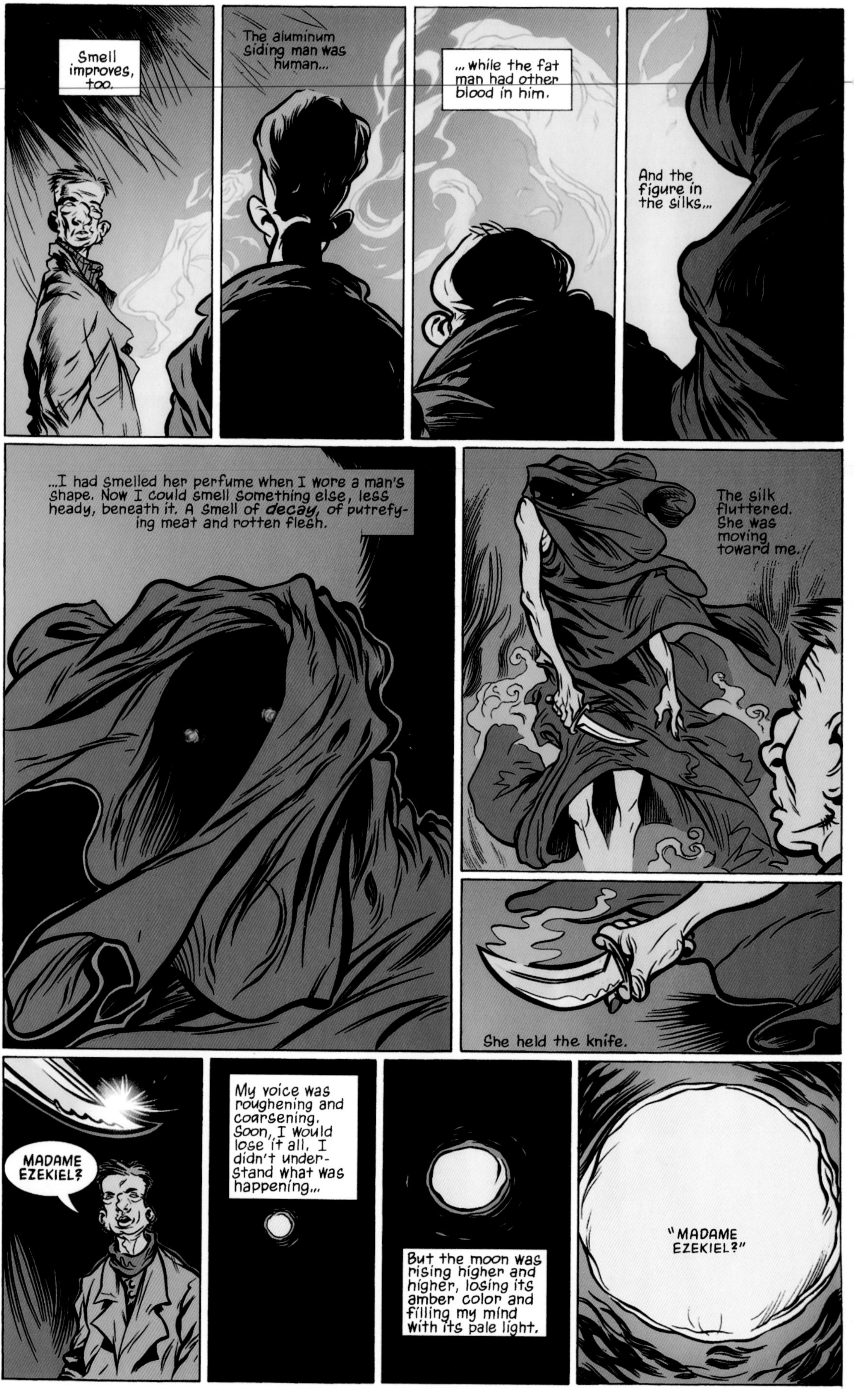
Smell improves, too.
The aluminum siding man was human...
...while the fat man had other blood in him.
And the figure in the silks...
...I had smelled her perfume when I wore a man's shape. Now I could smell something else, less heady, beneath it. A smell of decay, of putrefying meat and rotten flesh.
The silk fluttered. She was moving toward me.
She held the knife.
MADAME EZEKIEL?
My voice was roughening and coarsening. Soon, I would lose it all. I didn't understand what was happening...
But the moon was rising higher and higher, losing its amber color and filling my mind with its pale light.
"MADAME EZEKIEL?"

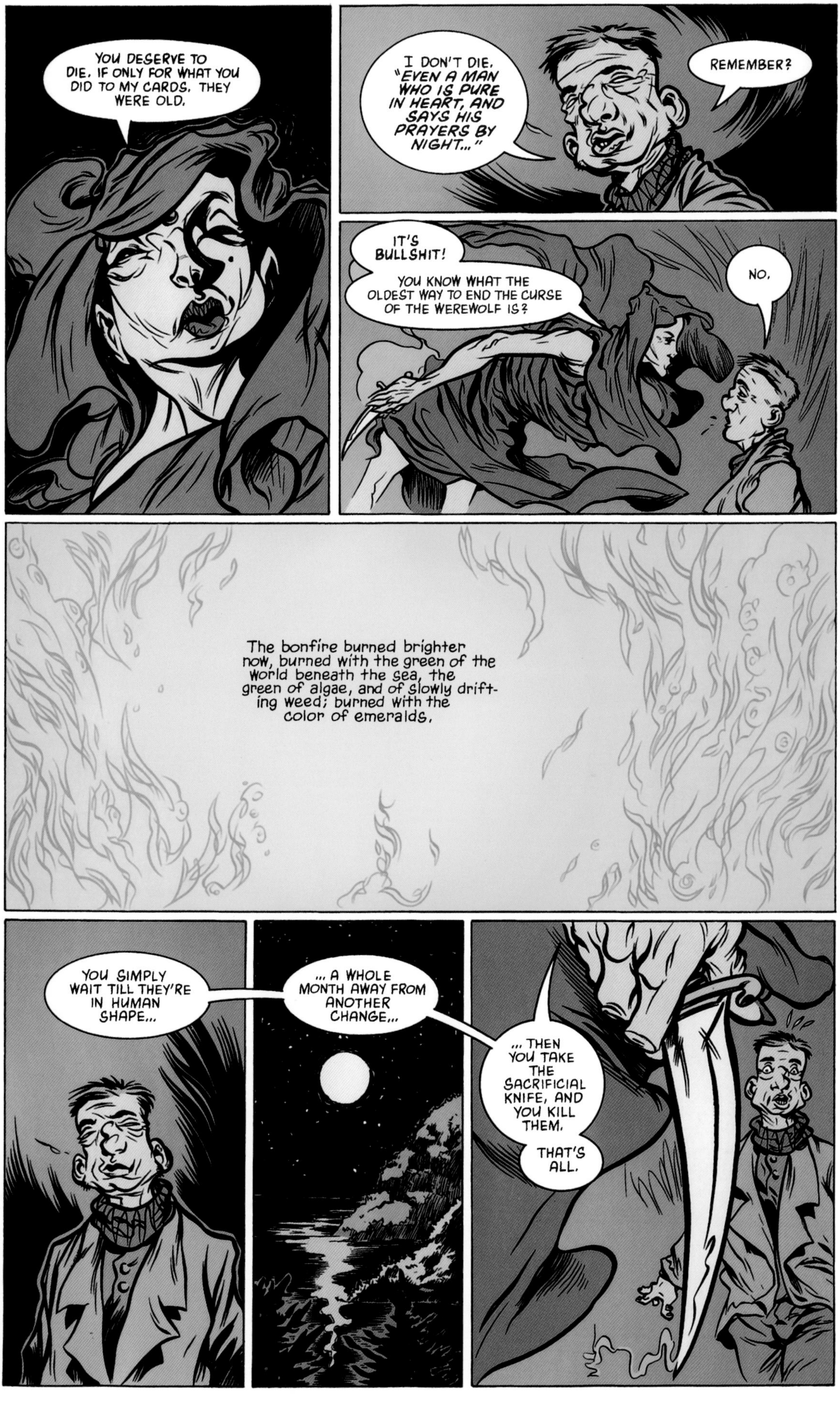
YOU DESERVE TO DIE, IF ONLY FOR WHAT YOU DID TO MY CARDS. THEY WERE OLD.
I DON'T DIE. "EVEN A MAN WHO IS PURE IN HEART, AND SAYS HIS PRAYERS BY NIGHT..."
REMEMBER?
IT'S BULLSHIT!
YOU KNOW WHAT THE OLDEST WAY TO END THE CURSE OF THE WEREWOLF IS?
NO.
The bonfire burned brighter now, burned with the green of the world beneath the sea, the green of algae, and of slowly drifting weed; burned with the color of emeralds.
YOU SIMPLY WAIT TILL THEY'RE IN HUMAN SHAPE...
... A WHOLE MONTH AWAY FROM ANOTHER CHANGE...
... THEN YOU TAKE THE SACRIFICIAL KNIFE, AND YOU KILL THEM.
THAT'S ALL.

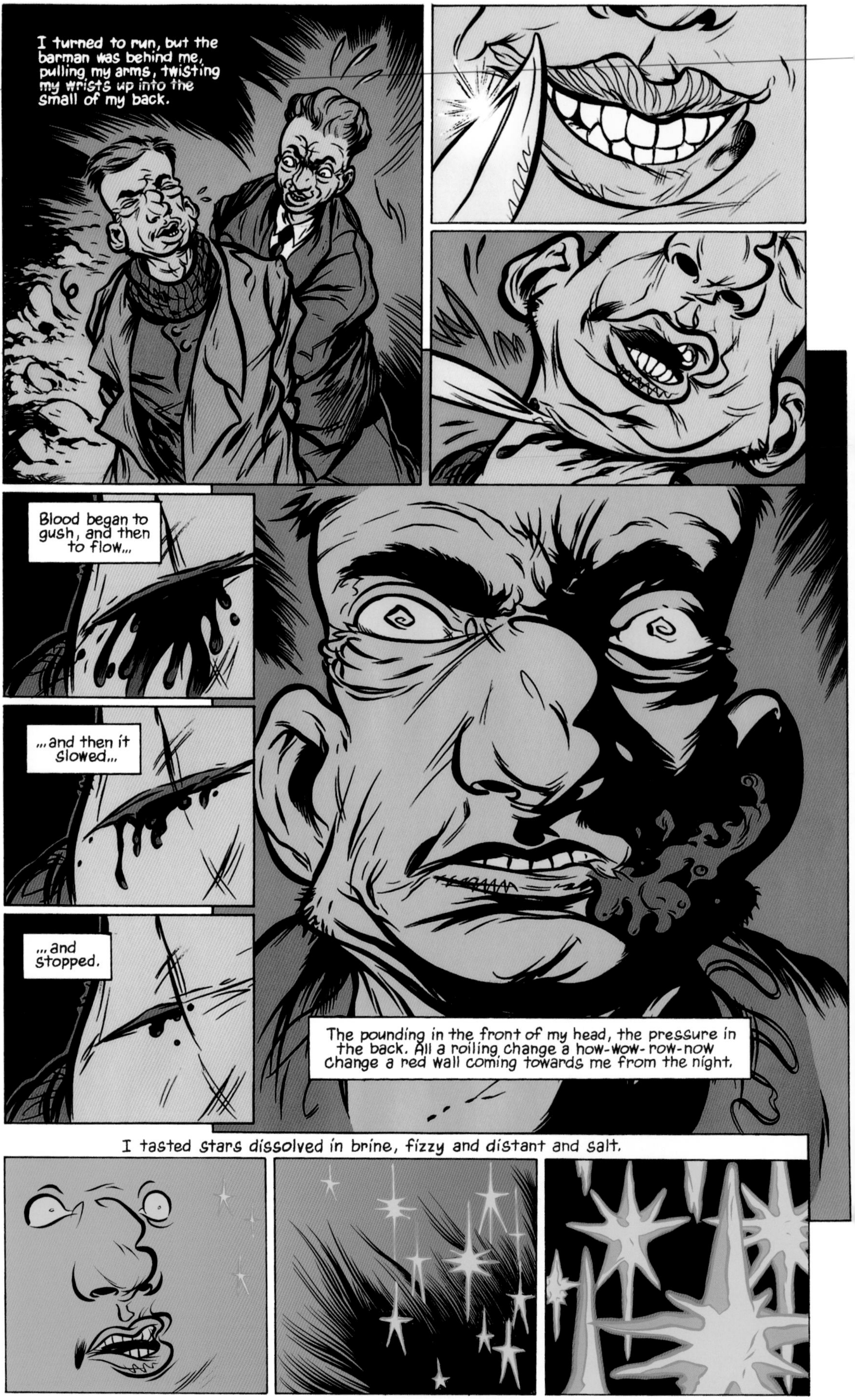
I turned to run, but the barman was behind me, pulling my arms, twisting my wrists up into the small of my back.
Blood began to gush, and then to flow...
...and then it slowed...
...and stopped.
The pounding in the front of my head, the pressure in the back. All a roiling change a how-wow-row-now change a red wall coming towards me from the night.
I tasted stars dissolved in brine, fizzy and distant and salt.

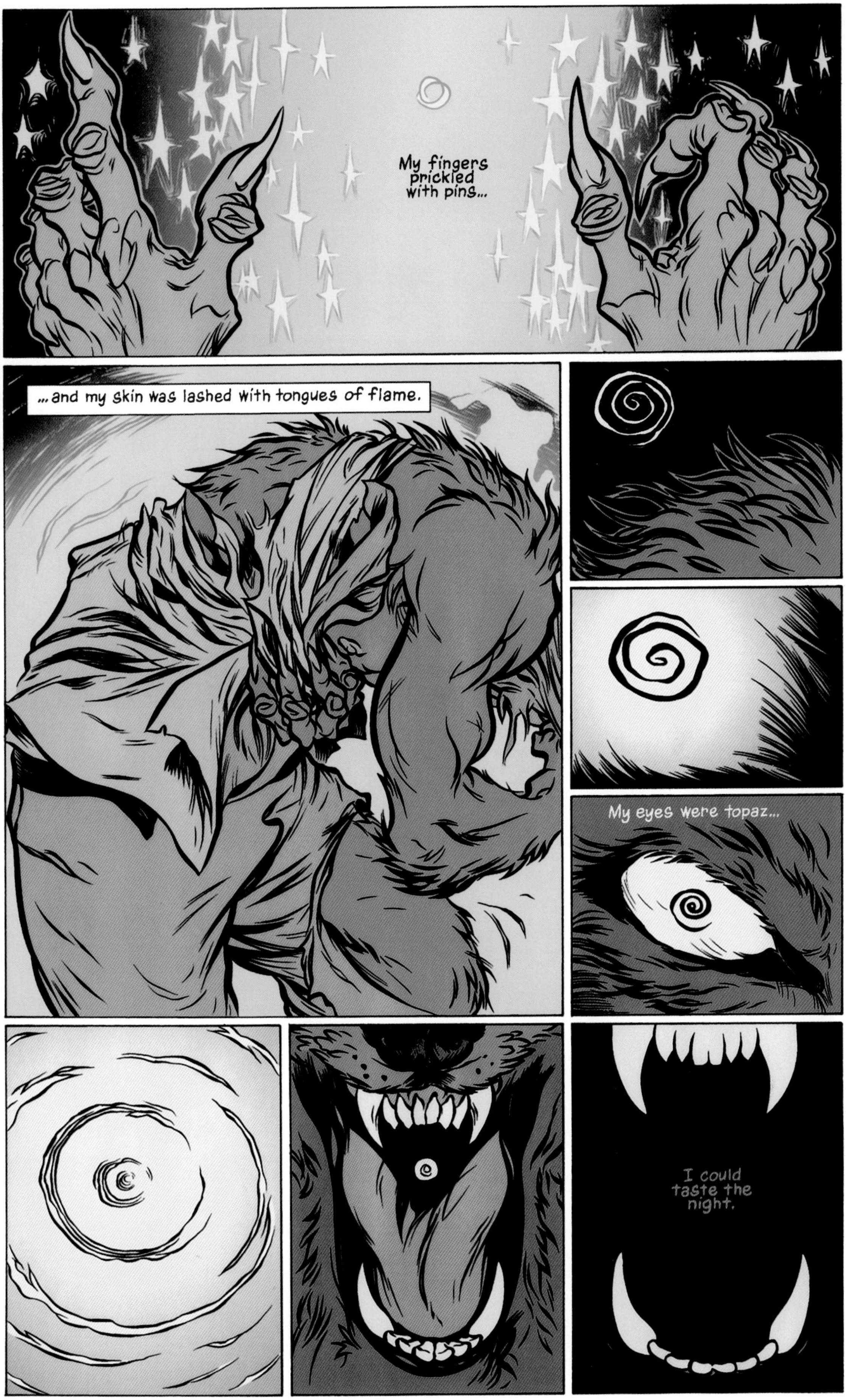
My fingers prickled with pins...
...and my skin was lashed with tongues of flame.
My eyes were topaz...
I could taste the night.

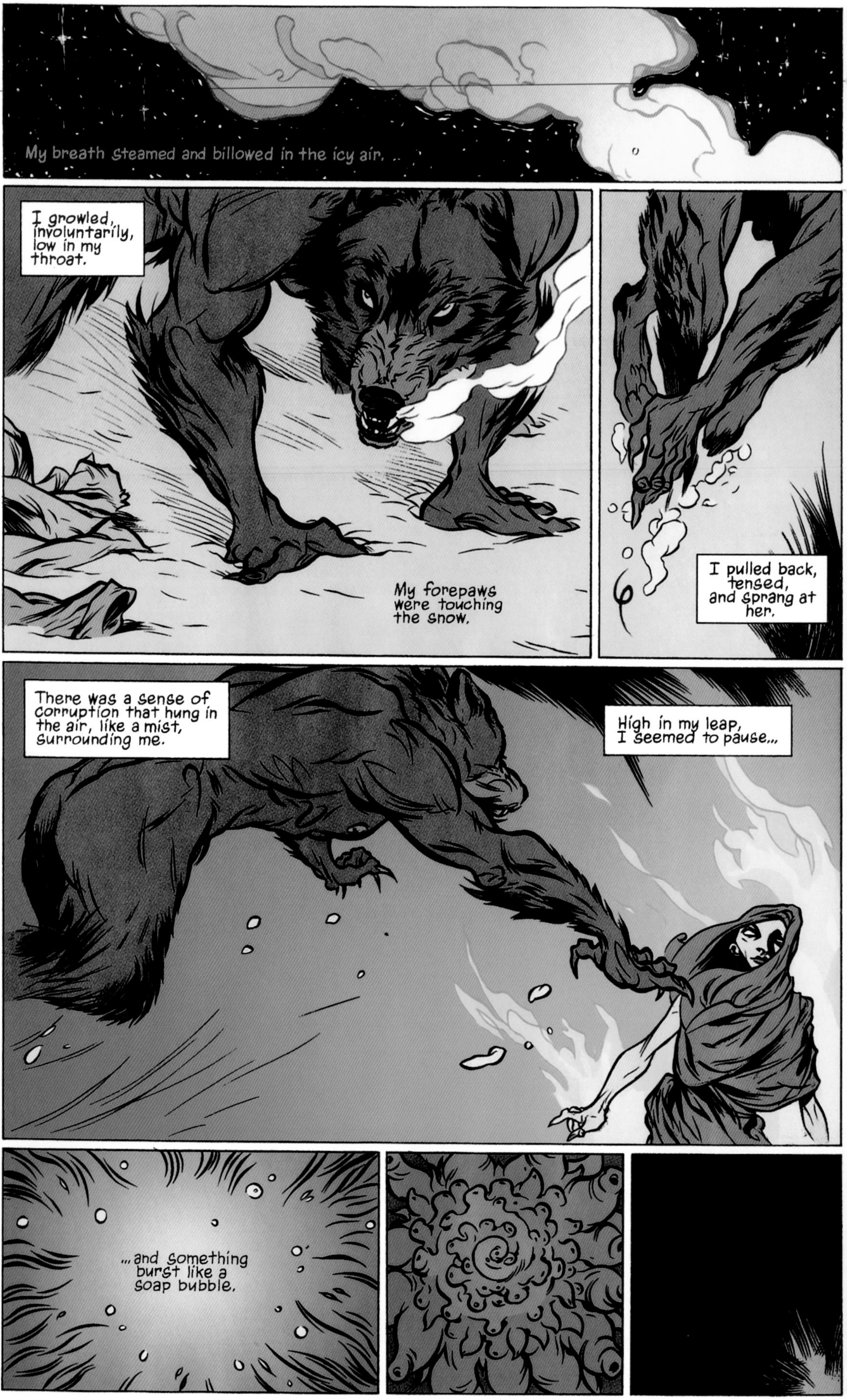
My breath steamed and billowed in the icy air.
I growled, involuntarily, low in my throat.
My forepaws were touching the snow.
I pulled back, tensed, and sprang at her.
There was a sense of corruption that hung in the air, like a mist, surrounding me.
High in my leap, I seemed to pause...
...and something burst like a soap bubble.

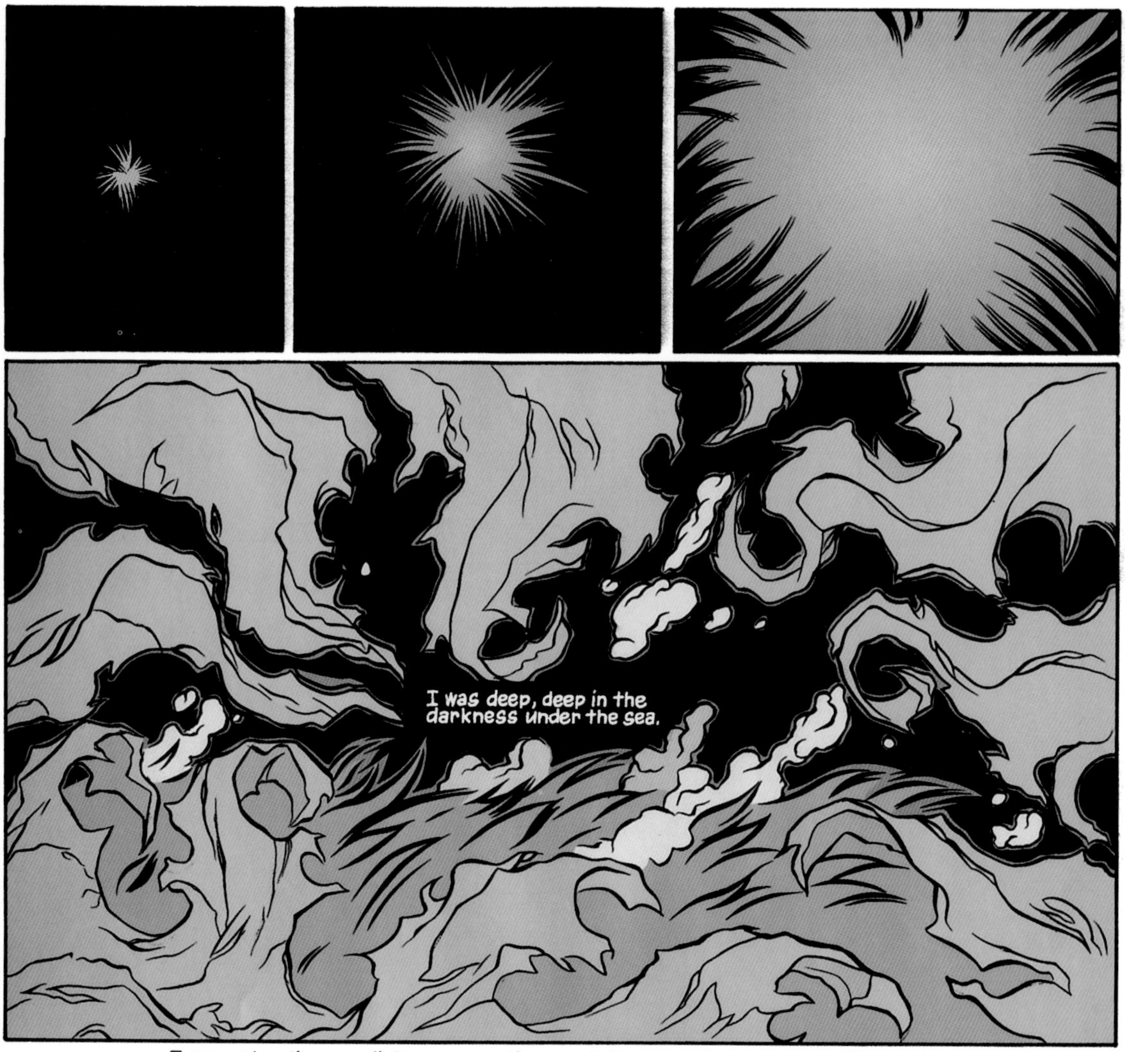
I was deep, deep in the darkness under the sea.

I was standing on all fours on a slimy rock floor, at the entrance of some kind of citadel, built of enormous, rough-hewn stones.

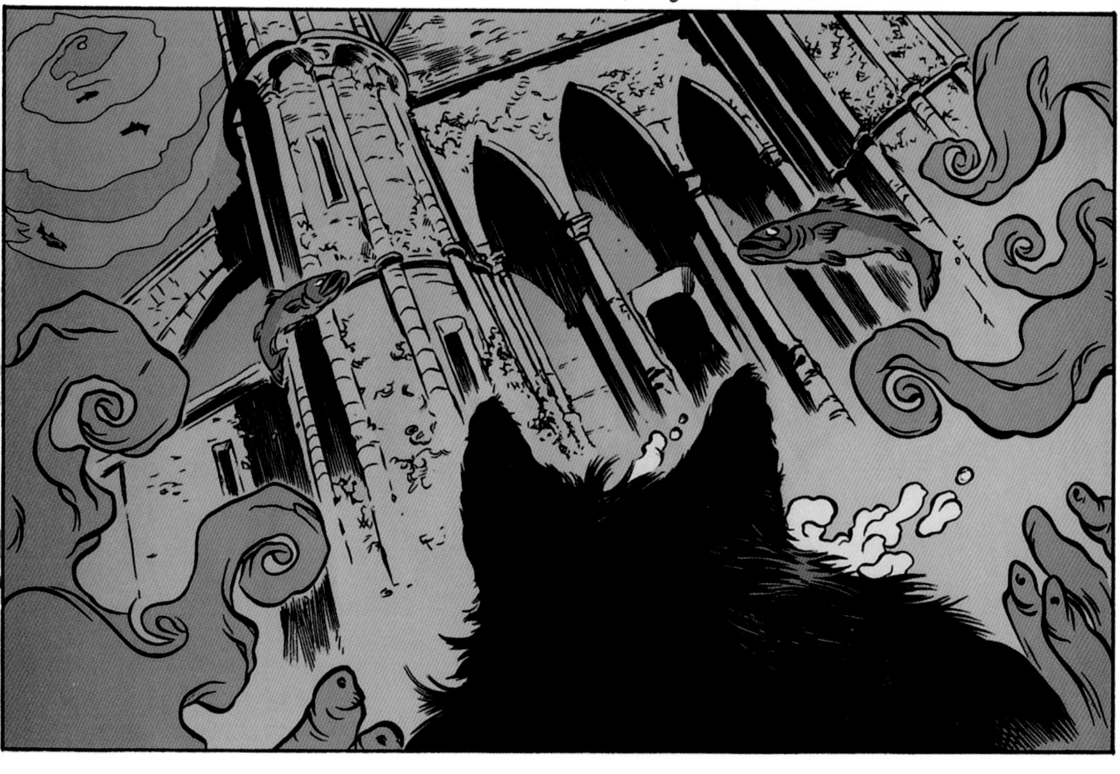

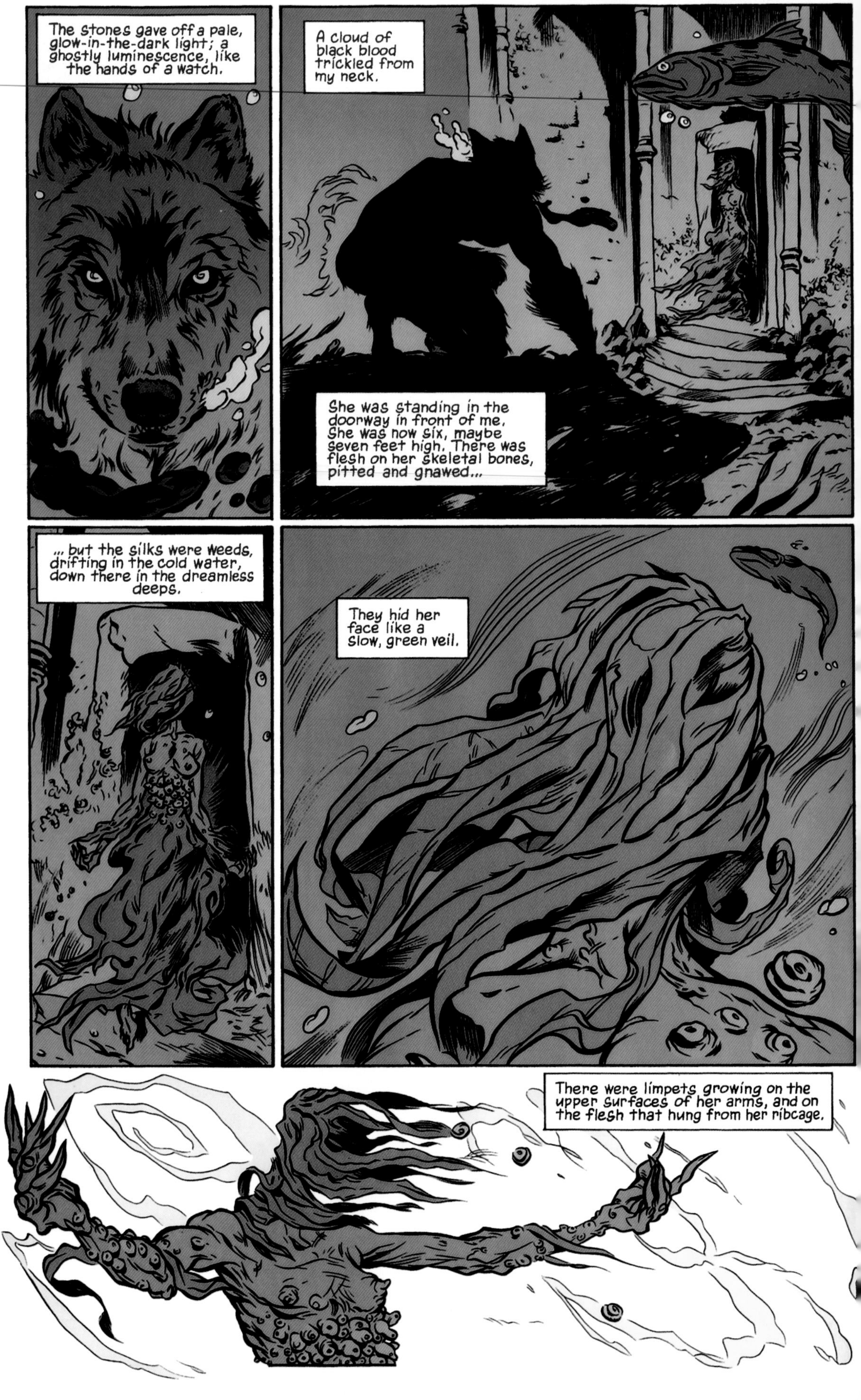

The stones gave off a pale, glow-in-the-dark light; a ghostly luminescence, like the hands of a watch.
A cloud of black blood trickled from my neck.
She was standing in the doorway in front of me. She was now six, maybe seven feet high. There was flesh on her skeletal bones, pitted and gnawed...
... but the silks were weeds, drifting in the cold water, down there in the dreamless deeps.
They hid her face like a slow, green veil.
There were limpets growing on the upper surfaces of her arms, and on the flesh that hung from her ribcage.

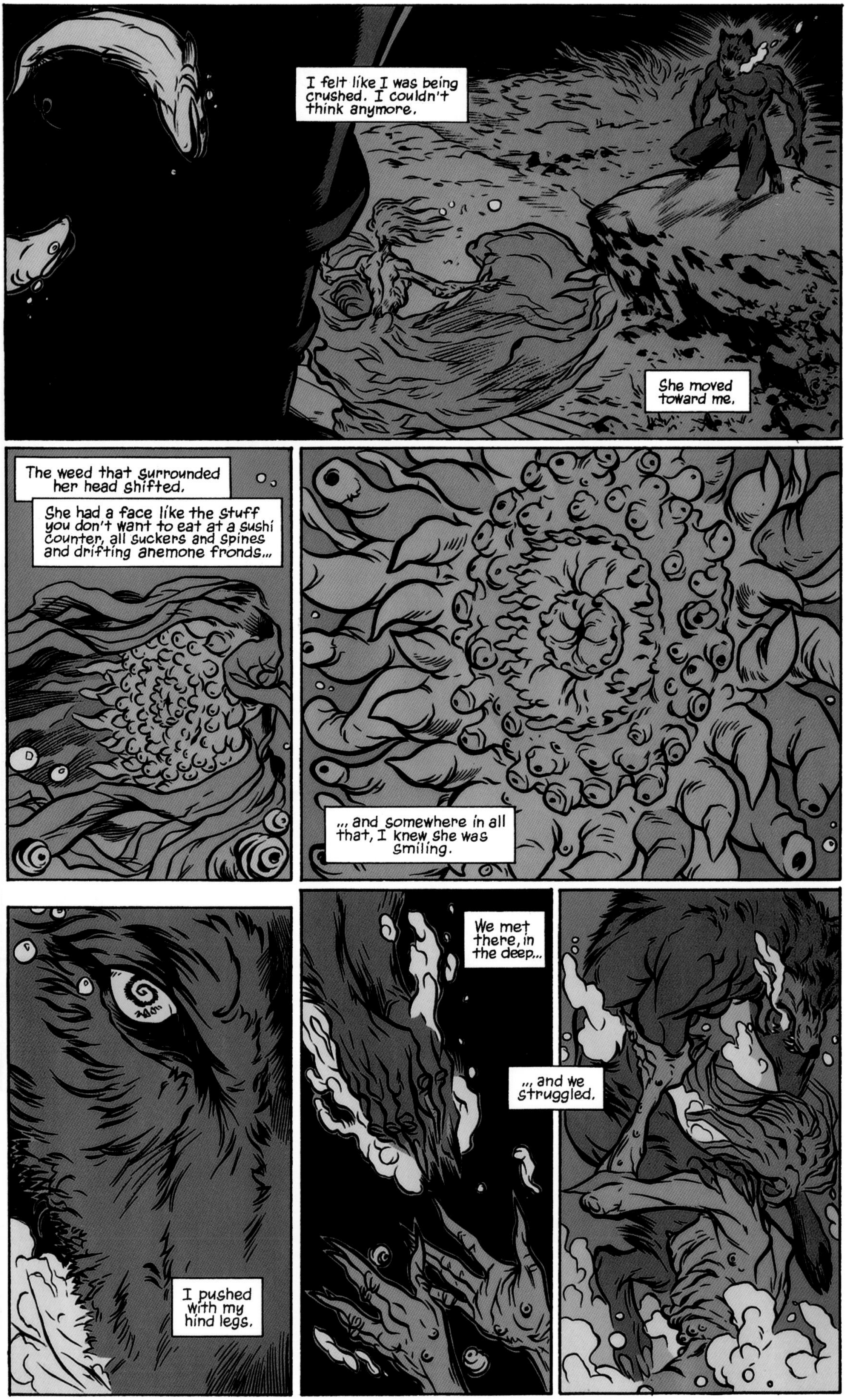
I felt like I was being crushed. I couldn't think anymore.
She moved toward me.
The weed that surrounded her head shifted.
She had a face like the stuff you don't want to eat at a sushi counter, all suckers and spines and drifting anemone fronds...
... and somewhere in all that, I knew she was smiling.
I pushed with my hind legs.
We met there, in the deep...
... and we struggled.

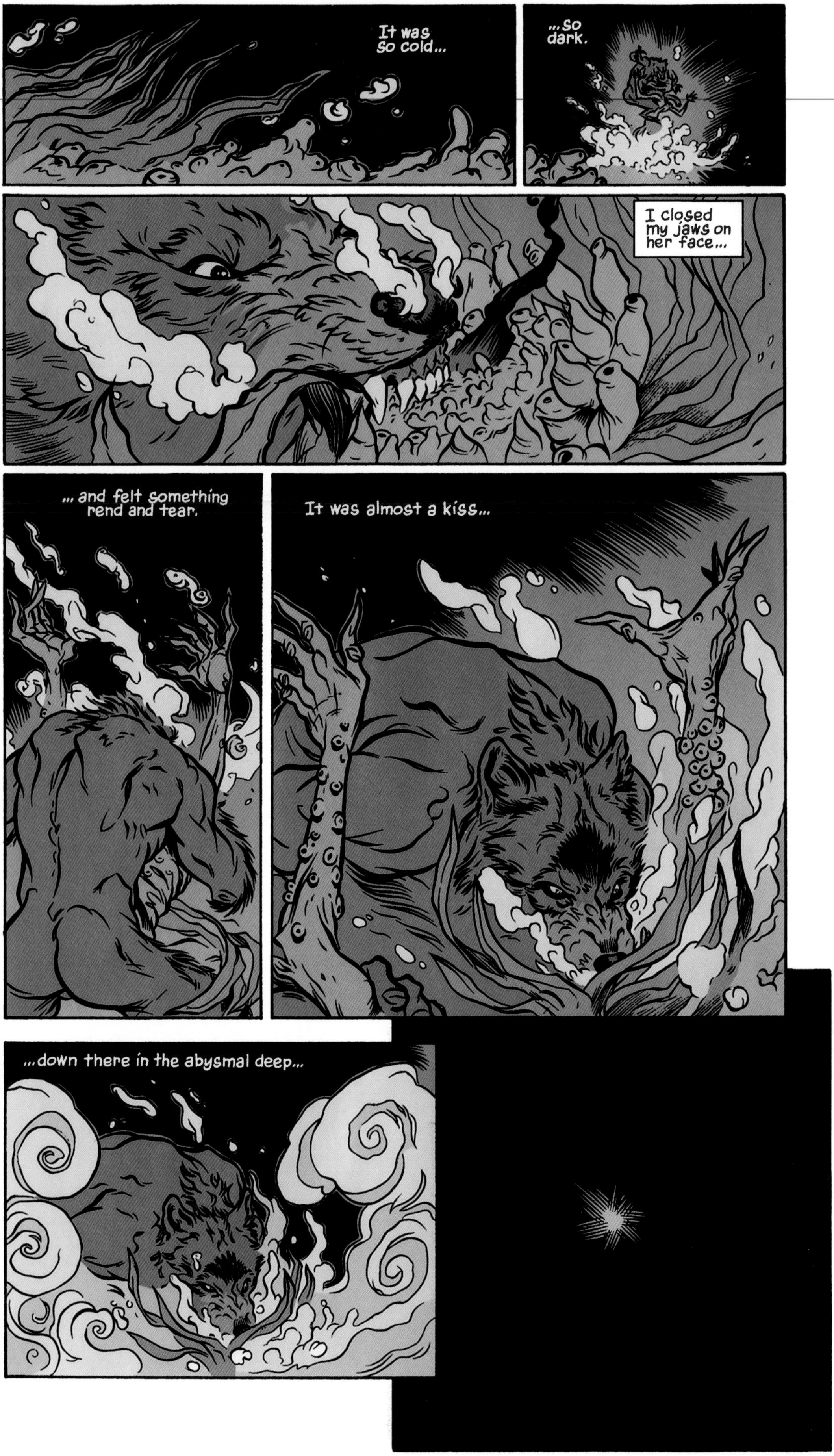
It was so cold...
...so dark.
I closed my jaws on her face...
...and felt something rend and tear.
It was almost a kiss...
...down there in the abysmal deep...

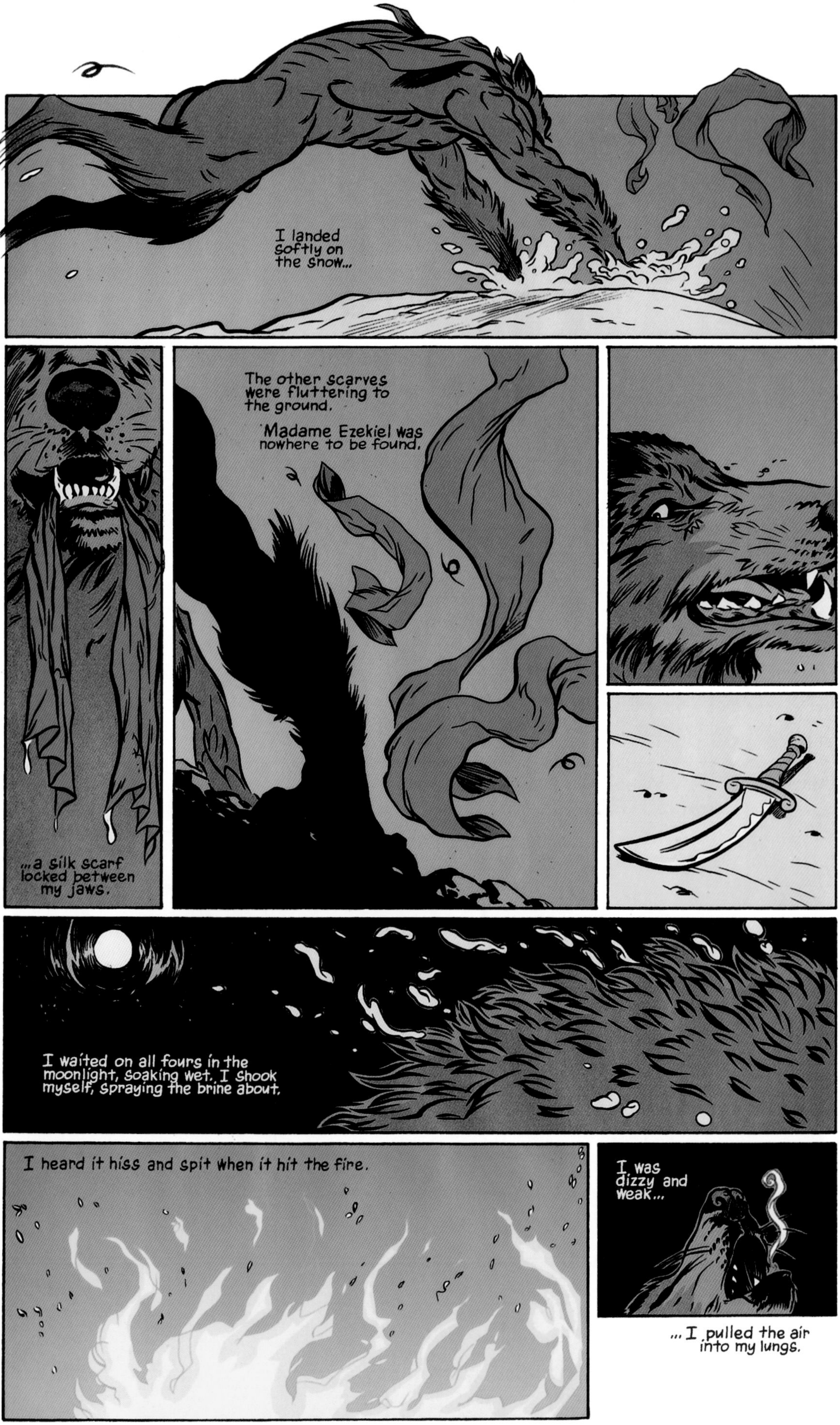

I landed softly on the snow...
...a silk scarf locked between my jaws.
The other scarves were fluttering to the ground.
Madame Ezekiel was nowhere to be found.
I waited on all fours in the moonlight, soaking wet. I shook myself, spraying the brine about.
I heard it hiss and spit when it hit the fire.
I was dizzy and weak...
... I pulled the air into my lungs.

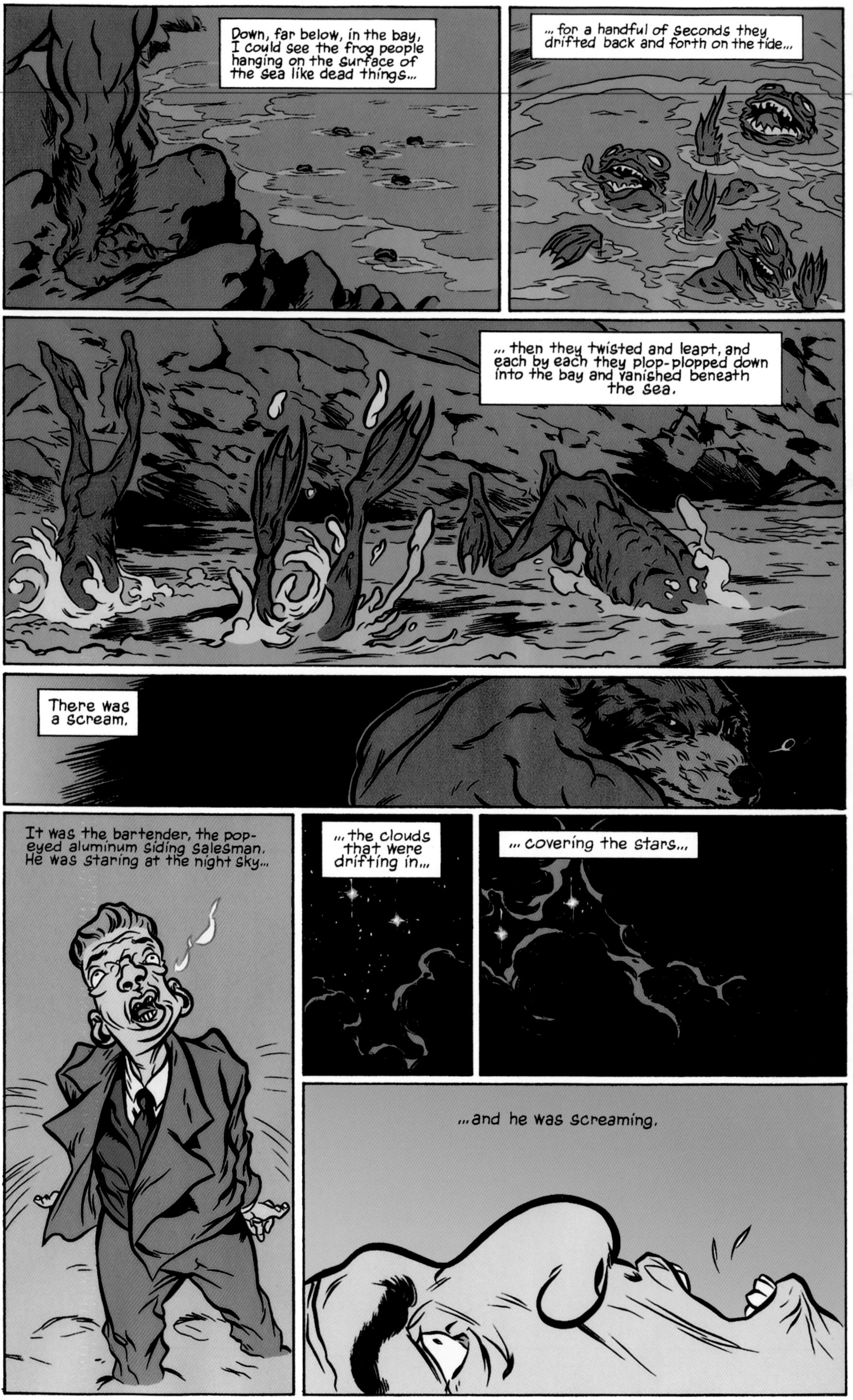
Down, far below, in the bay, I could see the frog people hanging on the surface of the sea like dead things...
... for a handful of seconds they drifted back and forth on the tide...
... then they twisted and leapt, and each by each they plop-plopped down into the bay and vanished beneath the sea.
There was a scream.
It was the bartender, the pop-eyed aluminum siding salesman. He was staring at the night sky...
... the clouds that were drifting in...
... covering the stars...
... and he was screaming.

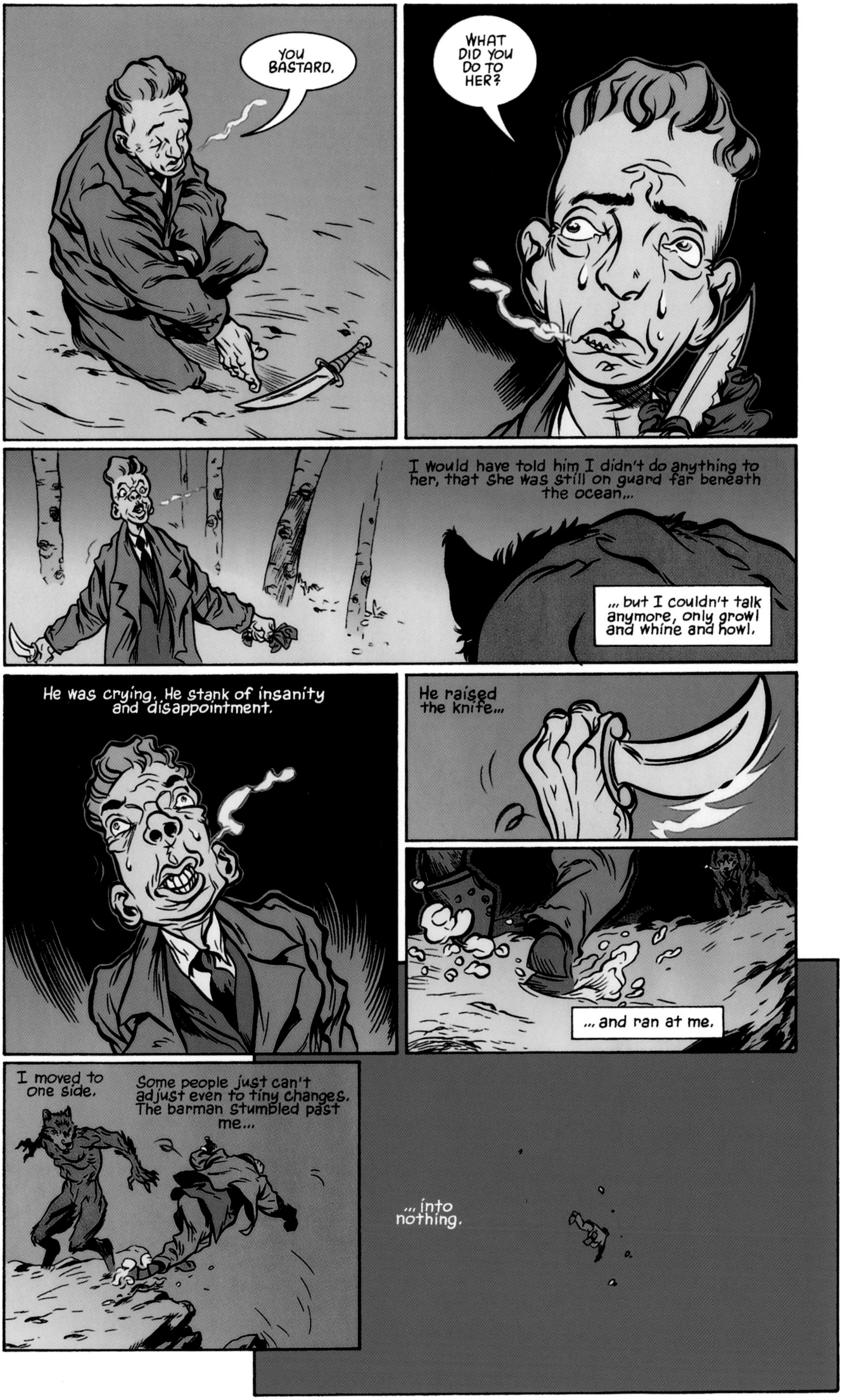
YOU BASTARD.
WHAT DID YOU DO TO HER?
I would have told him I didn't do anything to her, that she was still on guard far beneath the ocean...
... but I couldn't talk anymore, only growl and whine and howl.
He was crying. He stank of insanity and disappointment.
He raised the knife...
... and ran at me.
I moved to one side.
Some people just can't adjust even to tiny changes. The barman stumbled past me...
... into nothing.

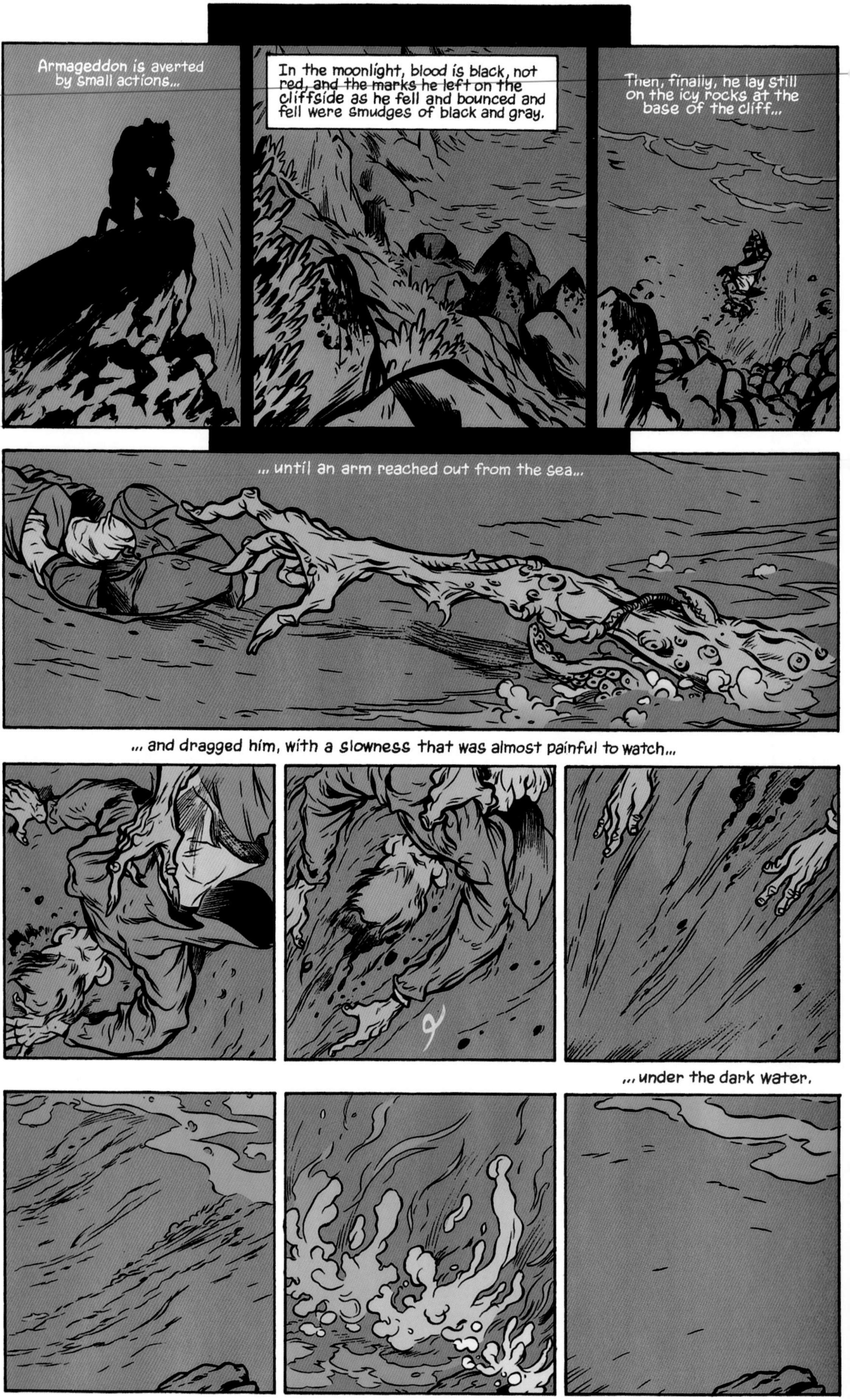
Armageddon is averted by small actions...
In the moonlight, blood is black, not red, and the marks he left on the cliffside as he fell and bounced and fell were smudges of black and gray.
Then, finally, he lay still on the icy rocks at the base of the cliff...
... until an arm reached out from the sea...
... and dragged him, with a slowness that was almost painful to watch...
... under the dark water.

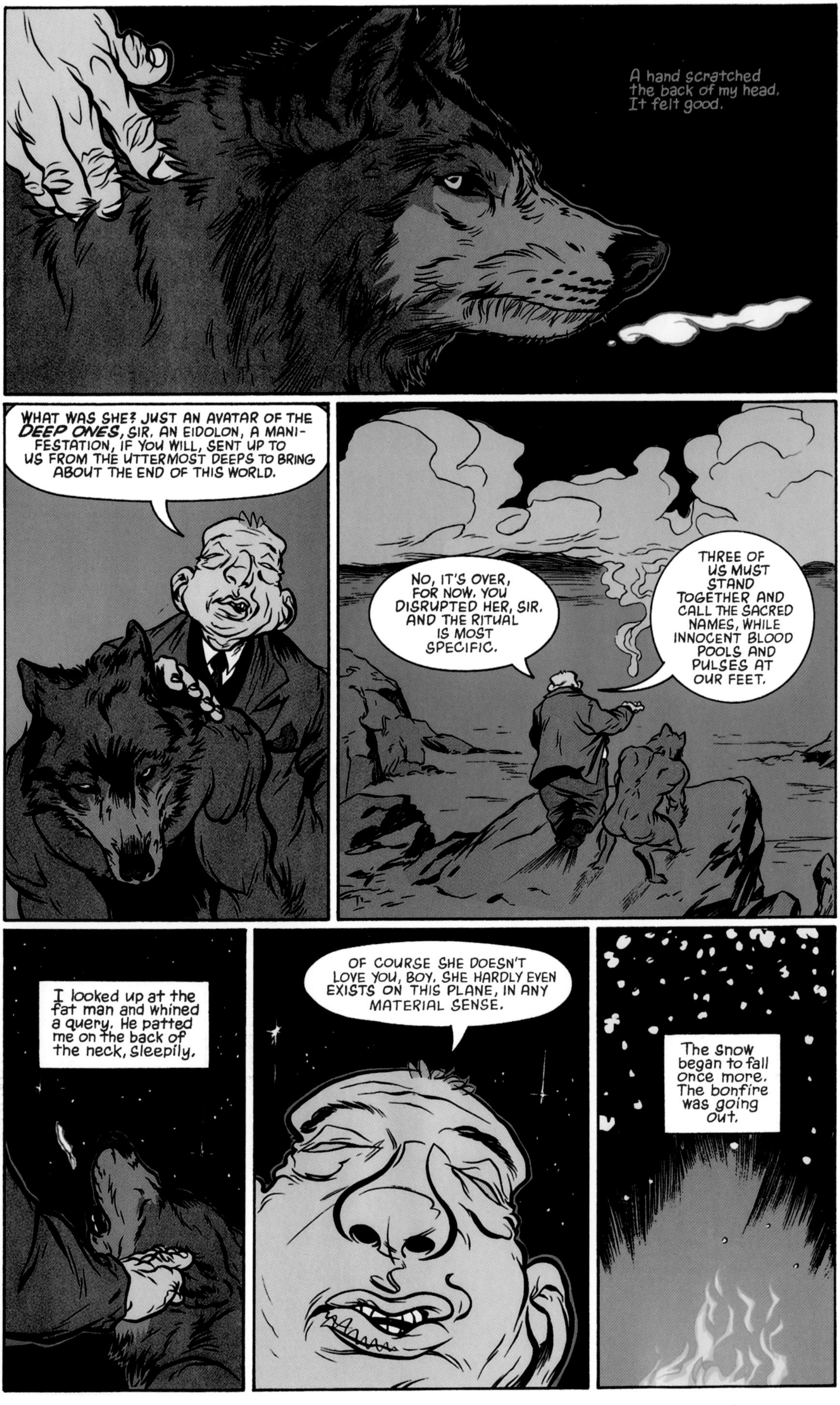
A hand scratched the back of my head. It felt good.
WHAT WAS SHE? JUST AN AVATAR OF THE DEEP ONES, SIR, AN EIDOLON, A MANIFESTATION, IF YOU WILL, SENT UP TO US FROM THE UTTERMOST DEEPS TO BRING ABOUT THE END OF THIS WORLD.
NO, IT'S OVER, FOR NOW. YOU DISRUPTED HER, SIR. AND THE RITUAL IS MOST SPECIFIC.
THREE OF US MUST STAND TOGETHER AND CALL THE SACRED NAMES, WHILE INNOCENT BLOOD POOLS AND PULSES AT OUR FEET.
I looked up at the fat man and whined a query. He patted me on the back of the neck, sleepily.
OF COURSE SHE DOESN'T LOVE YOU, BOY. SHE HARDLY EVEN EXISTS ON THIS PLANE, IN ANY MATERIAL SENSE.
The snow began to fall once more. The bonfire was going out.

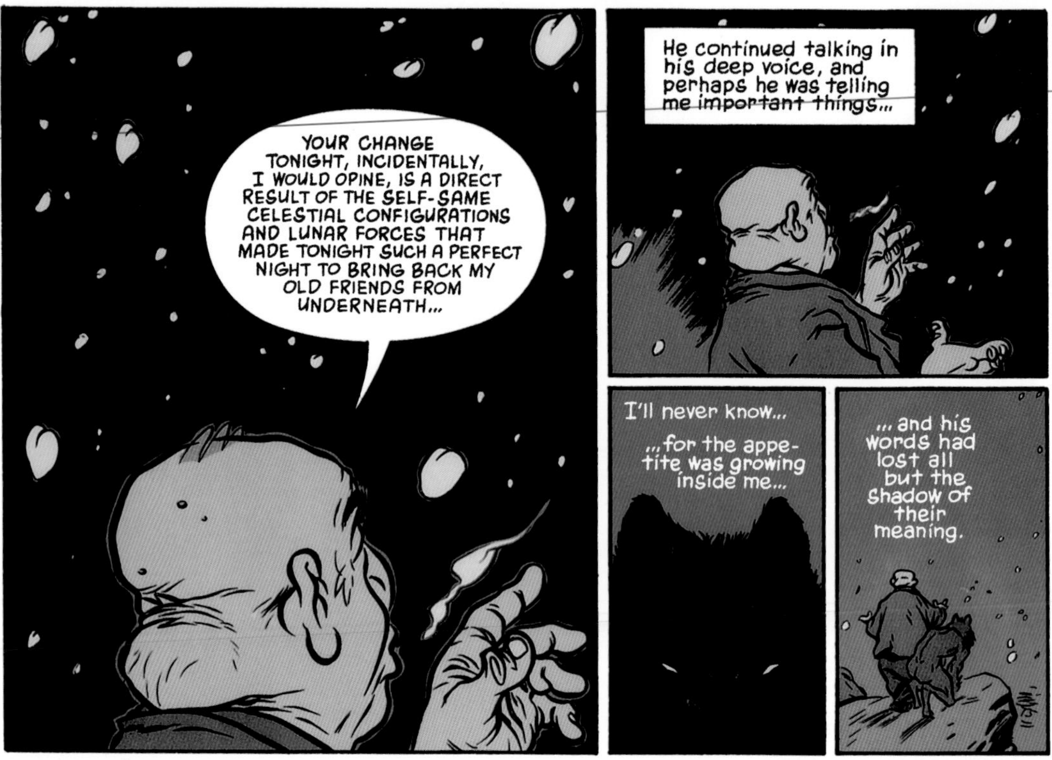
YOUR CHANGE TONIGHT, INCIDENTALLY, I WOULD OPINE, IS A DIRECT RESULT OF THE SELF-SAME CELESTIAL CONFIGURATIONS AND LUNAR FORCES THAT MADE TONIGHT SUCH A PERFECT NIGHT TO BRING BACK MY OLD FRIENDS FROM UNDERNEATH...
He continued talking in his deep voice, and perhaps he was telling me important things...
I'll never know...
...for the appetite was growing inside me...
...and his words had lost all but the shadow of their meaning.

I had no further interest in the sea or the clifftop or the fat man. There were deer running in the woods beyond the meadow: I could smell them on the winter night's air.

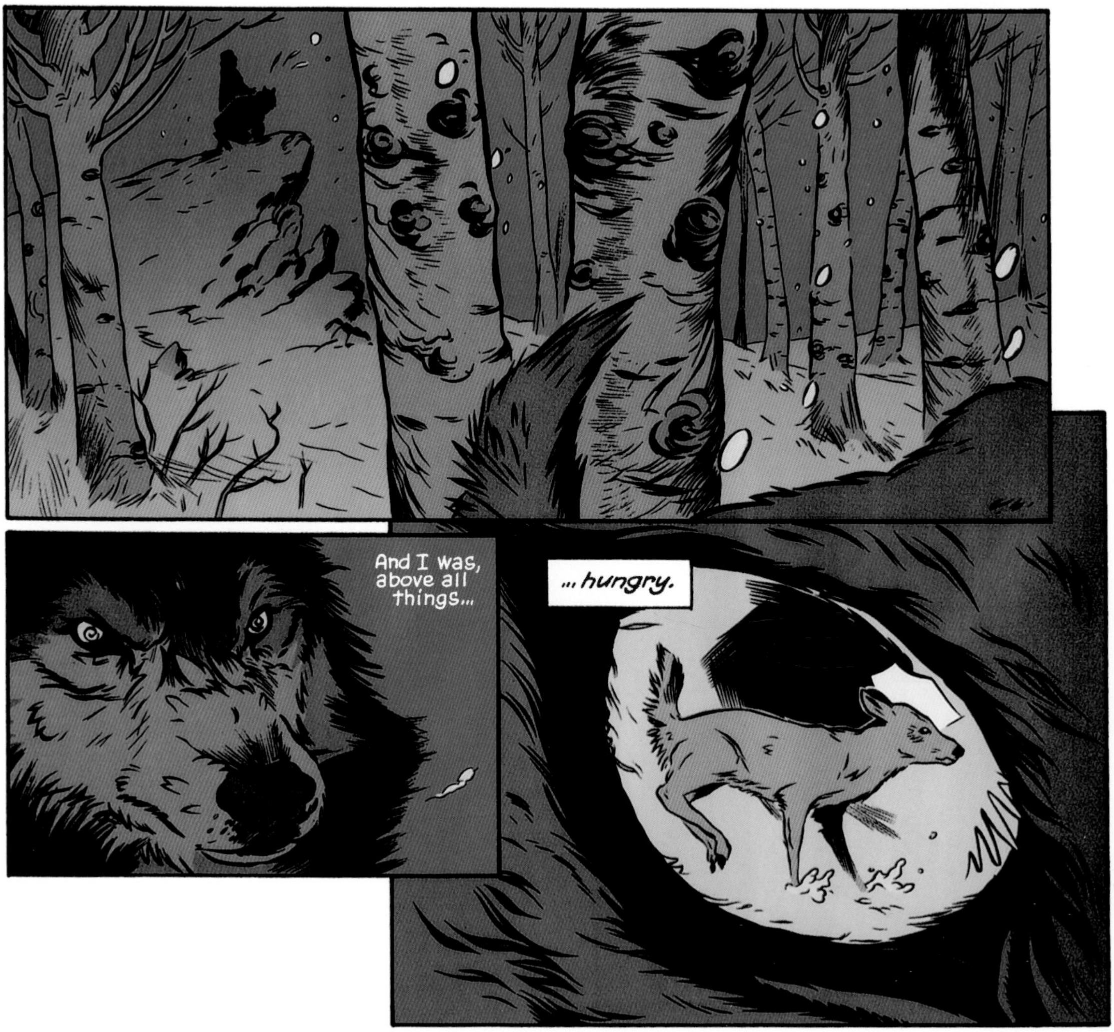
And I was, above all things...
...hungry.

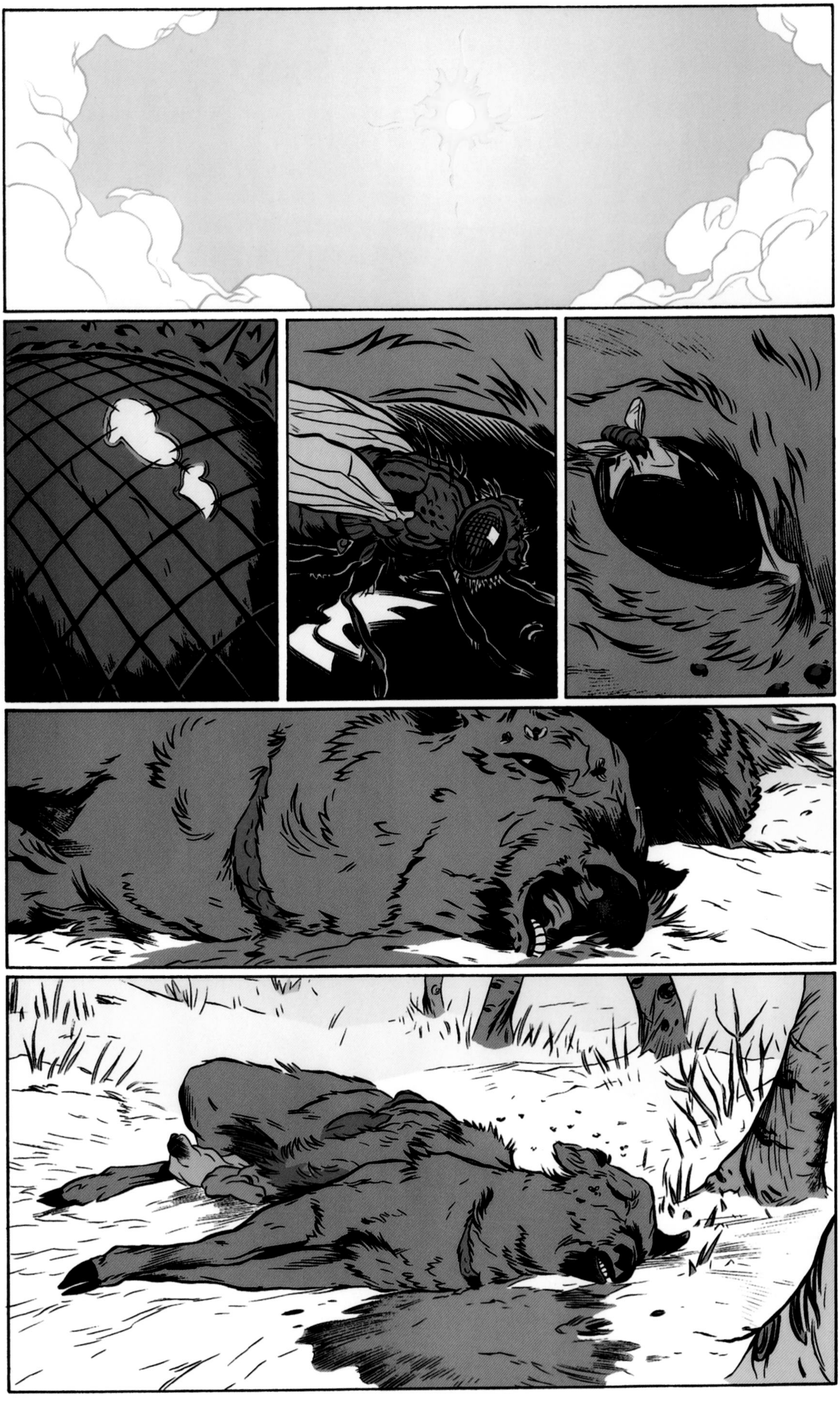

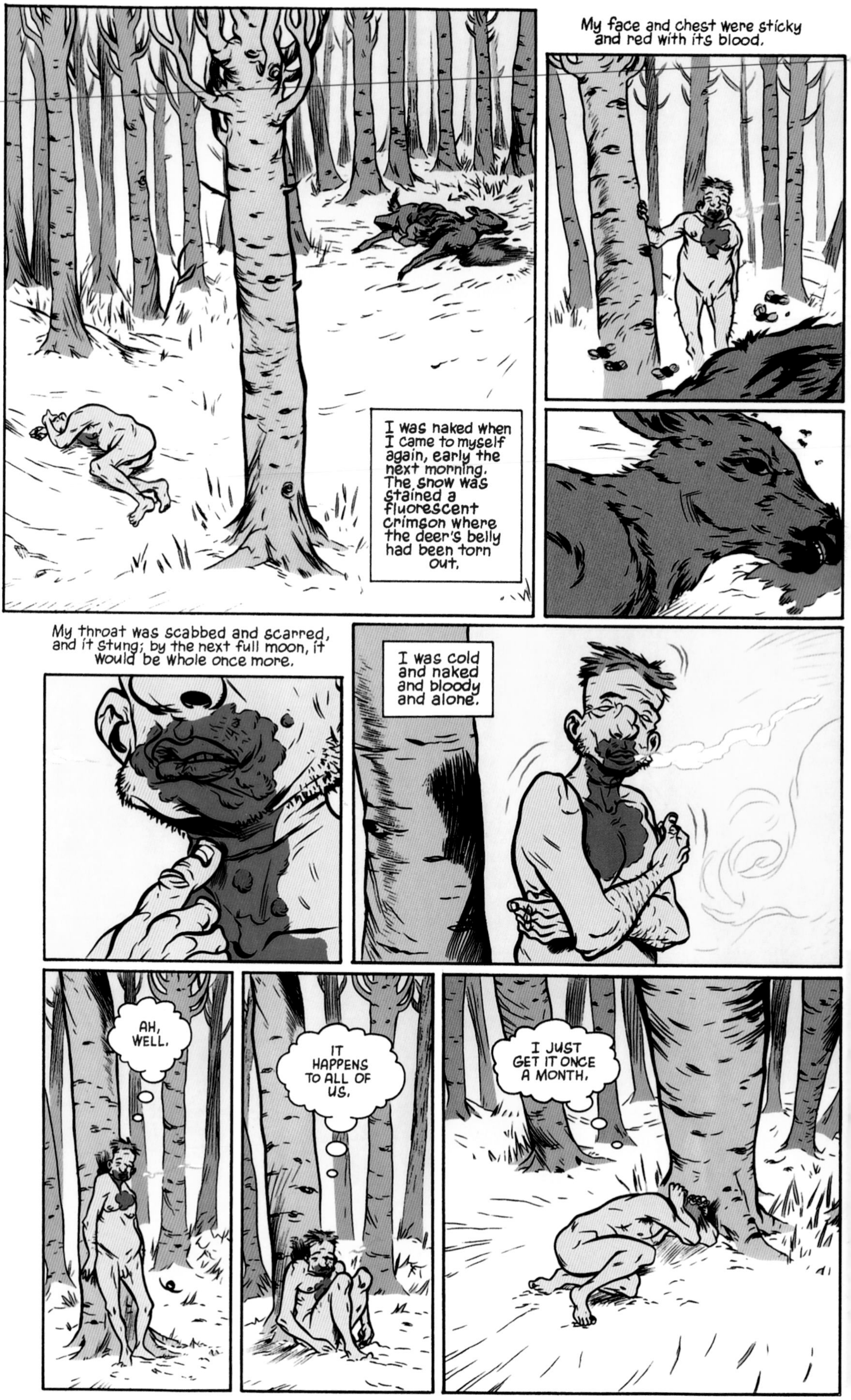
I was naked when I came to myself again, early the next morning. The snow was stained a fluorescent crimson where the deer's belly had been torn out.
My face and chest were sticky and red with its blood.
My throat was scabbed and scarred, and it stung; by the next full moon, it would be whole once more.
I was cold and naked and bloody and alone.
AH, WELL.
IT HAPPENS TO ALL OF US.
I JUST GET IT ONCE A MONTH.

I was painfully exhausted, but I would hold out until I found a deserted barn, or a cave, and then I was going to sleep for a couple of weeks.

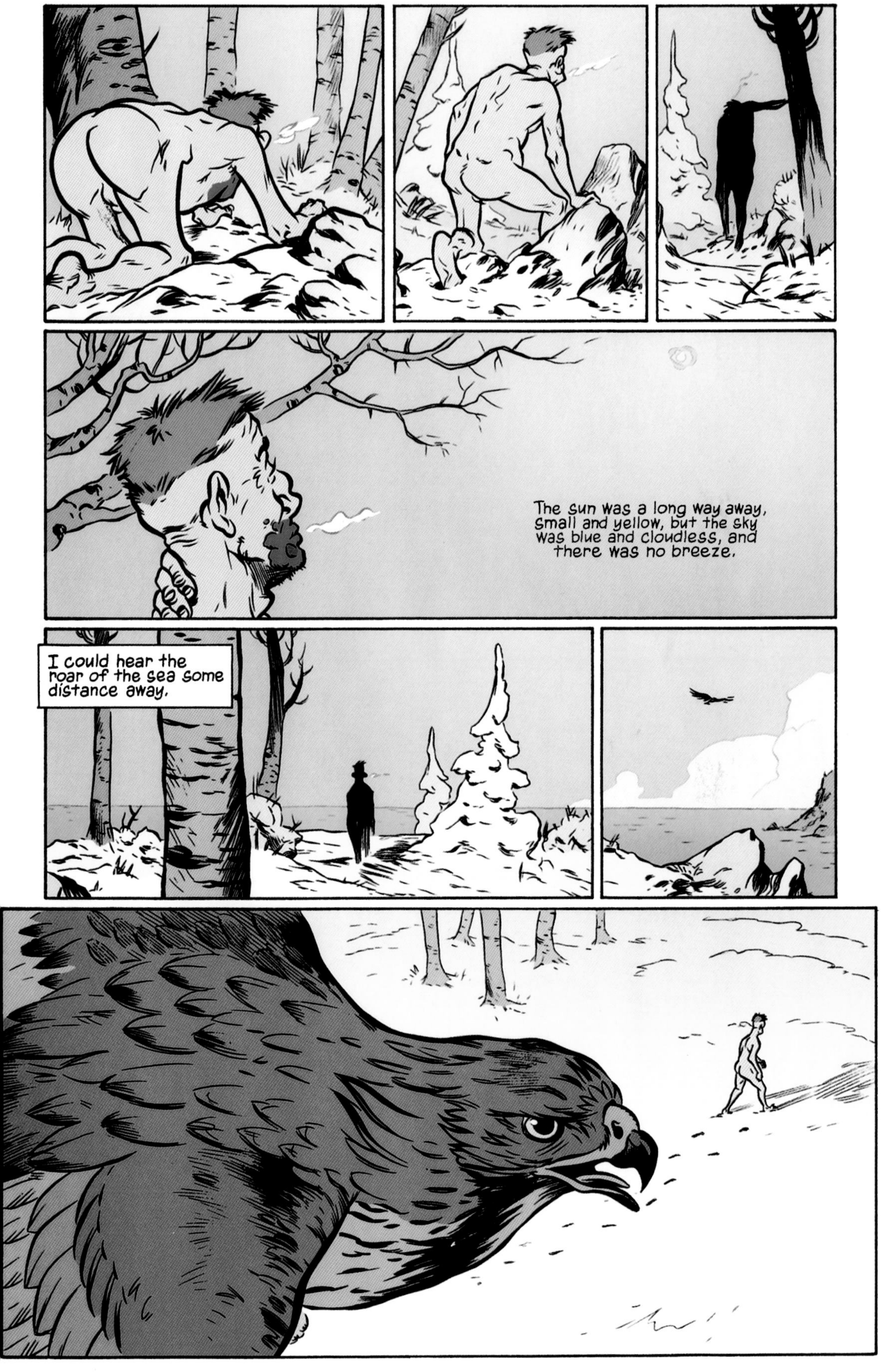
The sun was a long way away, small and yellow, but the sky was blue and cloudless, and there was no breeze.
I could hear the roar of the sea some distance away.

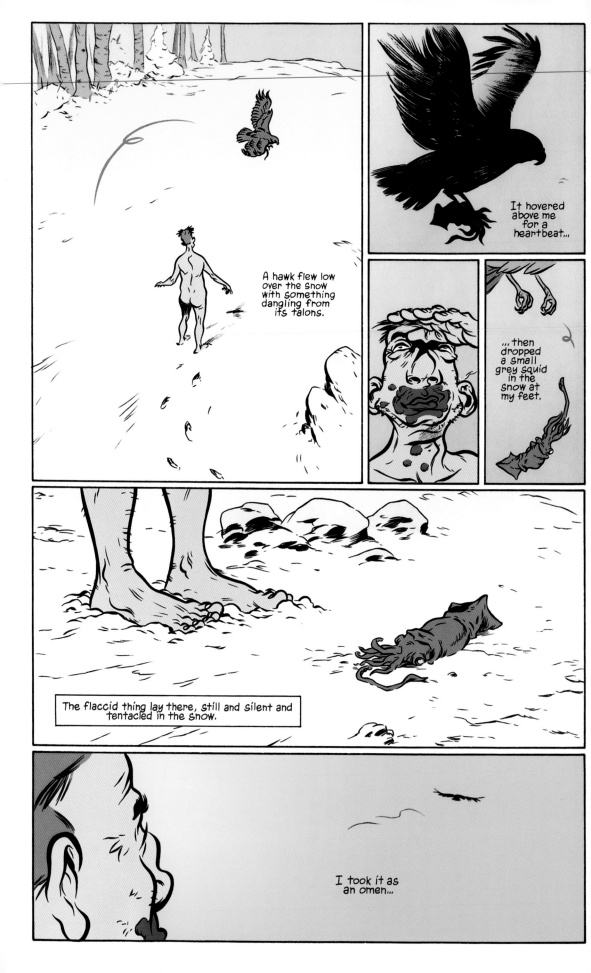

A hawk flew low over the snow with something dangling from its talons.

It hovered above me for a heartbeat...

...then dropped a small grey squid in the snow at my feet.

The flaccid thing lay there, still and silent and tentacled in the snow.

I took it as an omen...

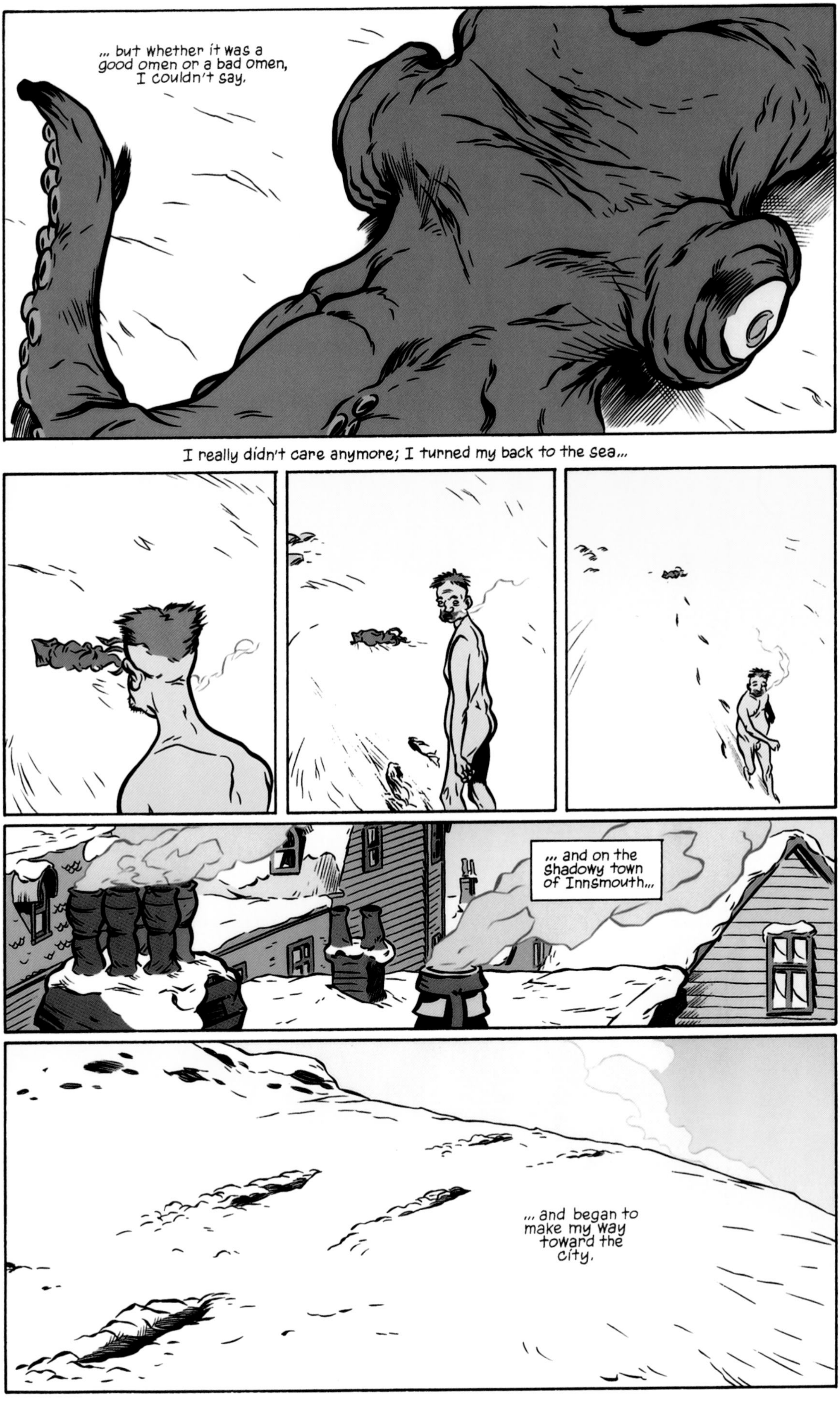
... but whether it was a good omen or a bad omen, I couldn't say.
I really didn't care anymore; I turned my back to the sea...
... and on the shadowy town of Innsmouth...
... and began to make my way toward the city.

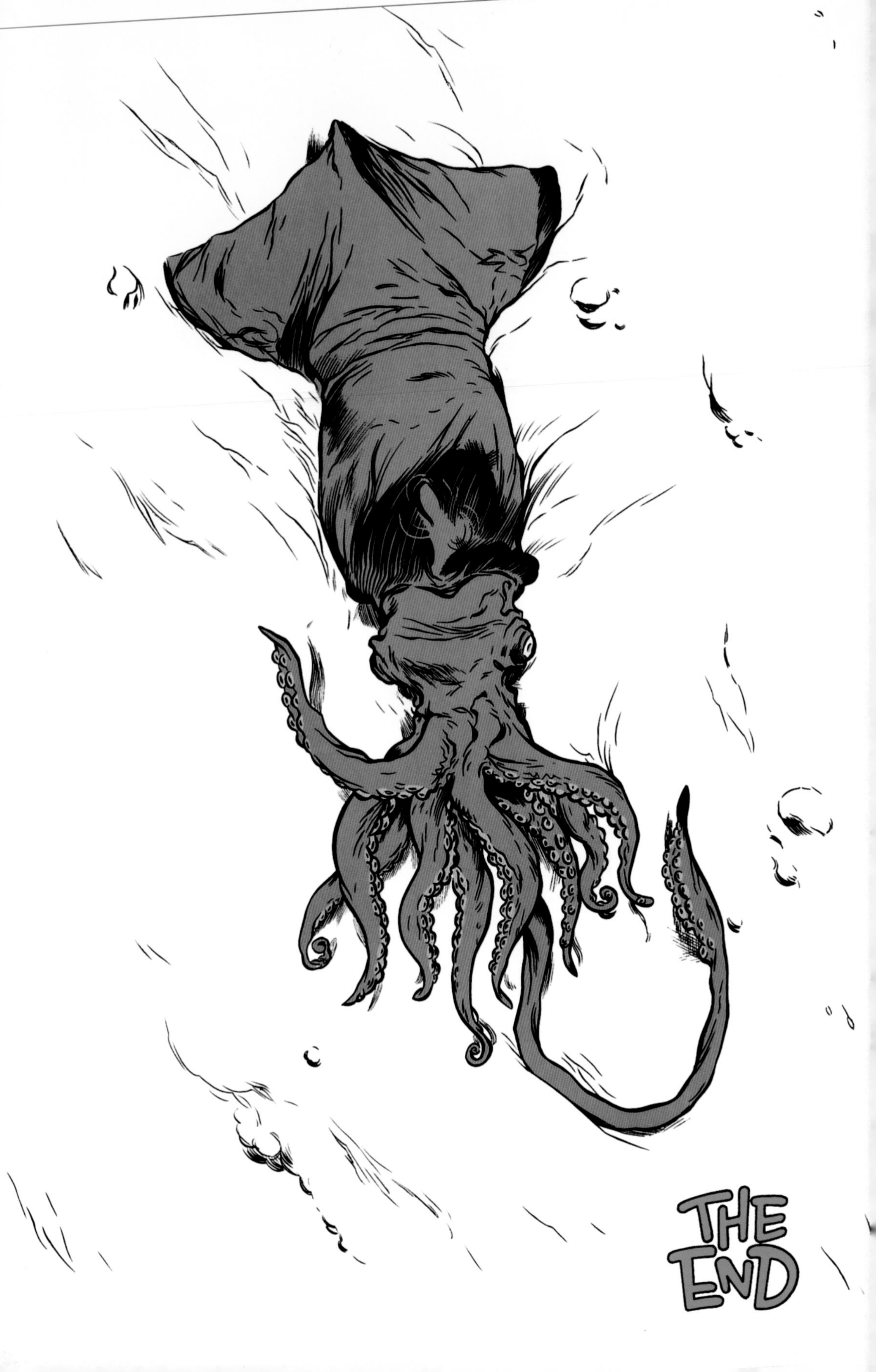
THE END

ONLY THE END OF THE WORLD AGAIN™

SKETCHBOOK

Featured in this sketchbook section are high-quality scans
of the original cover and inside front cover art followed by the
complete layouts drawn by P. Craig Russell and the complete
inks by Troy Nixey—scanned from the original artwork and
not digitally cleaned up to present a side-by-side
comparison of the actual, original artwork.

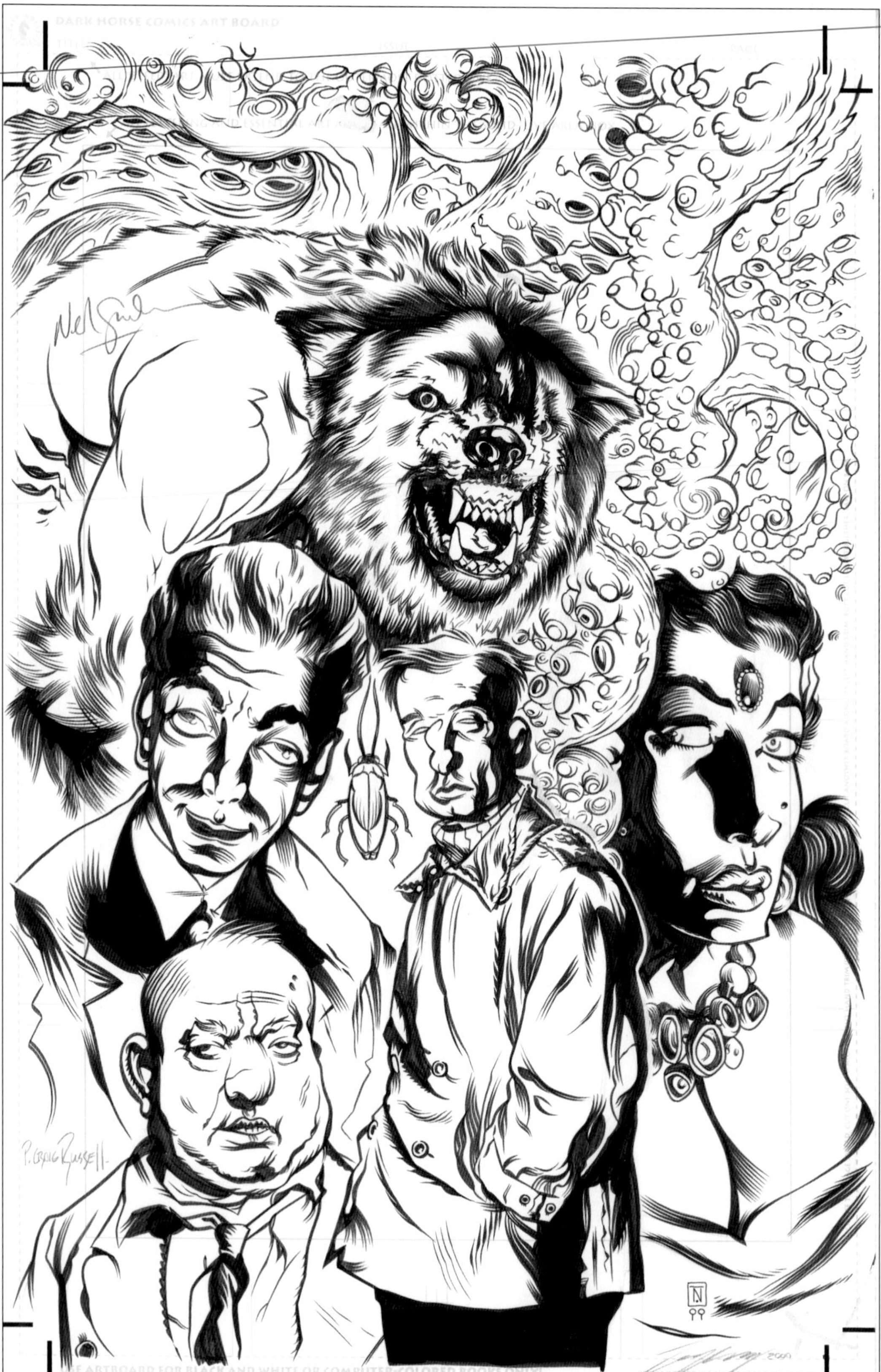
DARK HORSE COMICS ART BOARD
P. CRAIG RUSSELL
USE ARTBOARD FOR BLACK AND WHITE OR COMPUTER-COLORED BOOKS ONLY!

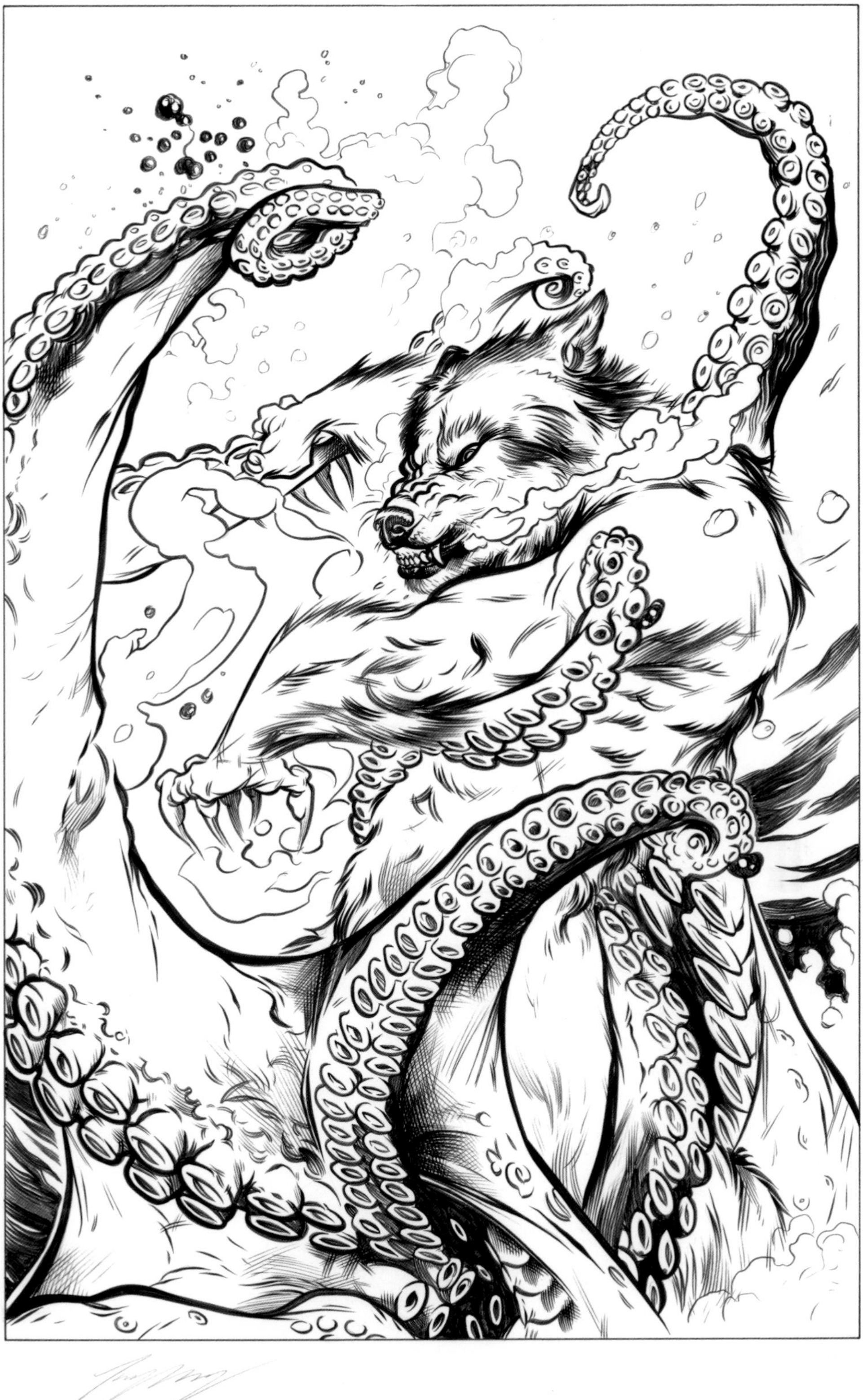

IT WAS A BAD DAY.

I WOKE UP NAKED IN THE BED,
WITH A CRAMP IN MY STOMACH,
FEELING MORE OR LESS LIKE
HELL, SOMETHING ABOUT THE
QUALITY OF THE LIGHT STRETCHED
AND METALLIC, LIKE THE COLOUR
OF A MIGRAINE, TOLD ME IT WAS
AFTERNOON.

THE ROOM WAS FREEZING...LIT-
ERALLY: THERE WAS A THIN CRUST
OF ICE ON THE INSIDE OF THE WIN-
DOWS. THE SHEETS ON THE BED
AROUND ME WERE RIPPED AND
CLAWED, AND THERE WAS ANI-
MAL HAIR IN THE BED.

IT ITCHED.

NEIL GAIMAN'S

ONLY THE END OF the WORLD AGAIN

ADAPTATION AND LAYOUTS by P. CRAIG RUSSELL
ART by TROY NIXEY
LETTERING by GALEN SHOWMAN

It was a bad day.

I woke up naked in the bed, with a cramp in my stomach, feeling more or less like hell. Something about the quality of the light, stretched and metallic, like the colour of a migraine, told me it was afternoon.

The room was freezing... literally: there was a thin crust of ice on the inside of the windows. The sheets on the bed around me were ripped and clawed, and there was animal hair in the bed.

It itched.

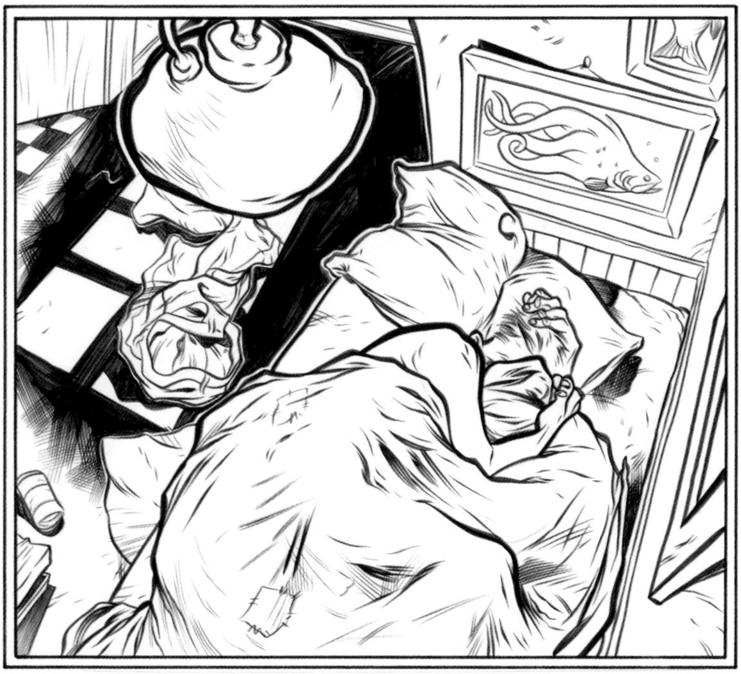

NEIL GAIMAN'S

ONLY THE END of the WORLD AGAIN

To STEFAN,
THANKS ALOT

ADAPTATION BY P. CRAIG RUSSELL
ARTWORK & LAYOUT BY TROY NIXEY
LETTERING BY SEAN KONOT

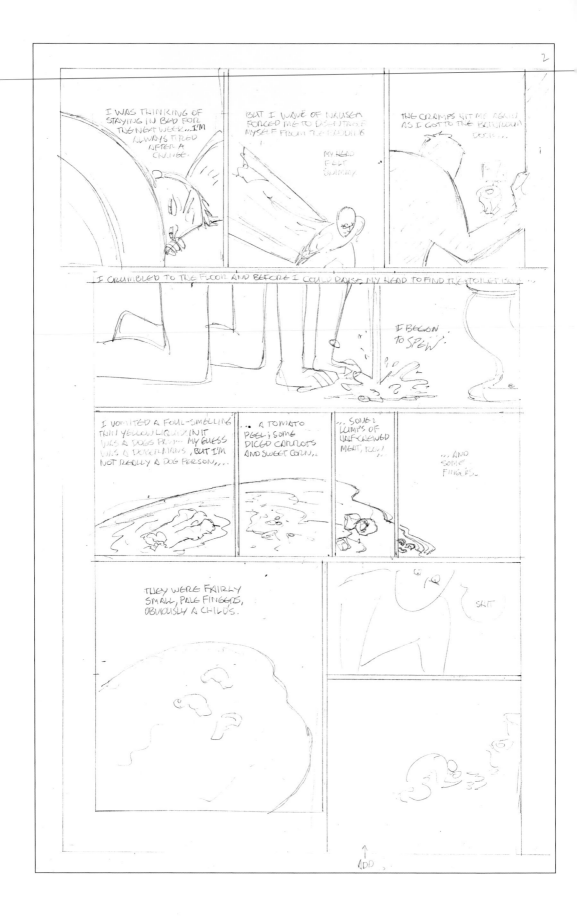

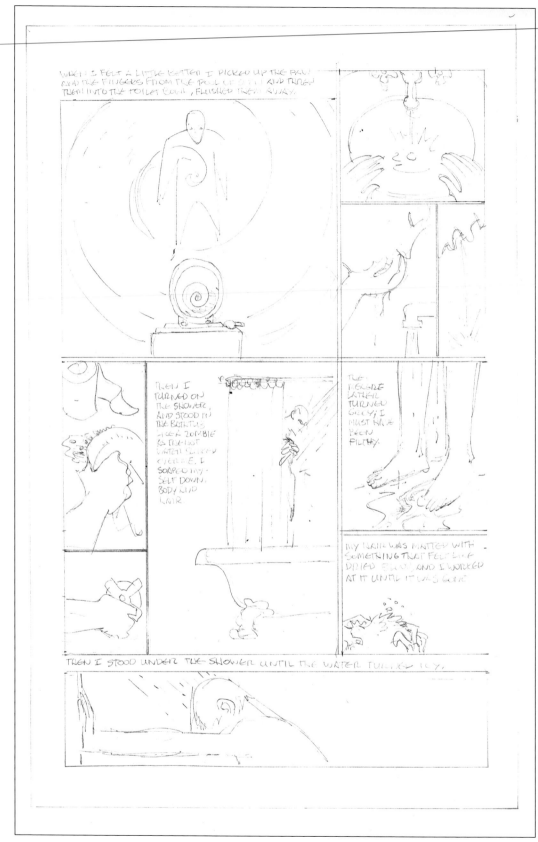

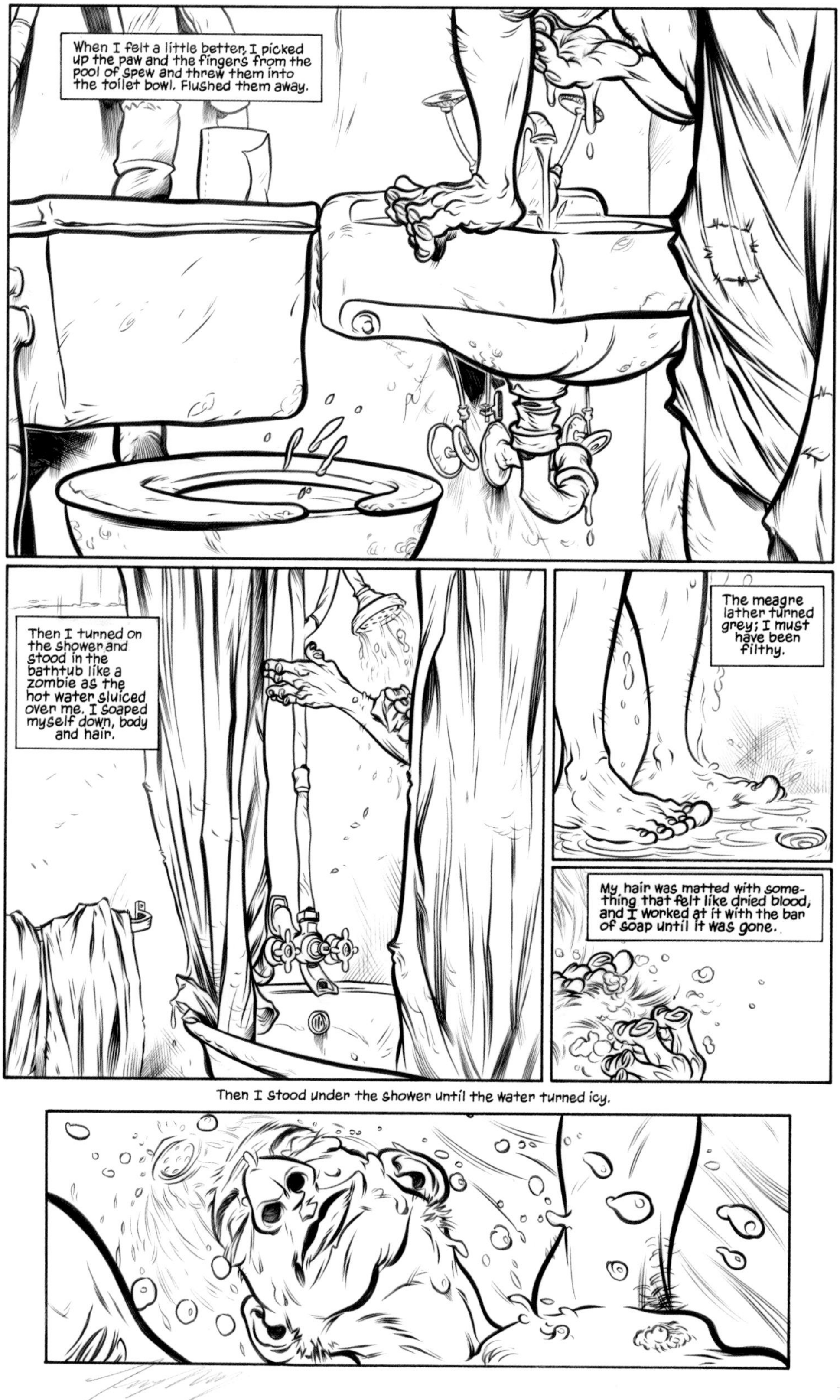
When I felt a little better, I picked up the paw and the fingers from the pool of spew and threw them into the toilet bowl. Flushed them away.
Then I turned on the shower and stood in the bathtub like a zombie as the hot water sluiced over me. I soaped myself down, body and hair.
The meagre lather turned grey; I must have been filthy.
My hair was matted with something that felt like dried blood, and I worked at it with the bar of soap until it was gone.
Then I stood under the shower until the water turned icy.

DRYING HAIR
AS HE LEAVES
BATHROOM

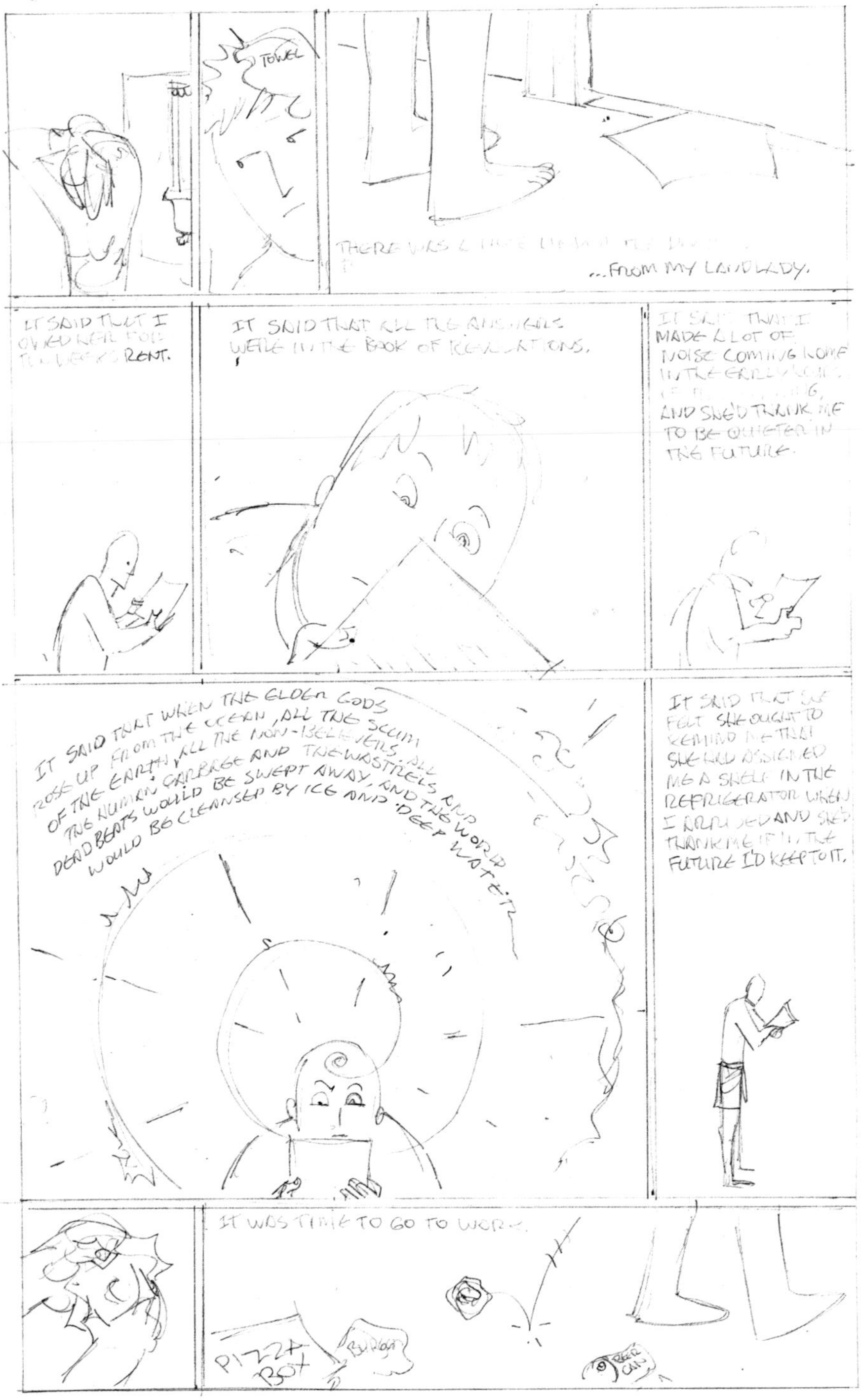

CRUMBLES
UP NOTE

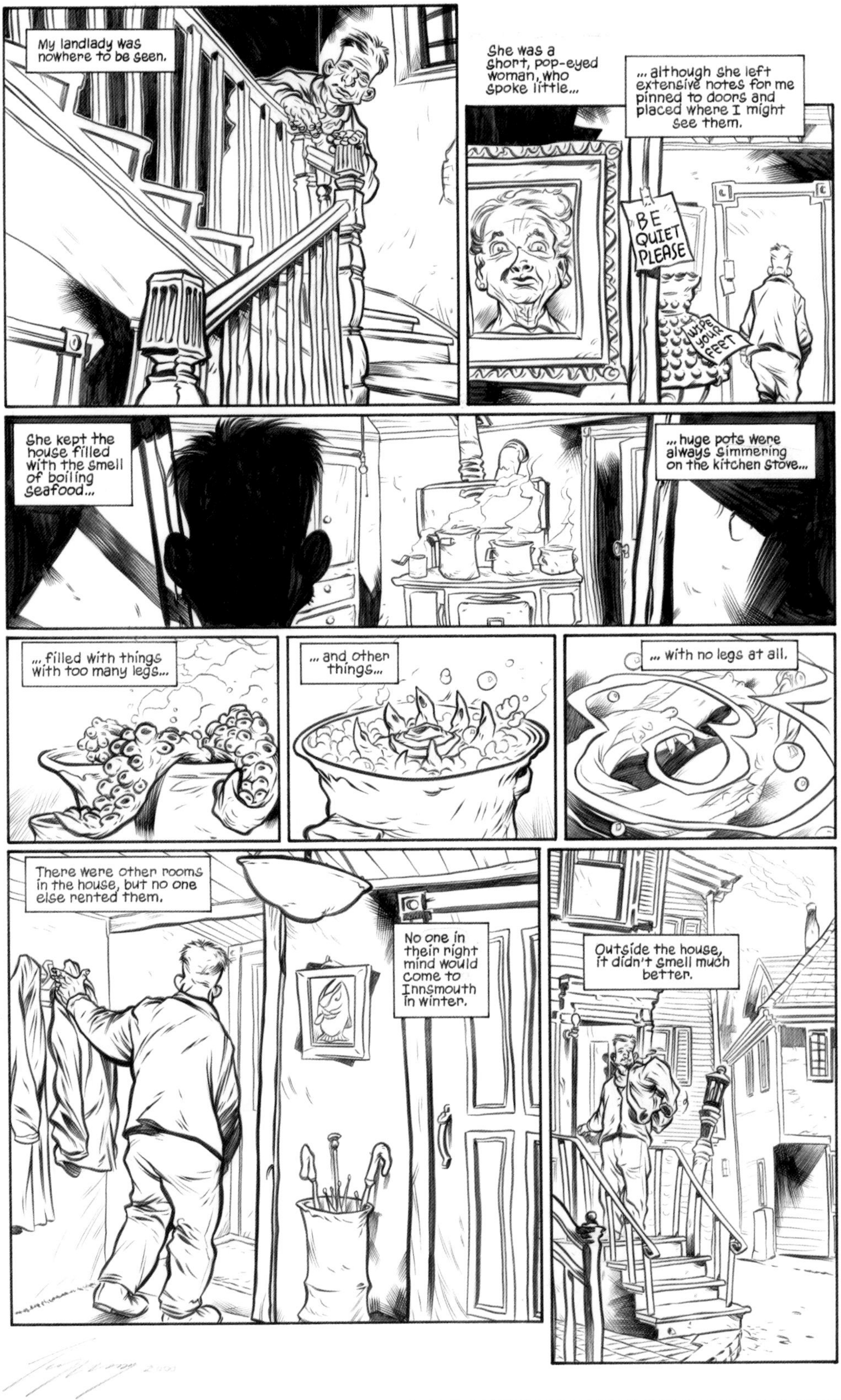
My landlady was nowhere to be seen.
She was a short, pop-eyed woman, who spoke little...
...although she left extensive notes for me pinned to doors and placed where I might see them.
BE QUIET PLEASE
WIPE YOUR FEET
She kept the house filled with the smell of boiling seafood...
...huge pots were always simmering on the kitchen stove...
...filled with things with too many legs...
...and other things...
...with no legs at all.
There were other rooms in the house, but no one else rented them.
No one in their right mind would come to Innsmouth in winter.
Outside the house, it didn't smell much better.

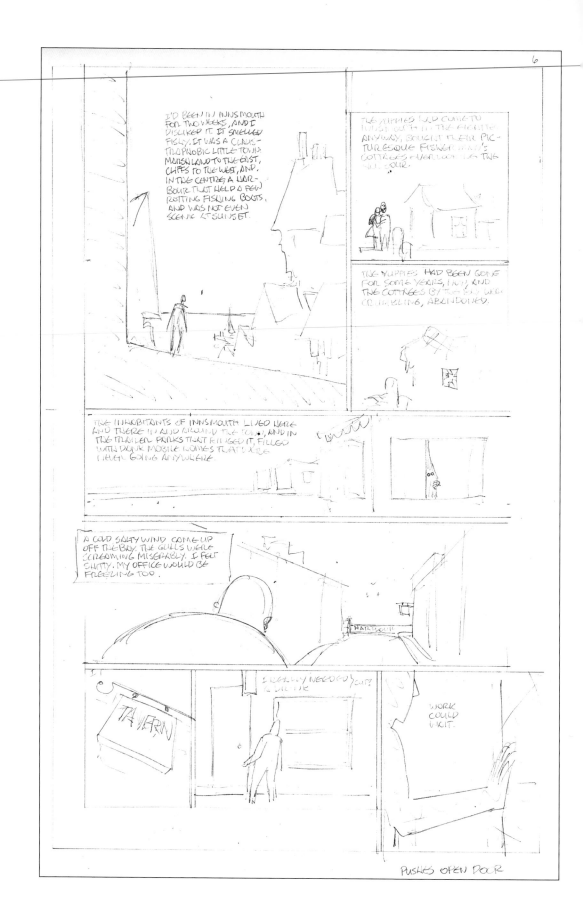

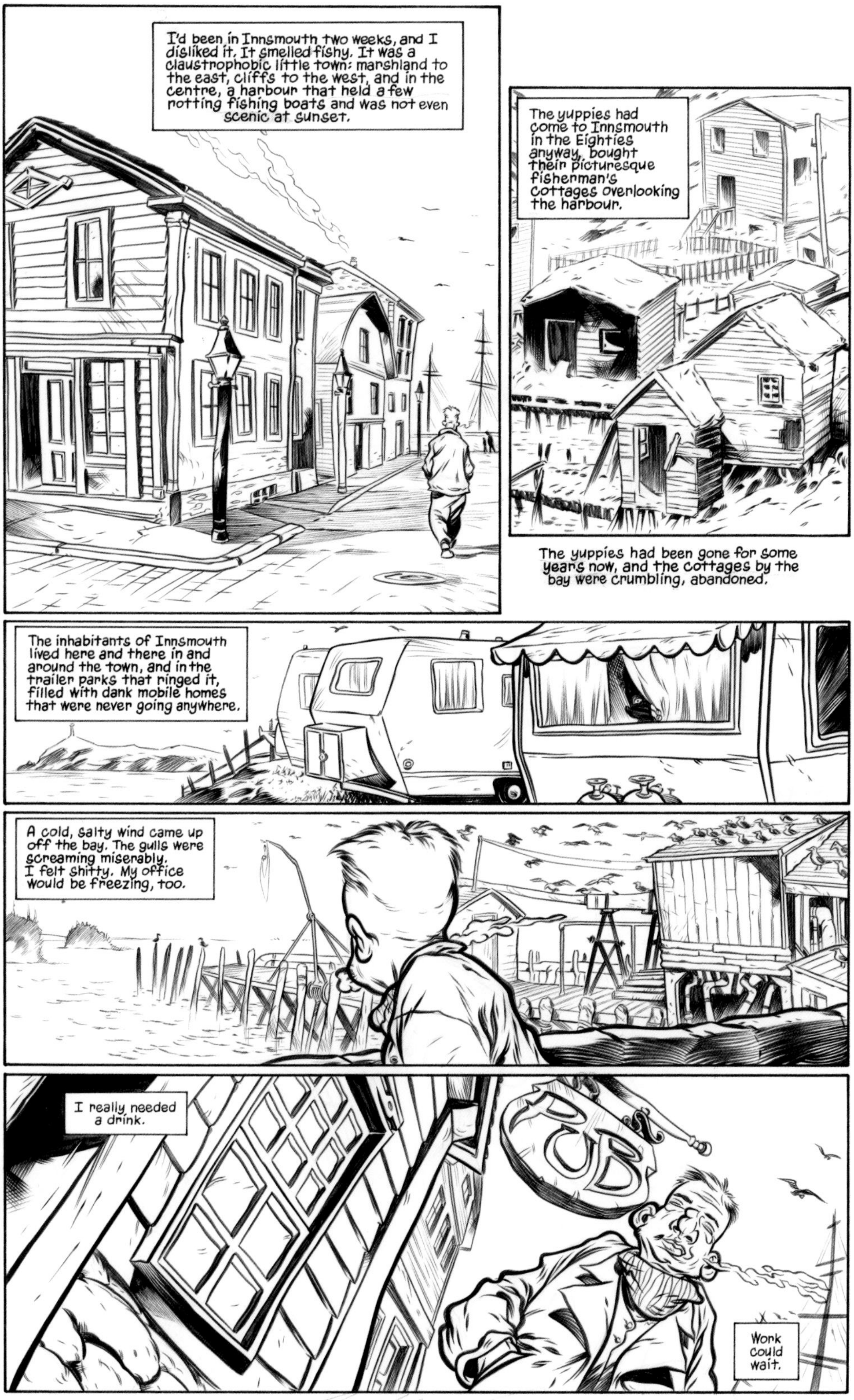
I'd been in Innsmouth two weeks, and I disliked it. It smelled fishy. It was a claustrophobic little town: marshland to the east, cliffs to the west, and in the centre, a harbour that held a few rotting fishing boats and was not even scenic at sunset.
The yuppies had come to Innsmouth in the Eighties anyway, bought their picturesque fisherman's cottages overlooking the harbour.
The yuppies had been gone for some years now, and the cottages by the bay were crumbling, abandoned.
The inhabitants of Innsmouth lived here and there in and around the town, and in the trailer parks that ringed it, filled with dank mobile homes that were never going anywhere.
A cold, salty wind came up off the bay. The gulls were screaming miserably. I felt shitty. My office would be freezing, too.
I really needed a drink.
PUB
Work could wait.

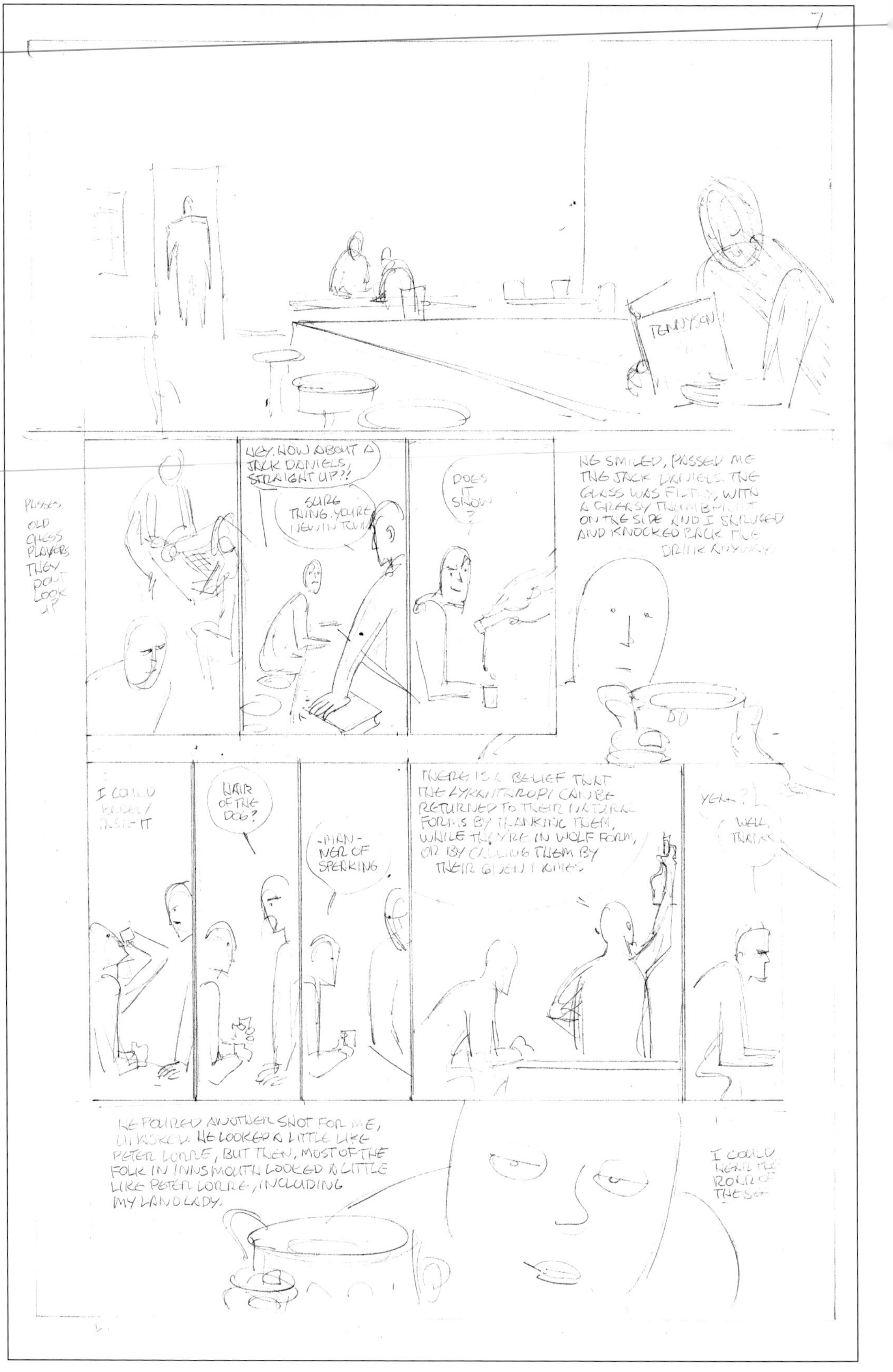
7
TENNYSON
PASSES OLD CHESS PLAYERS THEY DON'T LOOK UP
HEY. HOW ABOUT A JACK DANIELS, STRAIGHT UP?!
SURE THING. YOU'RE NEW IN TOWN
DOES IT SHOW?
HE SMILED, PASSED ME THE JACK DANIELS. THE GLASS WAS FILTHY, WITH A GREASY THUMBPRINT ON THE SIDE AND I SHRUGGED AND KNOCKED BACK THE DRINK ANYWAY.
I COULD
HAIR OF THE DOG?
-MAN-NER OF SPEAKING
THERE IS A BELIEF THAT THE LYKANTHROPI CAN BE RETURNED TO THEIR NATURAL FORMS BY THANKING THEM, WHILE THEY'RE IN WOLF FORM, OR BY CALLING THEM BY THEIR GIVEN NAMES
YEAH?
WELL, THANKS
HE POURED ANOTHER SHOT FOR ME, UNASKED. HE LOOKED A LITTLE LIKE PETER LORRE, BUT THEN, MOST OF THE FOLK IN INNSMOUTH LOOKED A LITTLE LIKE PETER LORRE, INCLUDING MY LANDLADY.
I COULD HEAR THE ROAR OF THE SE

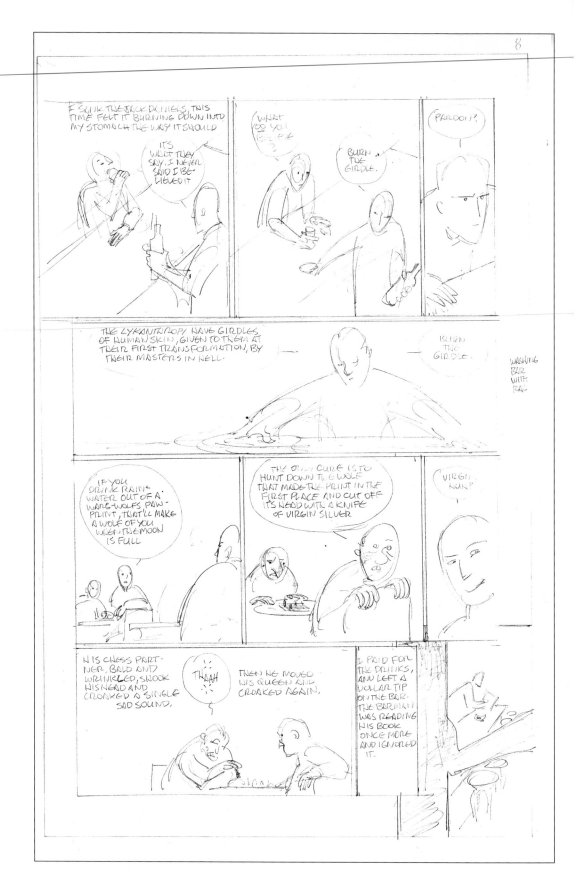

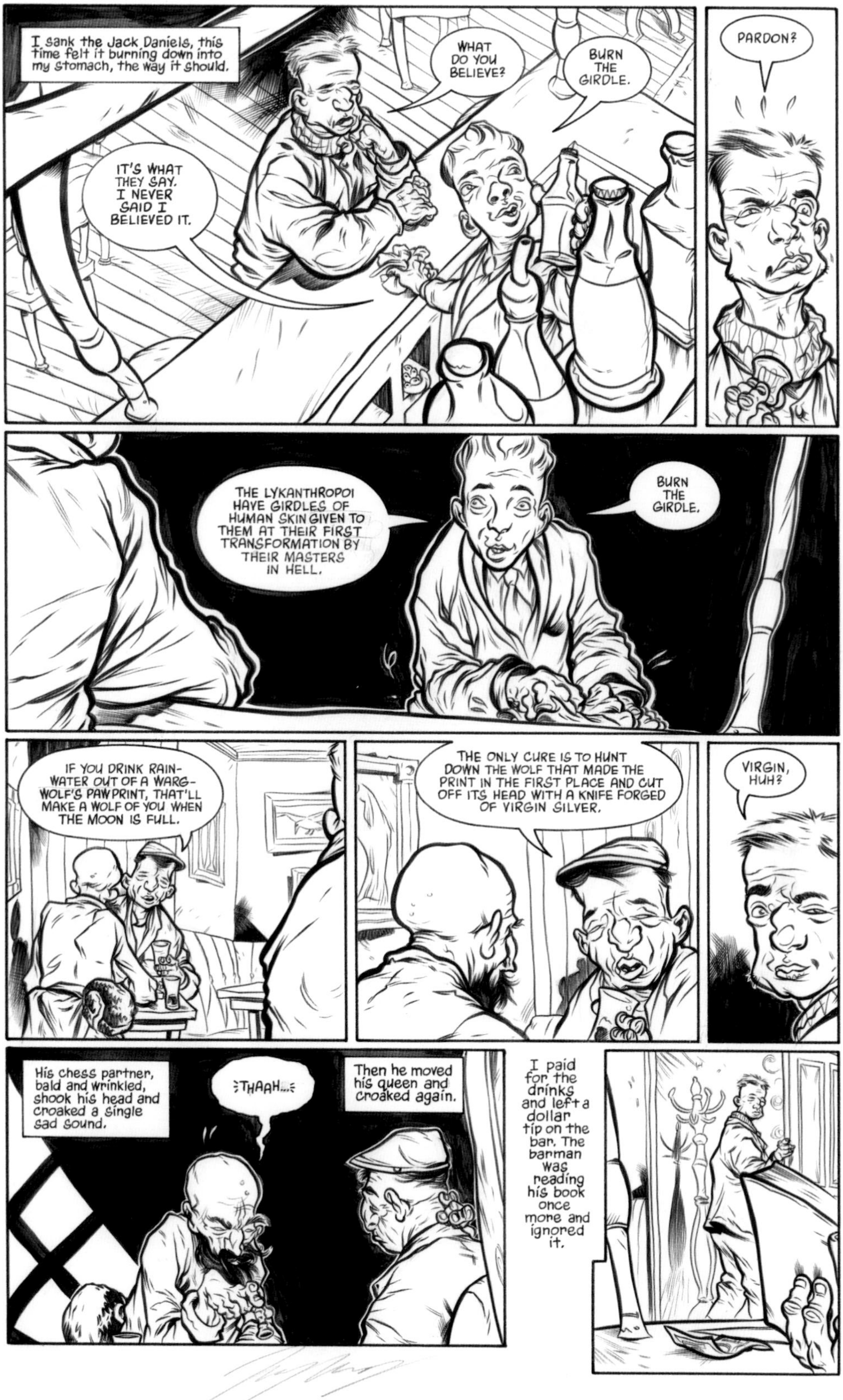
I sank the Jack Daniels, this time felt it burning down into my stomach, the way it should.
WHAT DO YOU BELIEVE?
BURN THE GIRDLE.
IT'S WHAT THEY SAY. I NEVER SAID I BELIEVED IT.
PARDON?
THE LYKANTHROPOI HAVE GIRDLES OF HUMAN SKIN GIVEN TO THEM AT THEIR FIRST TRANSFORMATION BY THEIR MASTERS IN HELL.
BURN THE GIRDLE.
IF YOU DRINK RAIN-WATER OUT OF A WARG-WOLF'S PAWPRINT, THAT'LL MAKE A WOLF OF YOU WHEN THE MOON IS FULL.
THE ONLY CURE IS TO HUNT DOWN THE WOLF THAT MADE THE PRINT IN THE FIRST PLACE AND CUT OFF ITS HEAD WITH A KNIFE FORGED OF VIRGIN SILVER.
VIRGIN, HUH?
His chess partner, bald and wrinkled, shook his head and croaked a single sad sound.
THAAH...
Then he moved his queen and croaked again.
I paid for the drinks and left a dollar tip on the bar. The barman was reading his book once more and ignored it.

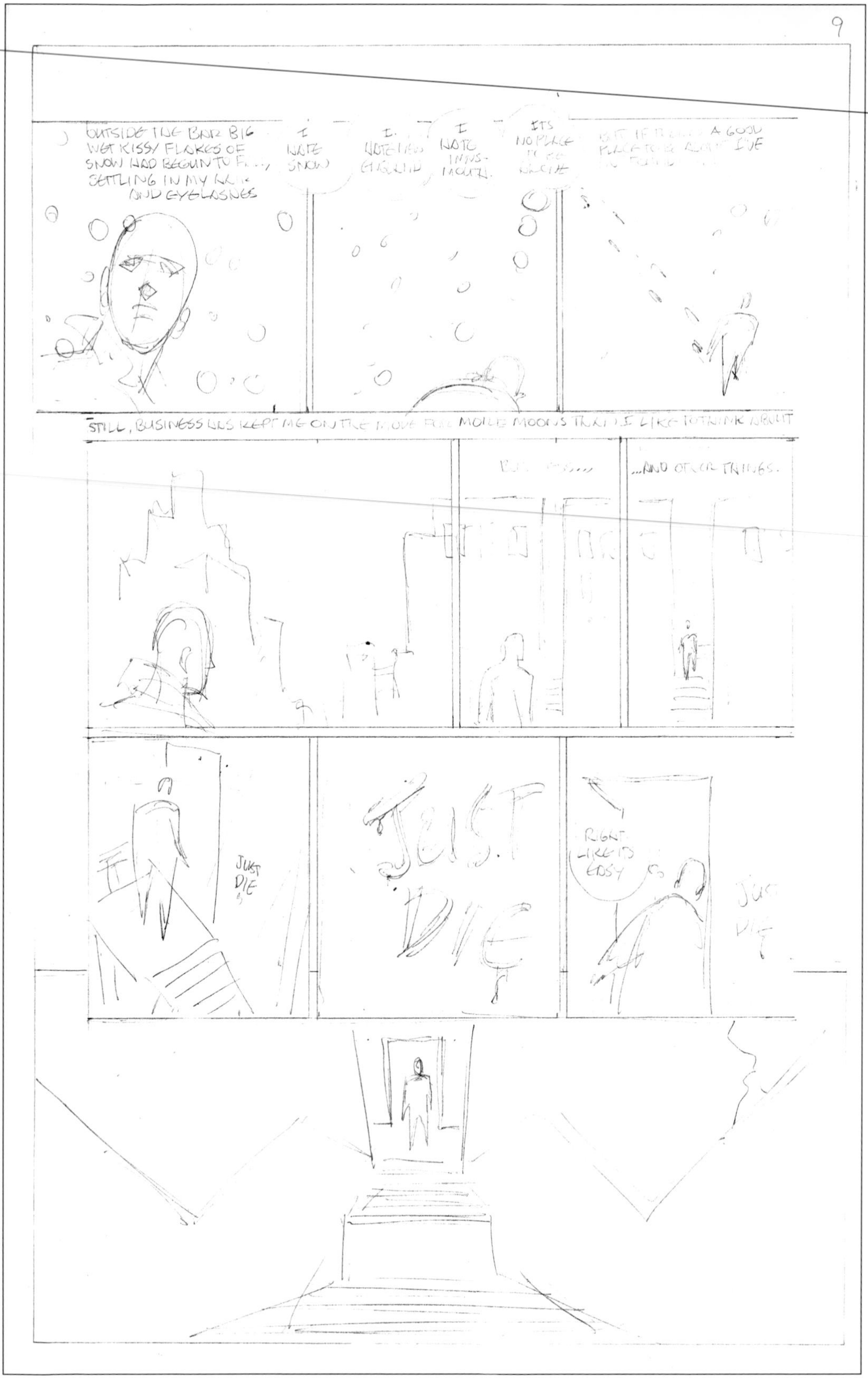
9
OUTSIDE THE BAR BIG WET KISSY FLAKES OF SNOW HAD BEGUN TO
SETTLING IN MY
AND
I HATE SNOW
I HATE
I HATE INNSMOUTH.
ITS NO PLACE
A GOOD PLACE
STILL, BUSINESS HAS KEPT ME ON THE MOVE MORE MOONS THAN I LIKE TO THINK ABOUT
...AND OTHER THINGS.
JUST DIE
JUST DIE
RIGHT. LIKE ITS EASY
JUST DIE

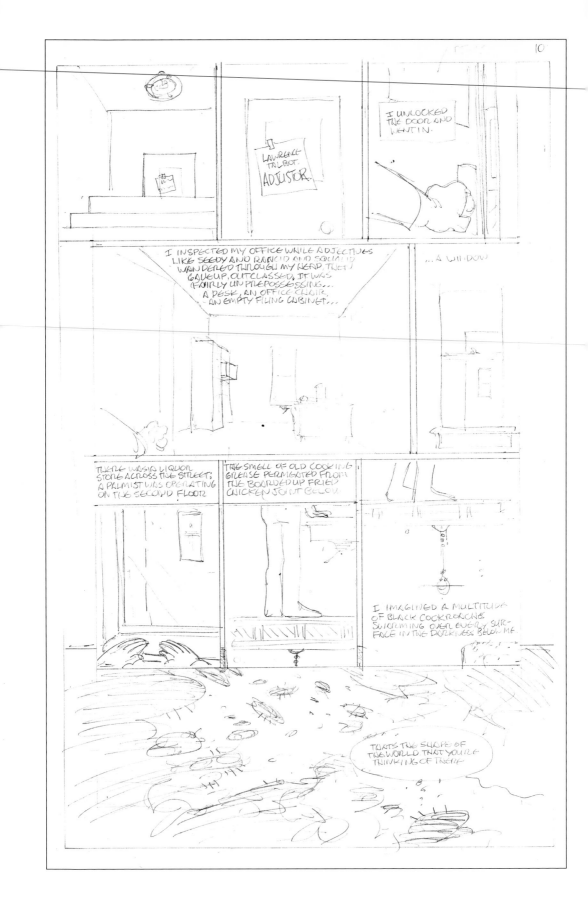

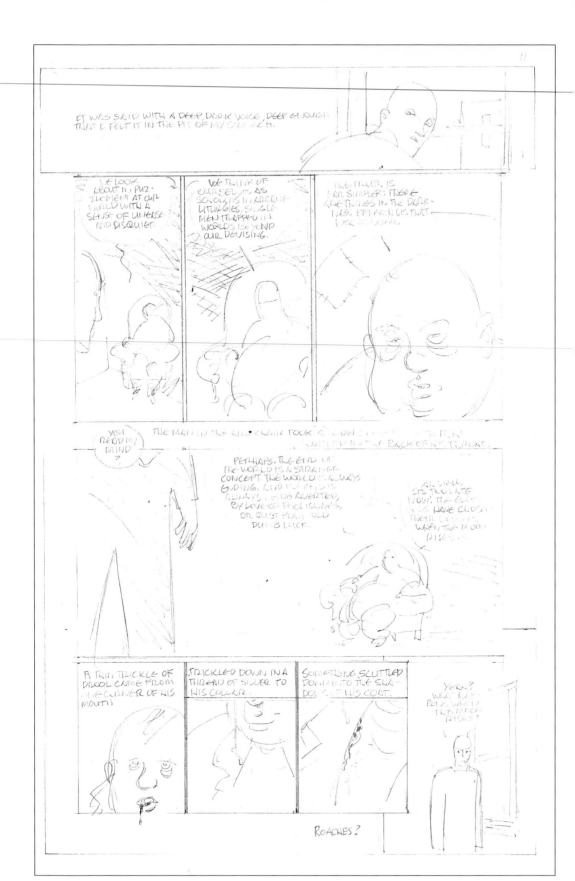

12

THE MAN IN THE GREAT CHAIR STIRRED, OPENED TWO LITTLE EYES, RED AND SWOLLEN, AND BLINKED, TRYING TO SEE

I DREAMED I HAD MANY MOUTHS

EVERY

MOUTH WAS

OPENING

AND CLOSING

INDEPENDENTLY.

SOME

MOUTHS

WERE TALKING

SOME

WHISPERING

SOME

EATING,

"SOME WRITING IN SILENCE"

HE LOOKED AROUND...

WIPED THE SPITTLE FROM THE CORNER OF HIS MOUTH...

SAT BACK IN THE CHAIR, BLINKING PUZZLEDLY.

WHO ARE YOU?

I'M THE GUY THAT RENTS THIS OFFICE.

BRRRPP

SORRY

RISES OUT OF CHAIR

HIS VOICE WAS ODDLY SMALL AND BREATHY FOR SUCH A HUGE MAN. HE LOOKED ME UP AND DOWN BLEARILY

SILVER BULLETS... OLD FASHIONED REMEDY.

YEAH. THAT'S SO OBVIOUS... MUST BE WHY I DIDN'T THINK OF IT. I COULD JUST KICK MYSELF. I REALLY COULD.

YOU'RE MAKING FUN OF AN OLD MAN.

NOT REALLY. I'M SORRY. NOW, GET OUT OF HERE, SOME OF US HAVE WORK TO DO.

HE SHAMBLED

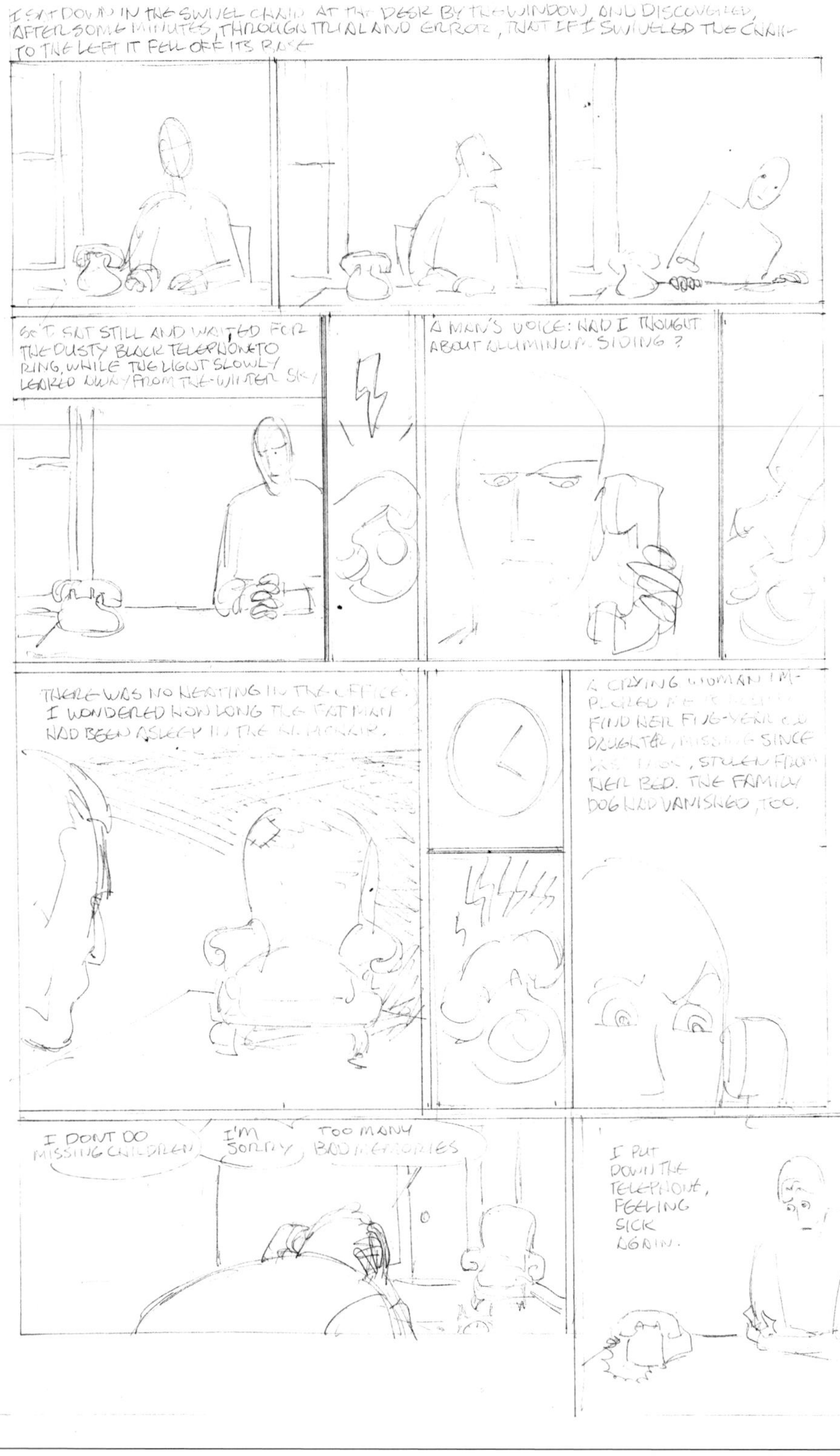
I SAT DOWN IN THE SWIVEL CHAIR AT THE DESK BY THE WINDOW, AND DISCOVERED, AFTER SOME MINUTES, THROUGH TRIAL AND ERROR, THAT IF I SWIVELED THE CHAIR TO THE LEFT IT FELL OFF ITS BASE
SO I SAT STILL AND WAITED FOR THE DUSTY BLACK TELEPHONE TO RING, WHILE THE LIGHT SLOWLY LEAKED AWAY FROM THE WINTER SKY
A MAN'S VOICE: HAD I THOUGHT ABOUT ALUMINUM SIDING?
THERE WAS NO HEATING IN THE OFFICE. I WONDERED HOW LONG THE FAT MAN HAD BEEN ASLEEP IN THE
A CRYING WOMAN IM-PLORED ME
FIND HER FIVE-YEAR
DAUGHTER,
, STOLEN FROM HER BED. THE FAMILY DOG HAD VANISHED, TOO.
I DONT DO MISSING CHILDREN
I'M SORRY
TOO MANY BAD MEMORIES
I PUT DOWN THE TELEPHONE, FEELING SICK AGAIN.

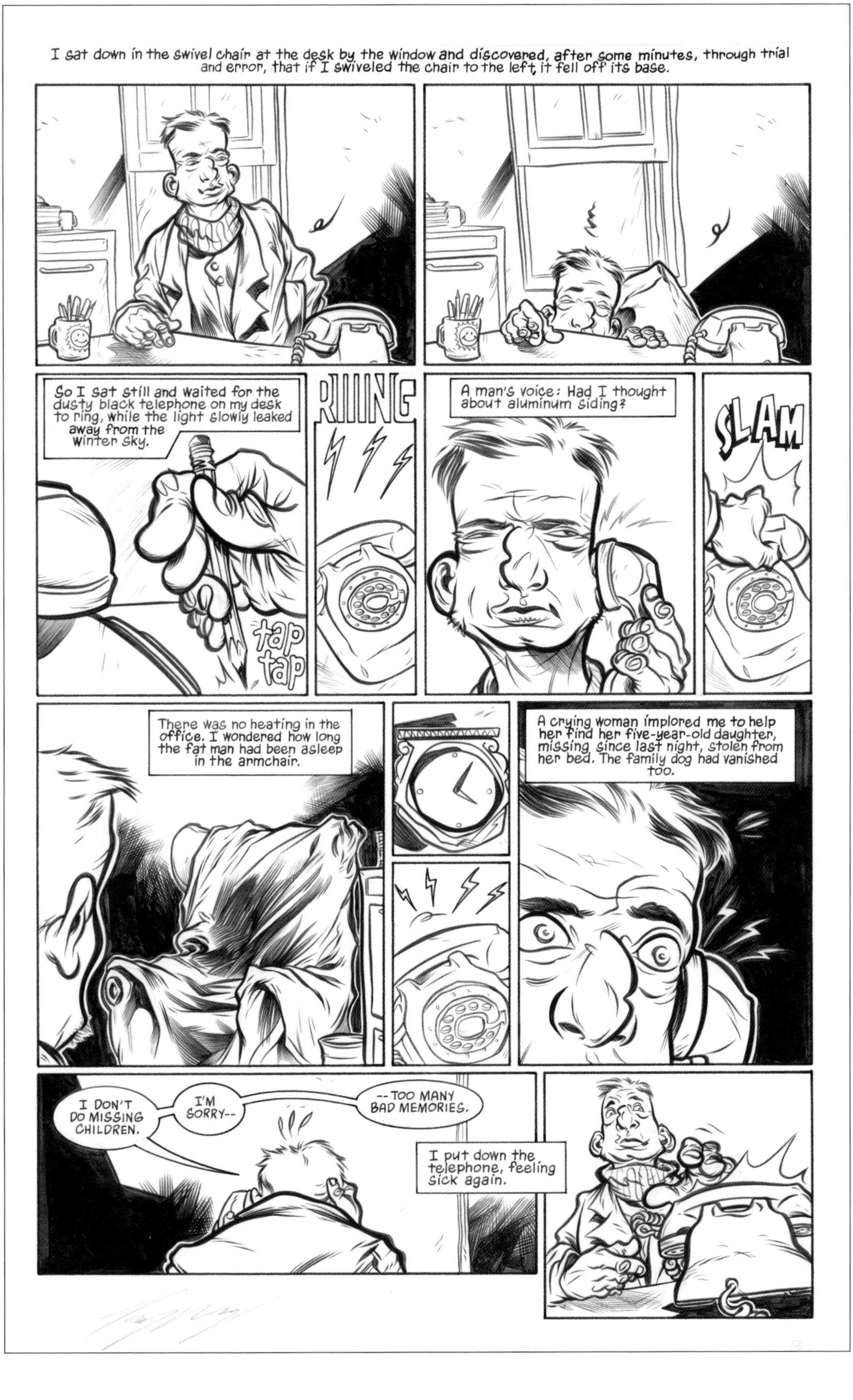

I sat down in the swivel chair at the desk by the window and discovered, after some minutes, through trial and error, that if I swiveled the chair to the left, it fell off its base.
So I sat still and waited for the dusty black telephone on my desk to ring, while the light slowly leaked away from the winter sky.
tap tap
RIIING
A man's voice: Had I thought about aluminum siding?
SLAM
There was no heating in the office. I wondered how long the fat man had been asleep in the armchair.
A crying woman implored me to help her find her five-year-old daughter, missing since last night, stolen from her bed. The family dog had vanished too.
I DON'T DO MISSING CHILDREN.
I'M SORRY--
--TOO MANY BAD MEMORIES.
I put down the telephone, feeling sick again.

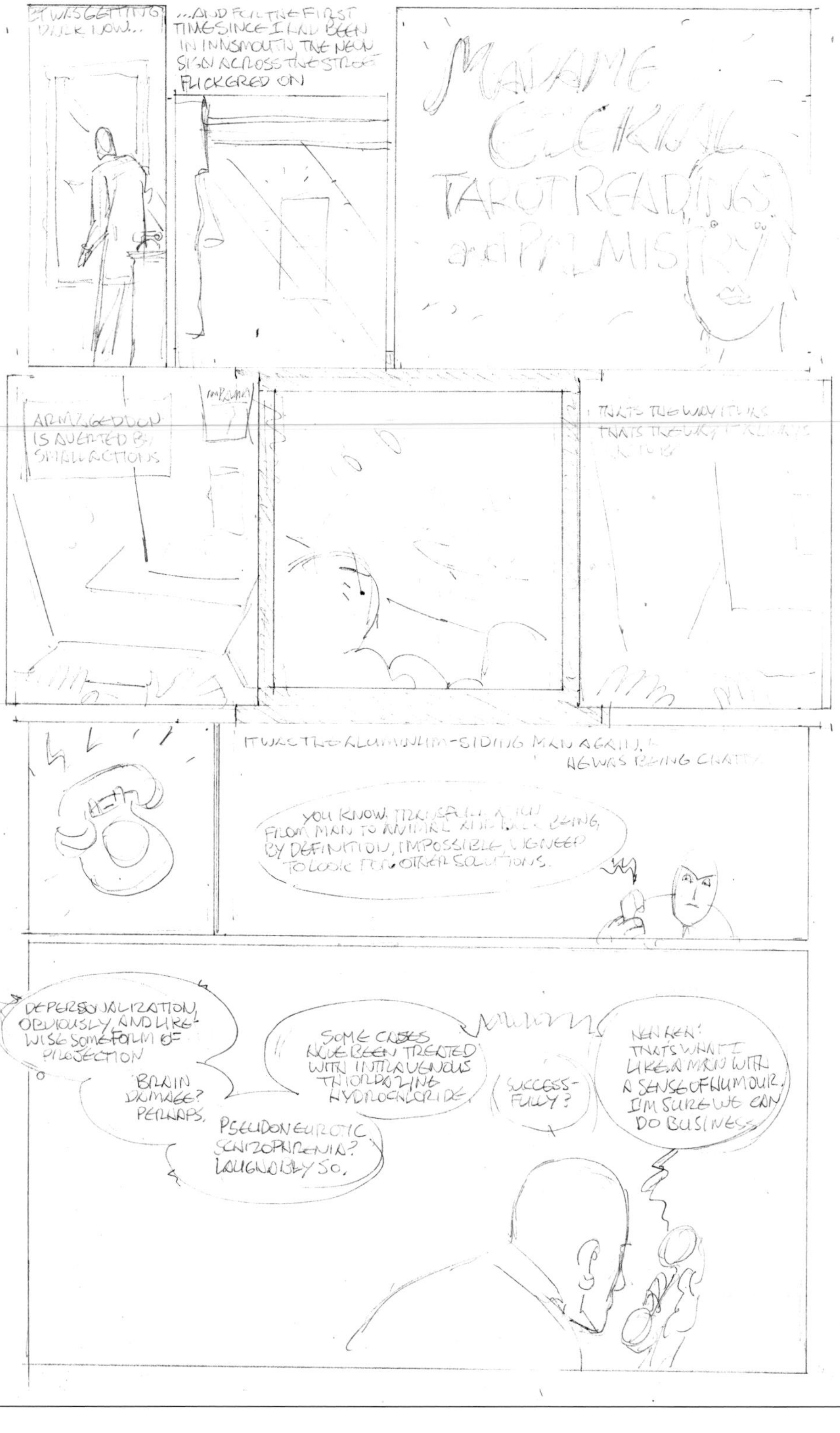
IT WAS GETTING DARK NOW...
...AND FOR THE FIRST TIME SINCE I HAD BEEN IN INNSMOUTH THE NEON SIGN ACROSS THE STREET FLICKERED ON
MADAME EZEKIEL TAROT READINGS and PALMISTRY
ARMAGEDDON IS AVERTED BY SMALL ACTIONS
BY DEFINITION, IMPOSSIBLE, WE NEED TO LOOK FOR OTHER SOLUTIONS.
DEPERSONALIZATION, OBVIOUSLY, AND LIKEWISE SOME FORM OF PROJECTION
BRAIN DAMAGE? PERHAPS.
PSEUDONEUROTIC SCHIZOPHRENIA? LAUGHABLY SO.
SOME CASES HAVE BEEN TREATED WITH INTRAVENOUS THIORIDAZINE HYDROCHLORIDE.
SUCCESSFULLY?
THATS WHAT I LIKE, A MAN WITH A SENSE OF HUMOUR. I'M SURE WE CAN DO BUSINESS

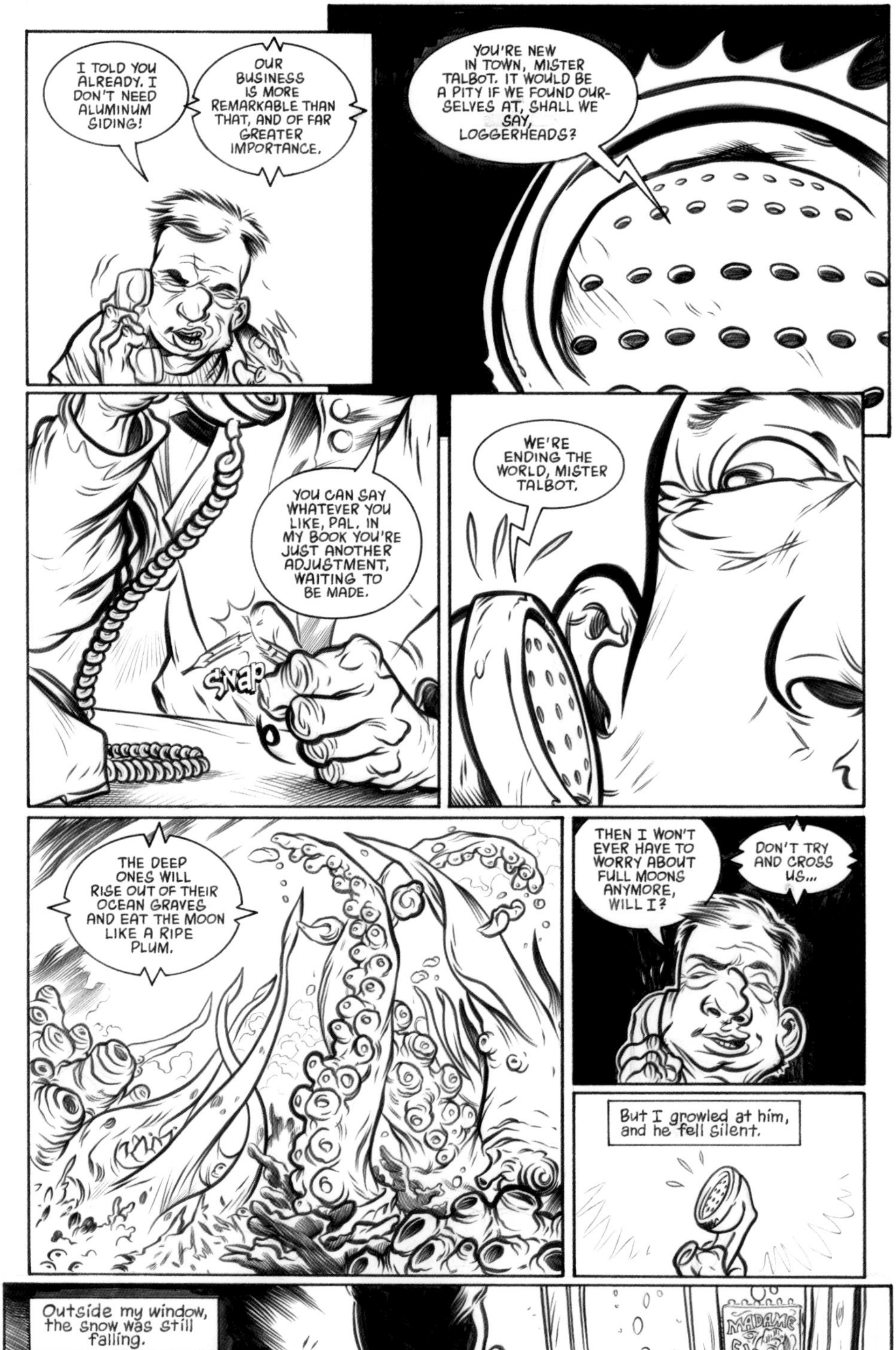
I TOLD YOU ALREADY. I DON'T NEED ALUMINUM SIDING!
OUR BUSINESS IS MORE REMARKABLE THAN THAT, AND OF FAR GREATER IMPORTANCE.
YOU'RE NEW IN TOWN, MISTER TALBOT. IT WOULD BE A PITY IF WE FOUND OURSELVES AT, SHALL WE SAY, LOGGERHEADS?
YOU CAN SAY WHATEVER YOU LIKE, PAL. IN MY BOOK YOU'RE JUST ANOTHER ADJUSTMENT, WAITING TO BE MADE.
SNAP
WE'RE ENDING THE WORLD, MISTER TALBOT.
THE DEEP ONES WILL RISE OUT OF THEIR OCEAN GRAVES AND EAT THE MOON LIKE A RIPE PLUM.
THEN I WON'T EVER HAVE TO WORRY ABOUT FULL MOONS ANYMORE, WILL I?
DON'T TRY AND CROSS US...
But I growled at him, and he fell silent.
Outside my window, the snow was still falling.
MADAME
READING
TO BE CONTINUED...

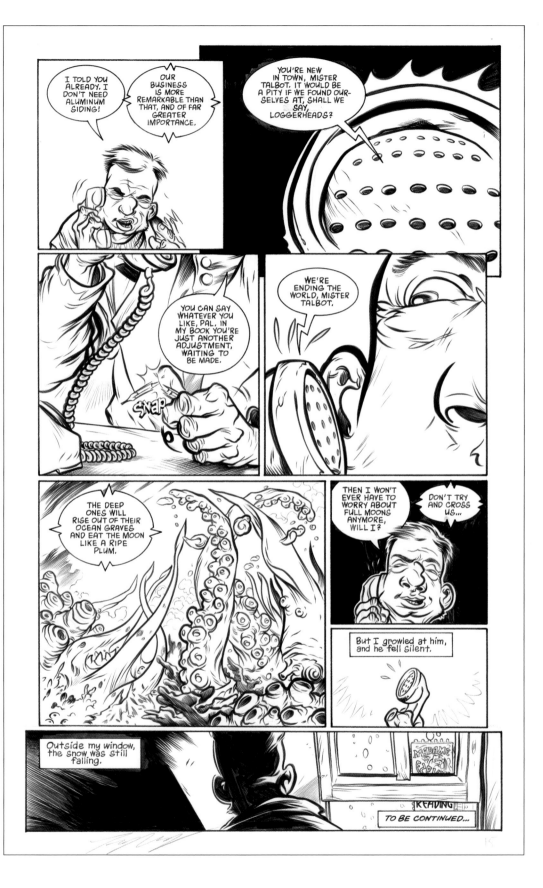

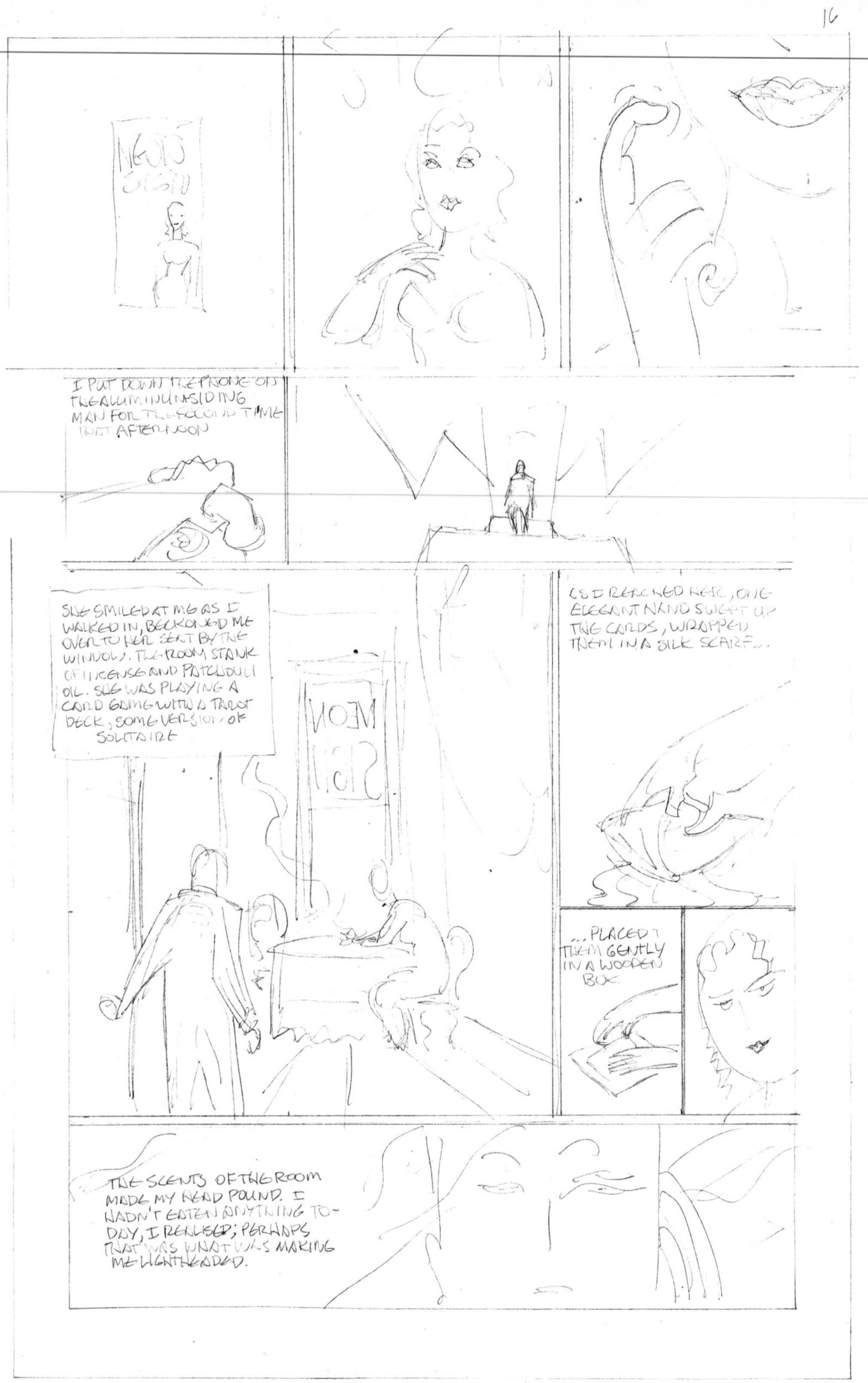
16
NEON SIGN
I PUT DOWN THE PHONE ON THE ALUMINIUM SIDING MAN FOR THE SECOND TIME THAT AFTERNOON
SHE SMILED AT ME AS I WALKED IN, BECKONED ME OVER TO HER SEAT BY THE WINDOW. THE ROOM STANK OF INCENSE AND PATCHOULI OIL. SHE WAS PLAYING A CARD GAME WITH A TAROT DECK, SOME VERSION OF SOLITAIRE
NEON SIGN
AS I REACHED HER, ONE ELEGANT HAND SWEPT UP THE CARDS, WRAPPED THEM IN A SILK SCARF...
...PLACED THEM GENTLY IN A WOODEN BOX.
THE SCENTS OF THE ROOM MADE MY HEAD POUND. I HADN'T EATEN ANYTHING TO-DAY, I REALISED; PERHAPS THAT WAS WHAT WAS MAKING ME LIGHTHEADED.

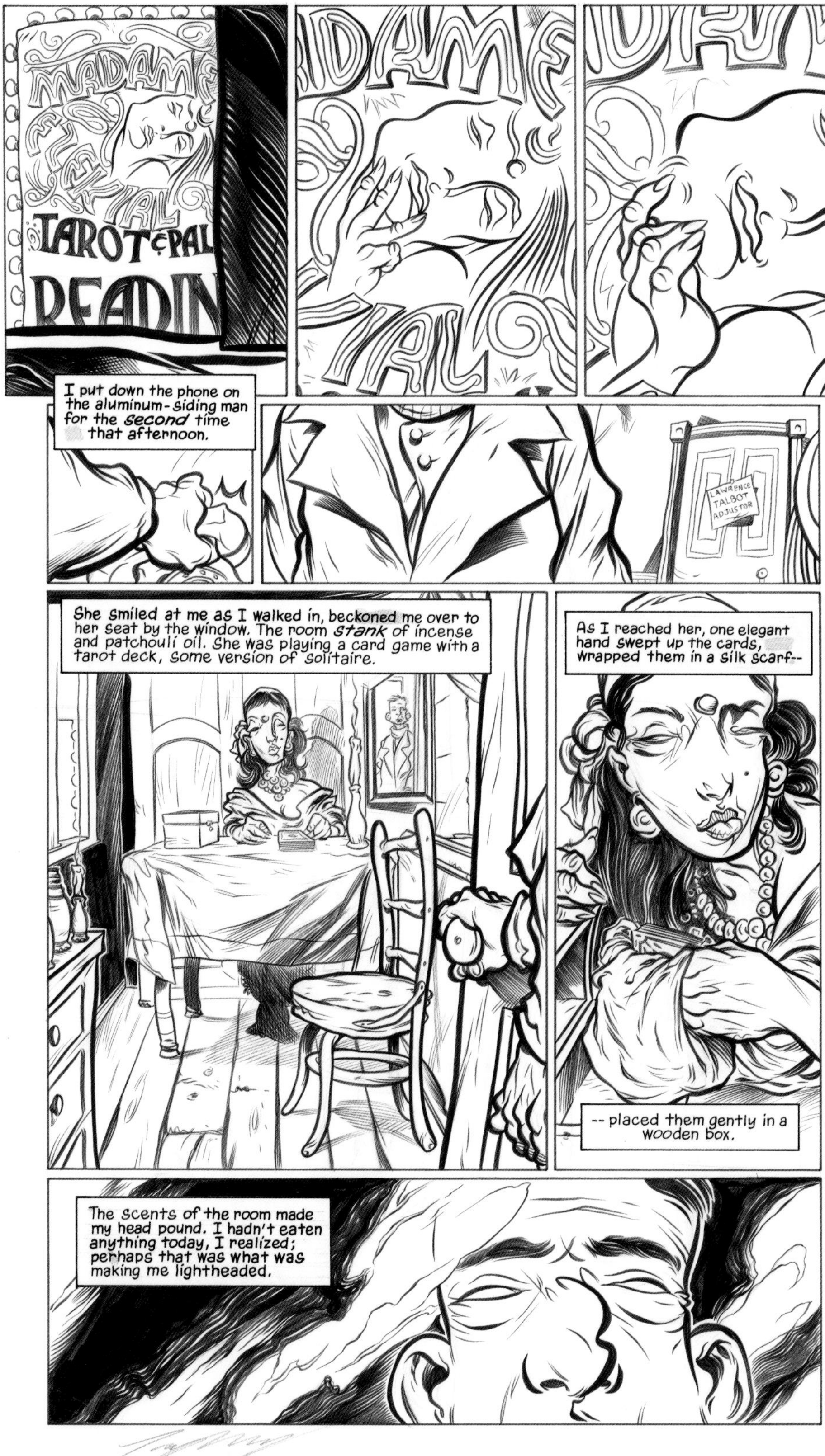
MADAME
TAROT & PAL
READIN
I put down the phone on the aluminum-siding man for the second time that afternoon.
LAWRENCE TALBOT ADJUSTOR
She smiled at me as I walked in, beckoned me over to her seat by the window. The room stank of incense and patchouli oil. She was playing a card game with a tarot deck, some version of solitaire.
As I reached her, one elegant hand swept up the cards, wrapped them in a silk scarf--
-- placed them gently in a wooden box.
The scents of the room made my head pound. I hadn't eaten anything today, I realized; perhaps that was what was making me lightheaded.

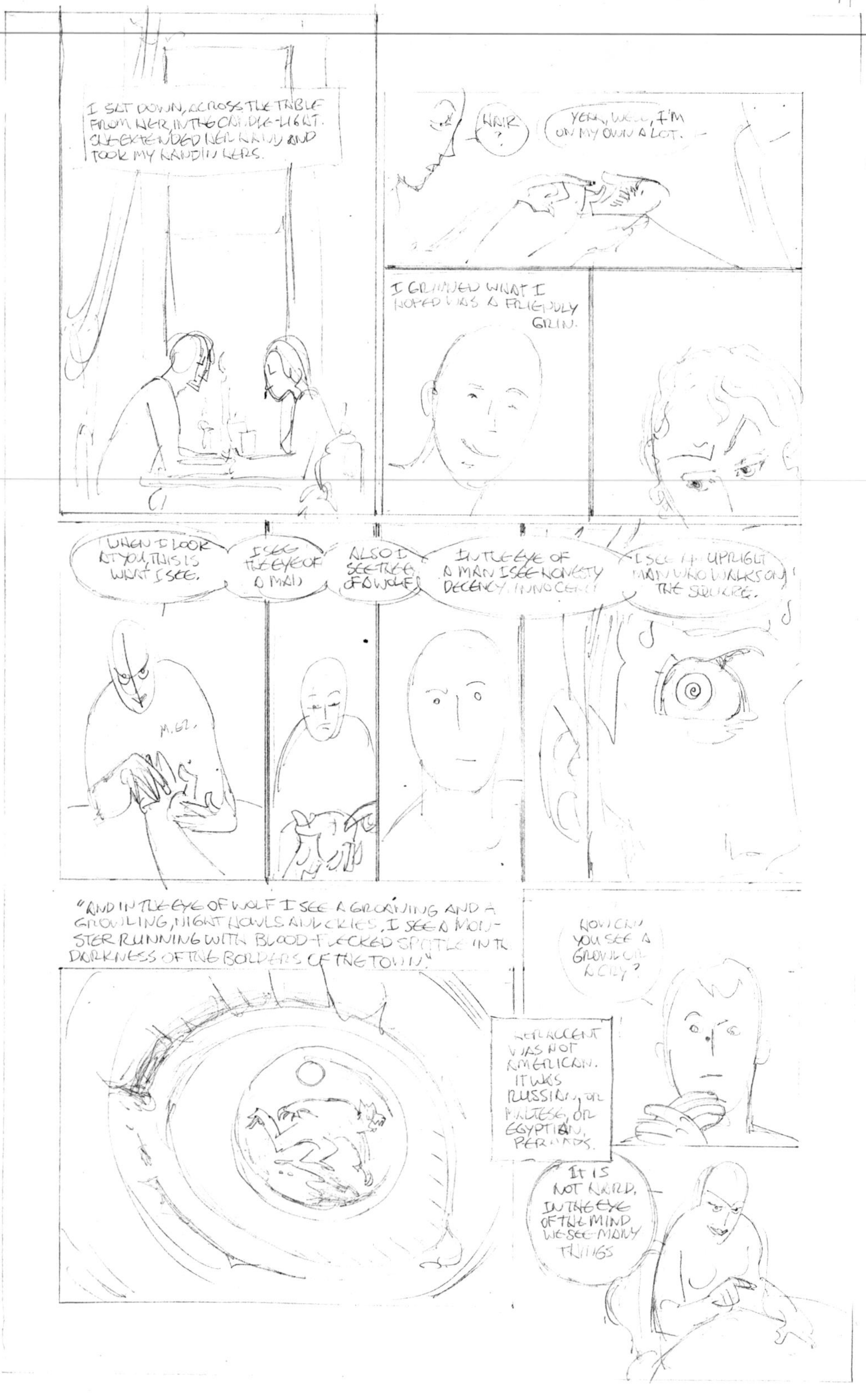
I SAT DOWN, ACROSS THE TABLE FROM HER, IN THE CANDLE-LIGHT. SHE EXTENDED HER HAND AND TOOK MY HAND IN HERS.
HAIR?
YEAH, WELL, I'M ON MY OWN A LOT.
I GRINNED WHAT I HOPED WAS A FRIENDLY GRIN.
WHEN I LOOK AT YOU, THIS IS WHAT I SEE.
I SEE THE EYE OF A MAN
ALSO I SEE THE EYE OF A WOLF
IN THE EYE OF A MAN I SEE HONESTY DECENCY, INNOCENCE
I SEE AN UPRIGHT MAN WHO WALKS ON THE SQUARE.
"AND IN THE EYE OF WOLF I SEE A GROANING AND A GROWLING, NIGHT HOWLS AND CRIES. I SEE A MONSTER RUNNING WITH BLOOD-FLECKED SPITTLE IN THE DARKNESS OF THE BORDERS OF THE TOWN."
HOW CAN YOU SEE A GROWL OR A CRY?
HER ACCENT WAS NOT AMERICAN. IT WAS RUSSIAN, OR MALTESE, OR EGYPTIAN, PERHAPS.
IT IS NOT HARD. IN THE EYE OF THE MIND WE SEE MANY THINGS

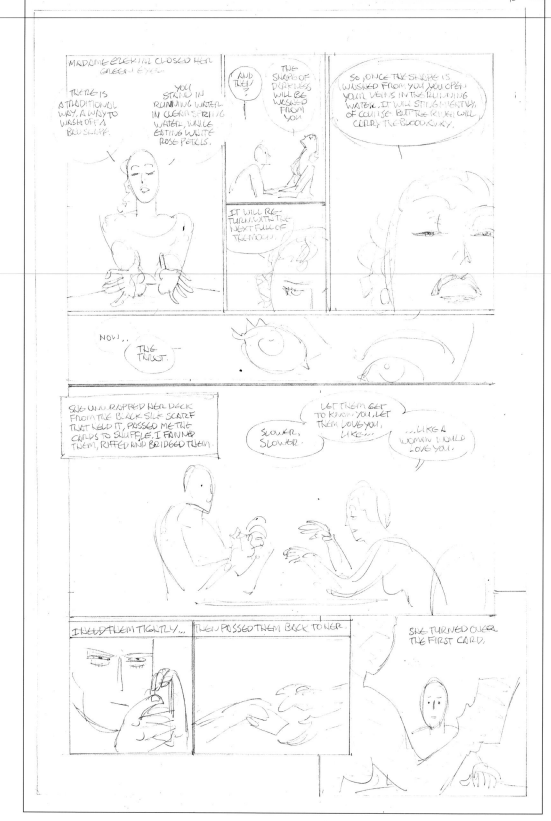

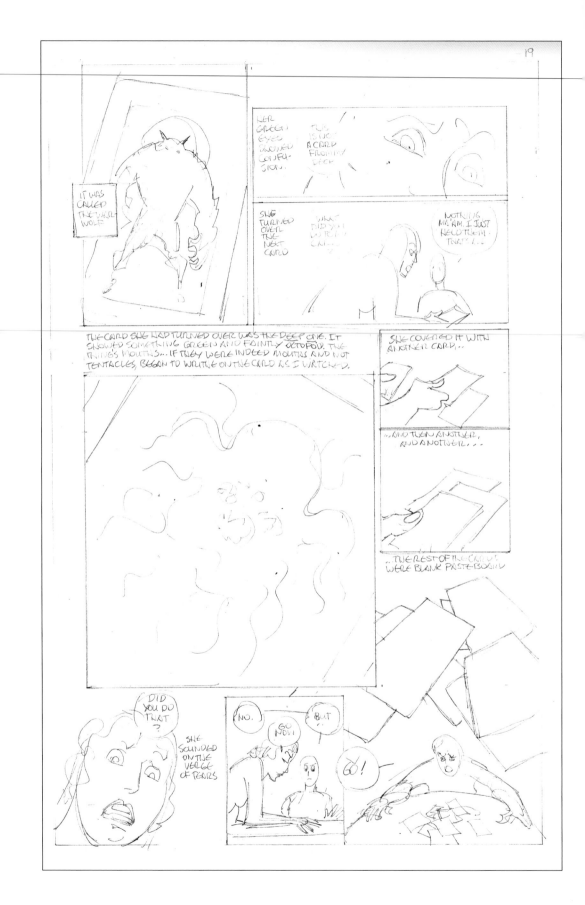

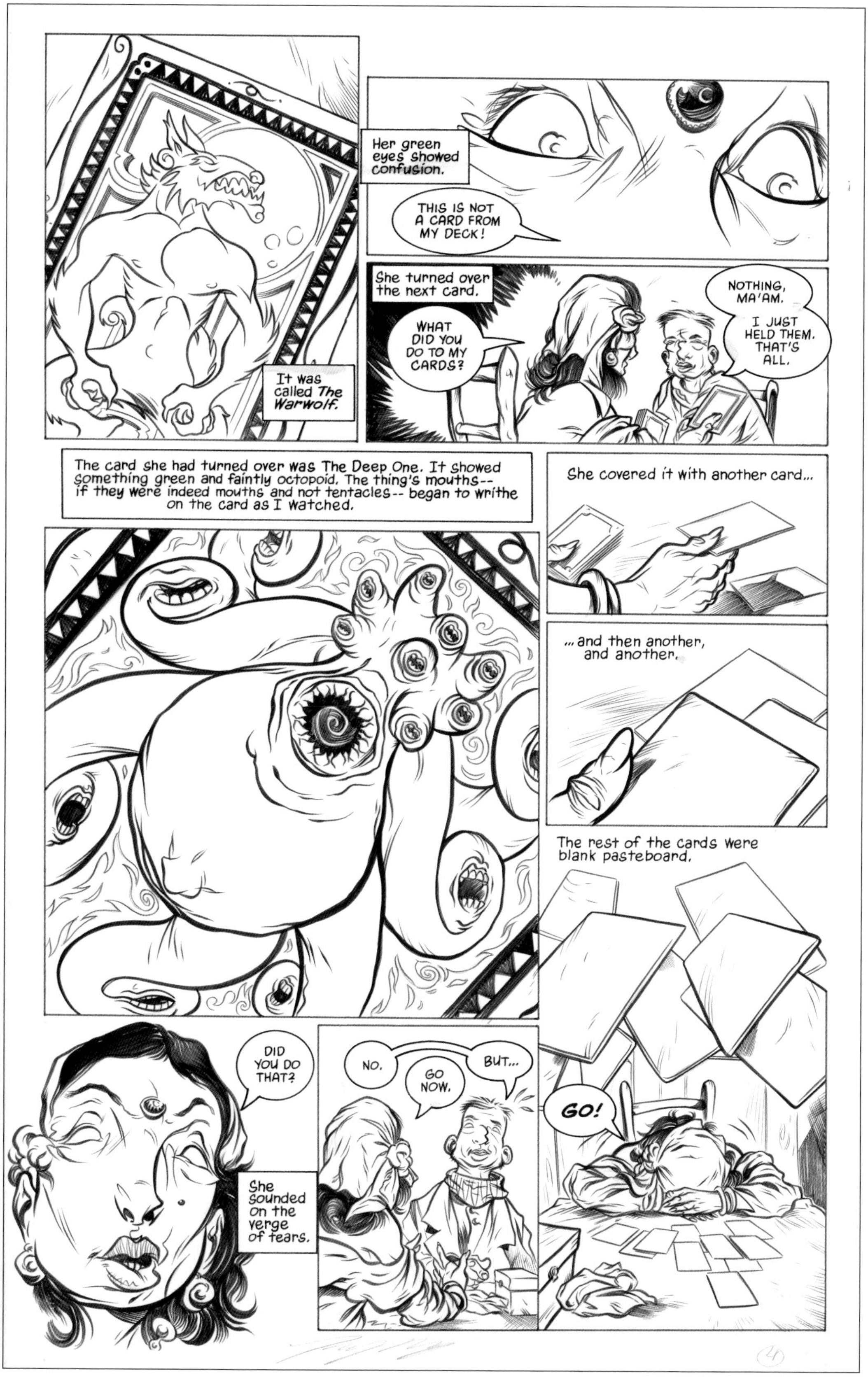
It was called *The Warwolf.*
Her green eyes showed confusion.
THIS IS NOT A CARD FROM MY DECK!
She turned over the next card.
WHAT DID YOU DO TO MY CARDS?
NOTHING, MA'AM.
I JUST HELD THEM. THAT'S ALL.
The card she had turned over was The Deep One. It showed something green and faintly octopoid. The thing's mouths-- if they were indeed mouths and not tentacles-- began to writhe on the card as I watched.
She covered it with another card...
...and then another, and another.
The rest of the cards were blank pasteboard.
DID YOU DO THAT?
She sounded on the verge of tears.
NO.
GO NOW.
BUT...
GO!

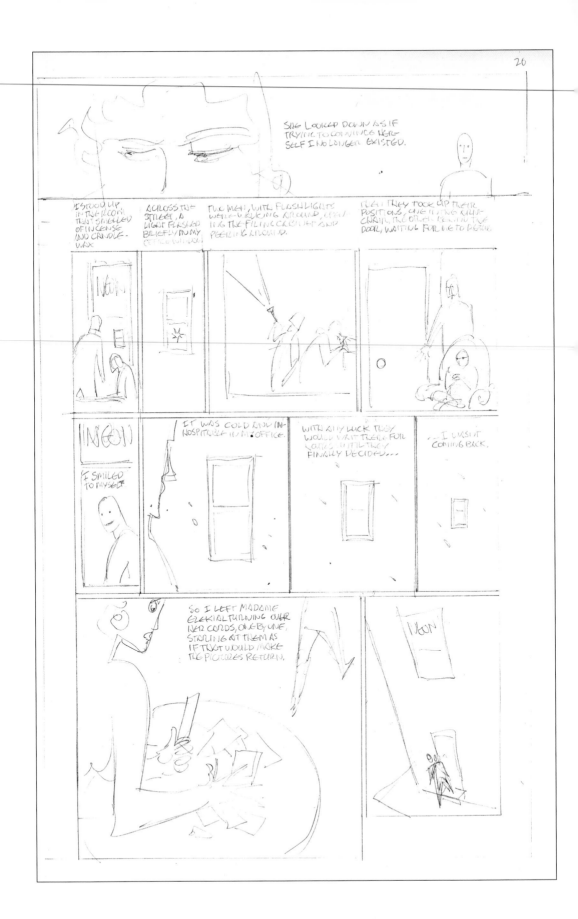

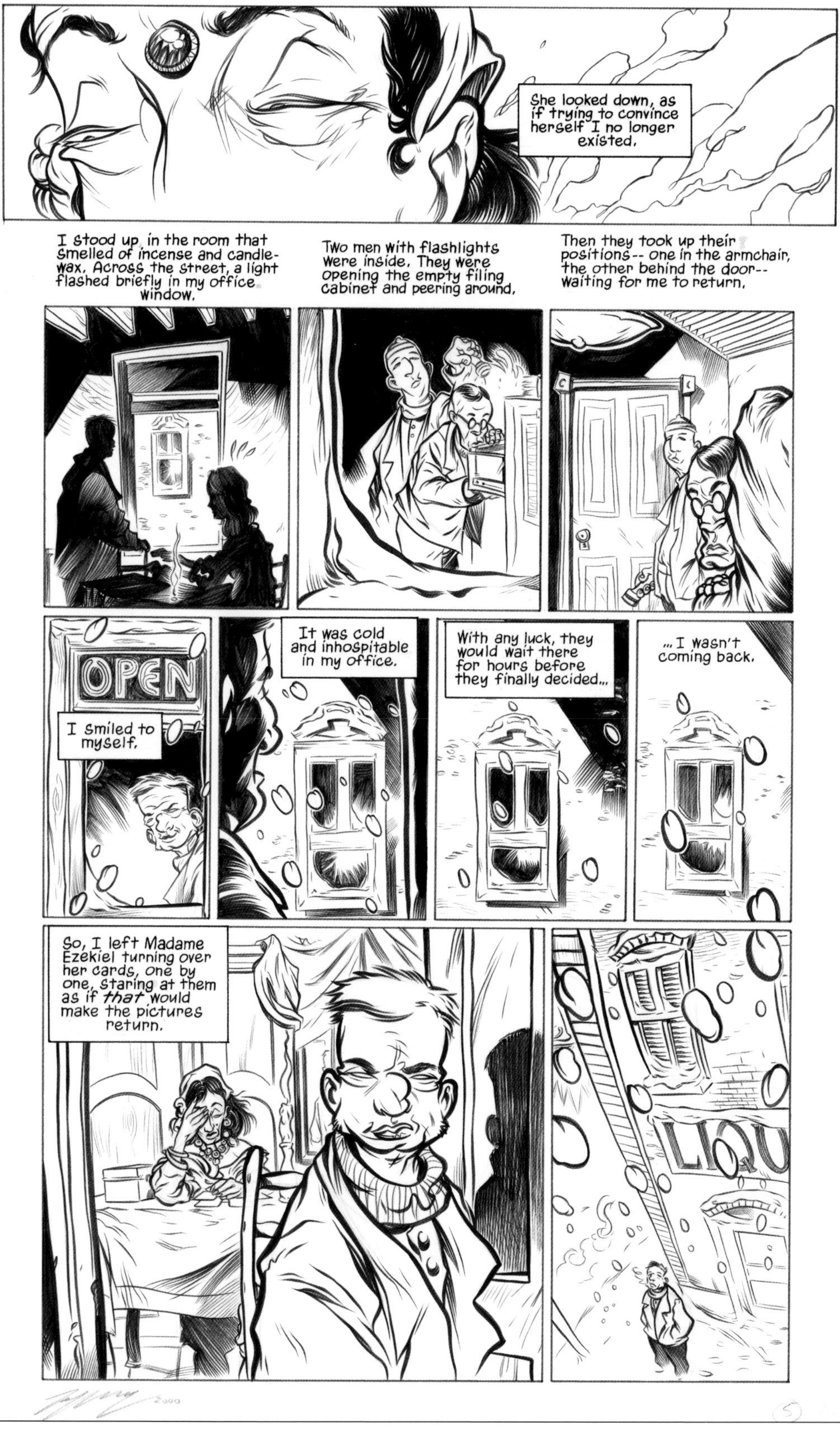
She looked down, as if trying to convince herself I no longer existed.
I stood up in the room that smelled of incense and candle-wax. Across the street, a light flashed briefly in my office window.
Two men with flashlights were inside. They were opening the empty filing cabinet and peering around.
Then they took up their positions -- one in the armchair, the other behind the door-- waiting for me to return.
OPEN
I smiled to myself.
It was cold and inhospitable in my office.
With any luck, they would wait there for hours before they finally decided...
...I wasn't coming back.
So, I left Madame Ezekiel turning over her cards, one by one, staring at them as if *that* would make the pictures return.
LIQU

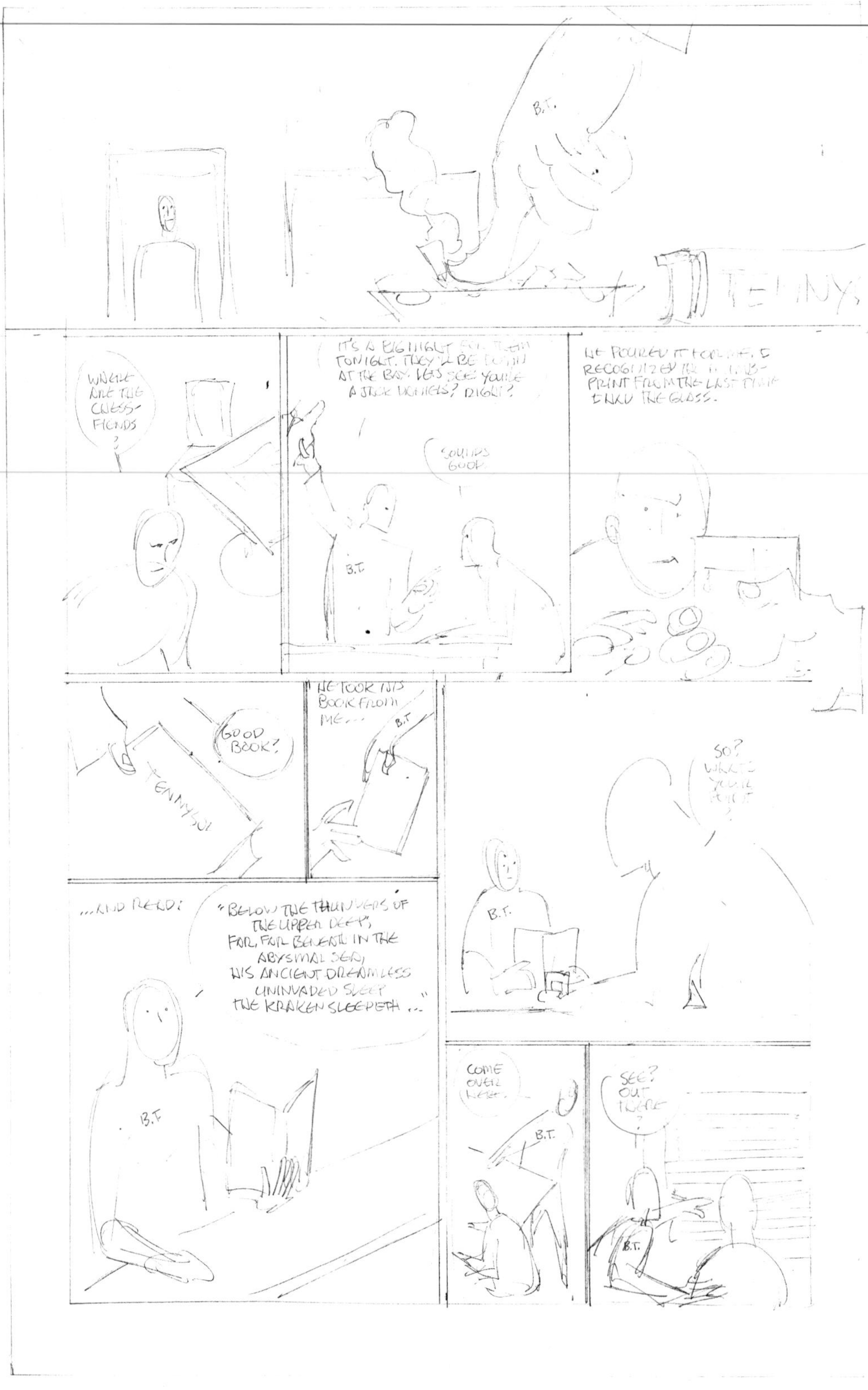
TENNYS
WHERE ARE THE CHESS-FIENDS?
IT'S A BIG NIGHT FOR THEM TONIGHT. THEY'LL BE DOWN AT THE BAY. LETS SEE: YOU'RE A JACK DANIELS, RIGHT?
SOUNDS GOOD
HE POURED IT FOR ME. I RECOGNIZED HIS THUMB-PRINT FROM THE LAST TIME I HAD THE GLASS.
GOOD BOOK?
TENNYSON
HE TOOK HIS BOOK FROM ME...
SO? WHAT'S YOUR POINT?
...AND READ:
"BELOW THE THUNDERS OF THE UPPER DEEP; FAR, FAR BENEATH IN THE ABYSMAL SEA, HIS ANCIENT DREAMLESS UNINVADED SLEEP THE KRAKEN SLEEPETH..."
COME OVER HERE.
SEE? OUT THERE?

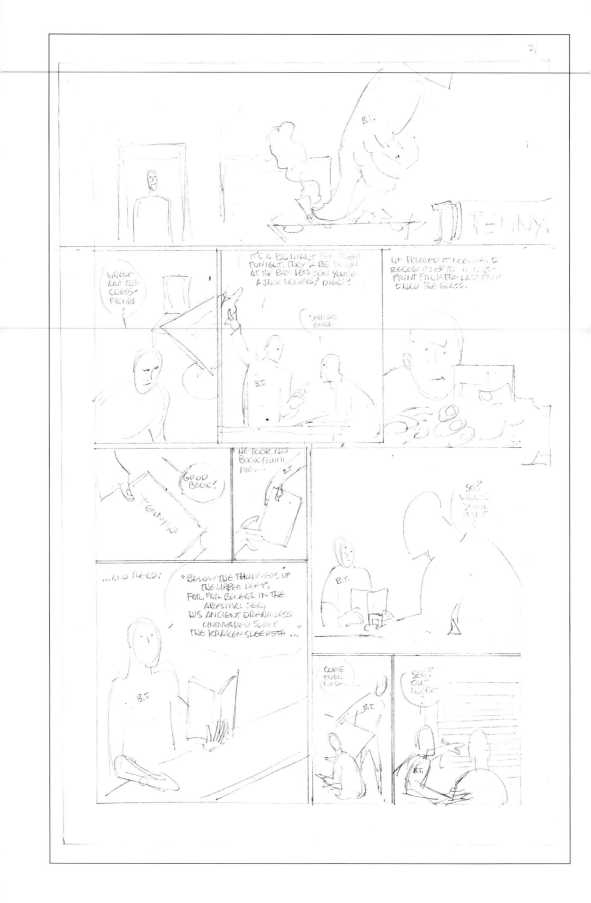

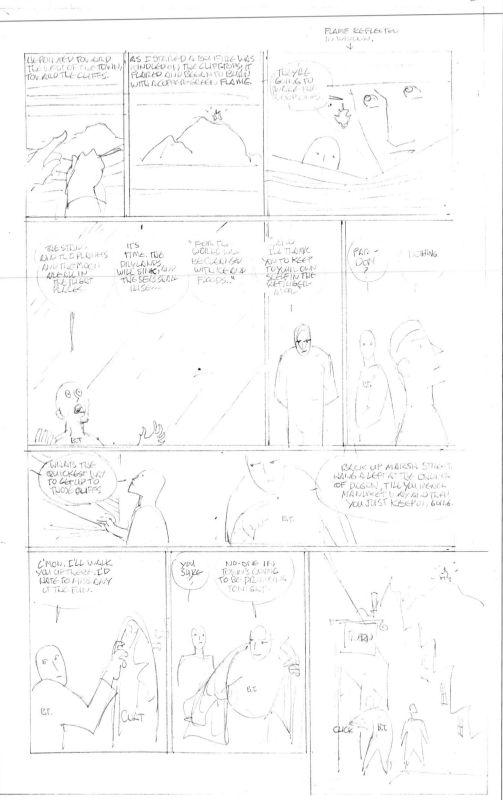

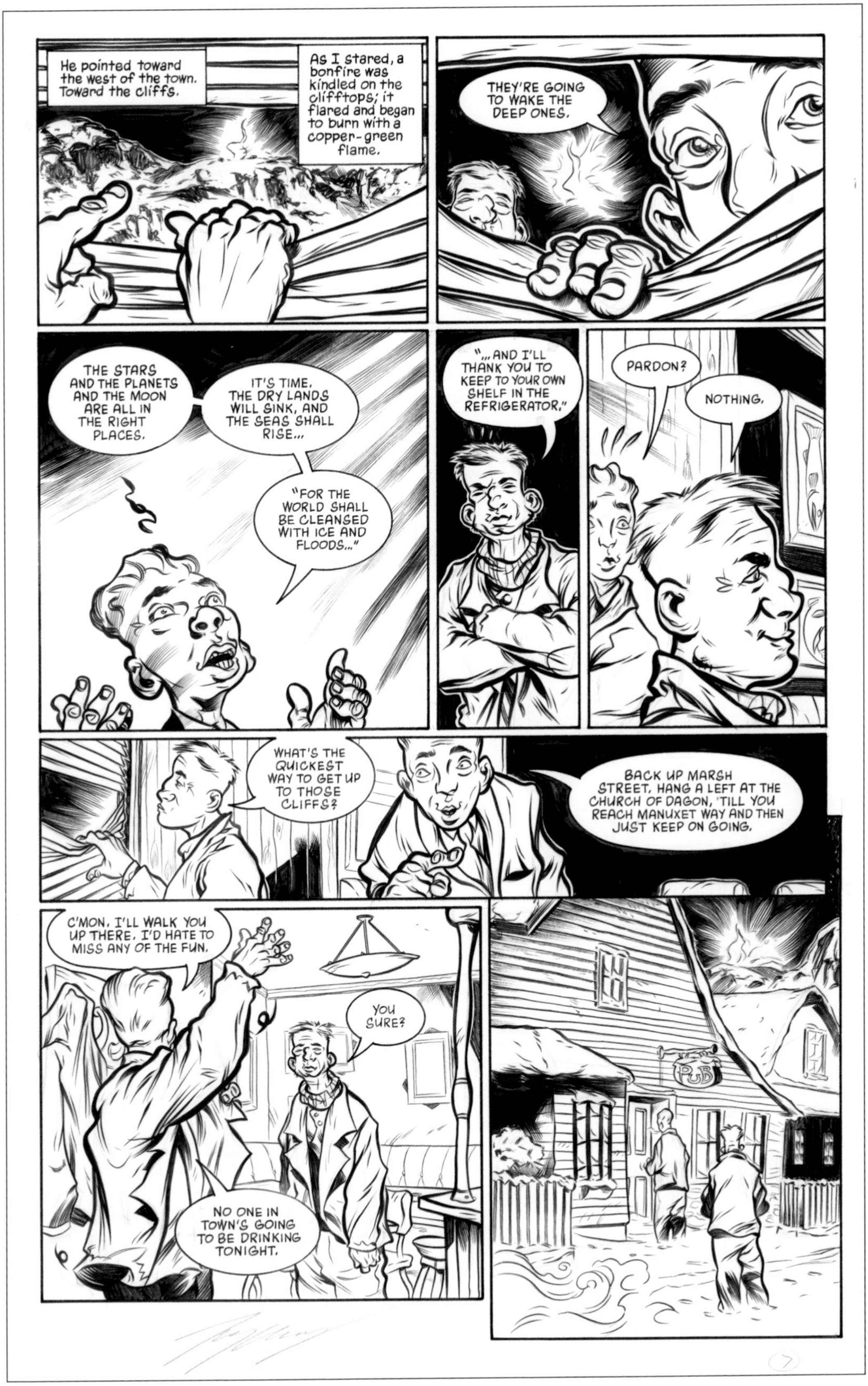
He pointed toward the west of the town. Toward the cliffs.
As I stared, a bonfire was kindled on the clifftops; it flared and began to burn with a copper-green flame.
THEY'RE GOING TO WAKE THE DEEP ONES.
THE STARS AND THE PLANETS AND THE MOON ARE ALL IN THE RIGHT PLACES.
IT'S TIME. THE DRY LANDS WILL SINK, AND THE SEAS SHALL RISE...
"FOR THE WORLD SHALL BE CLEANSED WITH ICE AND FLOODS..."
"...AND I'LL THANK YOU TO KEEP TO YOUR OWN SHELF IN THE REFRIGERATOR."
PARDON?
NOTHING.
WHAT'S THE QUICKEST WAY TO GET UP TO THOSE CLIFFS?
BACK UP MARSH STREET. HANG A LEFT AT THE CHURCH OF DAGON, 'TILL YOU REACH MANUXET WAY AND THEN JUST KEEP ON GOING.
C'MON. I'LL WALK YOU UP THERE. I'D HATE TO MISS ANY OF THE FUN.
YOU SURE?
NO ONE IN TOWN'S GOING TO BE DRINKING TONIGHT.
PUB
7

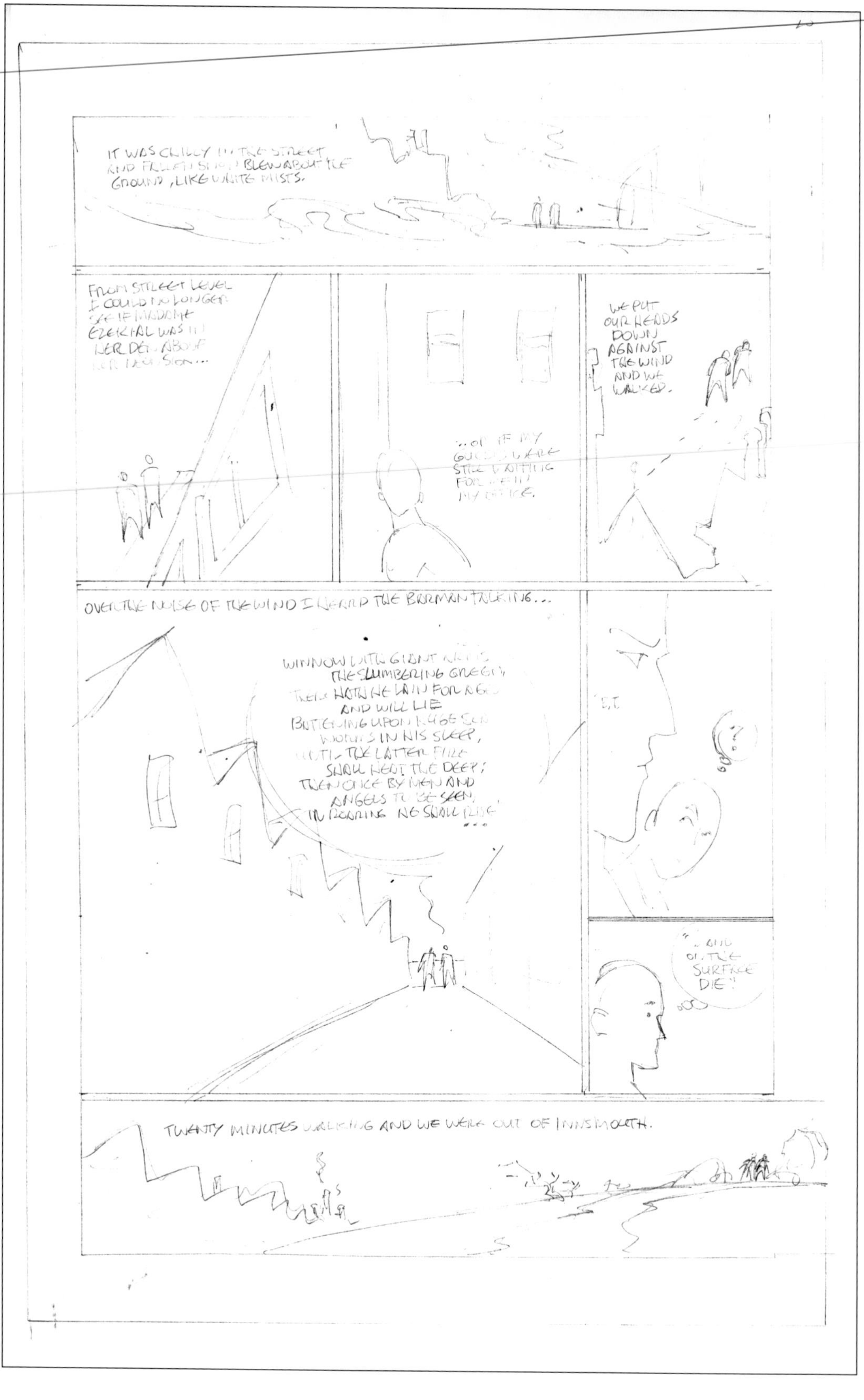

IT WAS CHILLY IN THE STREET AND FALLEN SNOW BLEW ABOUT THE GROUND, LIKE WHITE MISTS.
FROM STREET LEVEL I COULD NO LONGER SEE IF MADAME EZEKIAL WAS IN HER DEN ABOUT HER DECISION...
...OR IF MY GUESTS WERE STILL WAITING FOR ME IN MY OFFICE.
WE PUT OUR HEADS DOWN AGAINST THE WIND AND WE WALKED.
OVER THE NOISE OF THE WIND I HEARD THE BARMAN TALKING...
WINNOW WITH GIANT ARMS THE SLUMBERING GREEN. THERE HATH HE LAIN FOR AGES AND WILL LIE BATTENING UPON HUGE SEA WORMS IN HIS SLEEP, UNTIL THE LATTER FIRE SHALL HEAT THE DEEP; THEN ONCE BY MEN AND ANGELS TO BE SEEN, IN ROARING HE SHALL RISE...
"...AND ON THE SURFACE DIE."
TWENTY MINUTES WALKING AND WE WERE OUT OF INNSMOUTH.

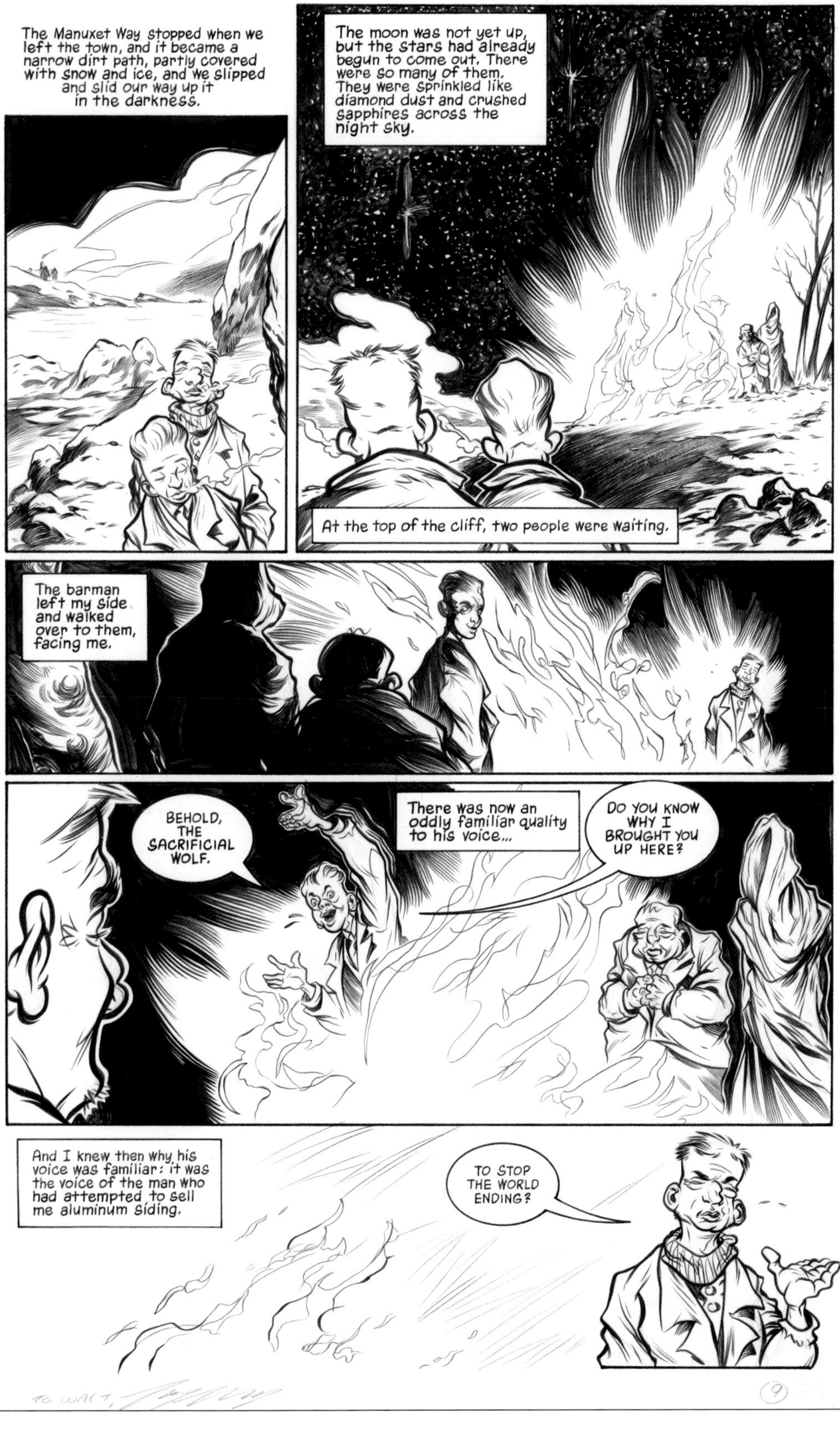

The Manuxet Way stopped when we left the town, and it became a narrow dirt path, partly covered with snow and ice, and we slipped and slid our way up it in the darkness.
The moon was not yet up, but the stars had already begun to come out. There were so many of them. They were sprinkled like diamond dust and crushed sapphires across the night sky.
At the top of the cliff, two people were waiting.
The barman left my side and walked over to them, facing me.
BEHOLD, THE SACRIFICIAL WOLF.
There was now an oddly familiar quality to his voice...
DO YOU KNOW WHY I BROUGHT YOU UP HERE?
And I knew then why his voice was familiar: it was the voice of the man who had attempted to sell me aluminum siding.
TO STOP THE WORLD ENDING?

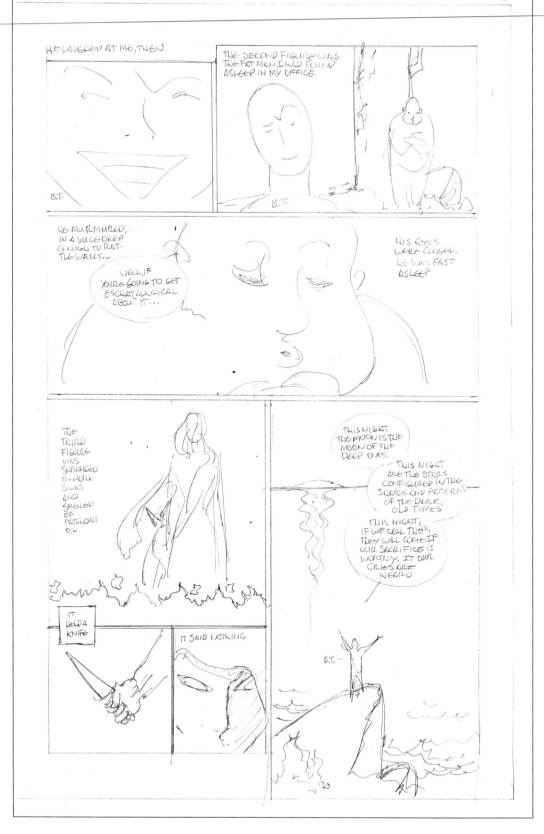

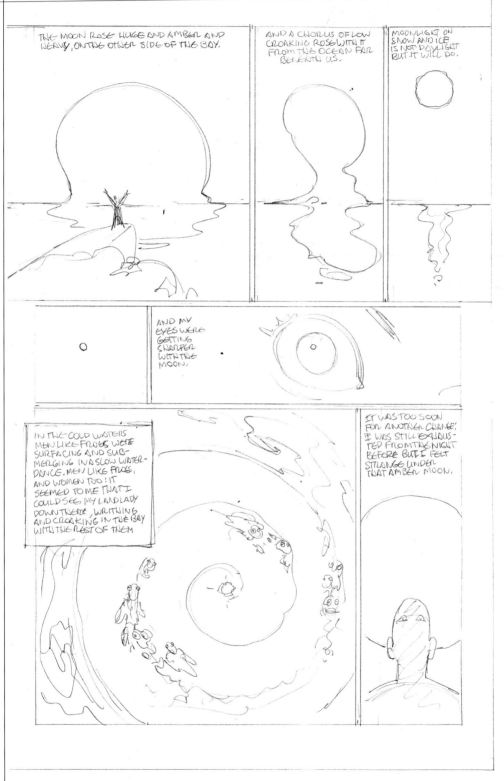

THE MOON ROSE HUGE AND AMBER AND HEAVY, ON THE OTHER SIDE OF THE BAY.

AND A CHORUS OF LOW CROAKING ROSE WITH IT FROM THE OCEAN FAR BENEATH US.

MOONLIGHT ON SNOW AND ICE IS NOT DAYLIGHT BUT IT WILL DO.

AND MY EYES WERE GETTING SHARPER WITH THE MOON.

IN THE COLD WATERS MEN LIKE FROGS WERE SURFACING AND SUBMERGING IN A SLOW WATER-DANCE. MEN LIKE FROGS, AND WOMEN TOO: IT SEEMED TO ME THAT I COULD SEE MY LANDLADY DOWN THERE, WRITHING AND CROAKING IN THE BAY WITH THE REST OF THEM

IT WAS TOO SOON FOR ANOTHER CHANGE; I WAS STILL EXHAUSTED FROM THE NIGHT BEFORE BUT I FELT STRANGE UNDER THAT AMBER MOON.

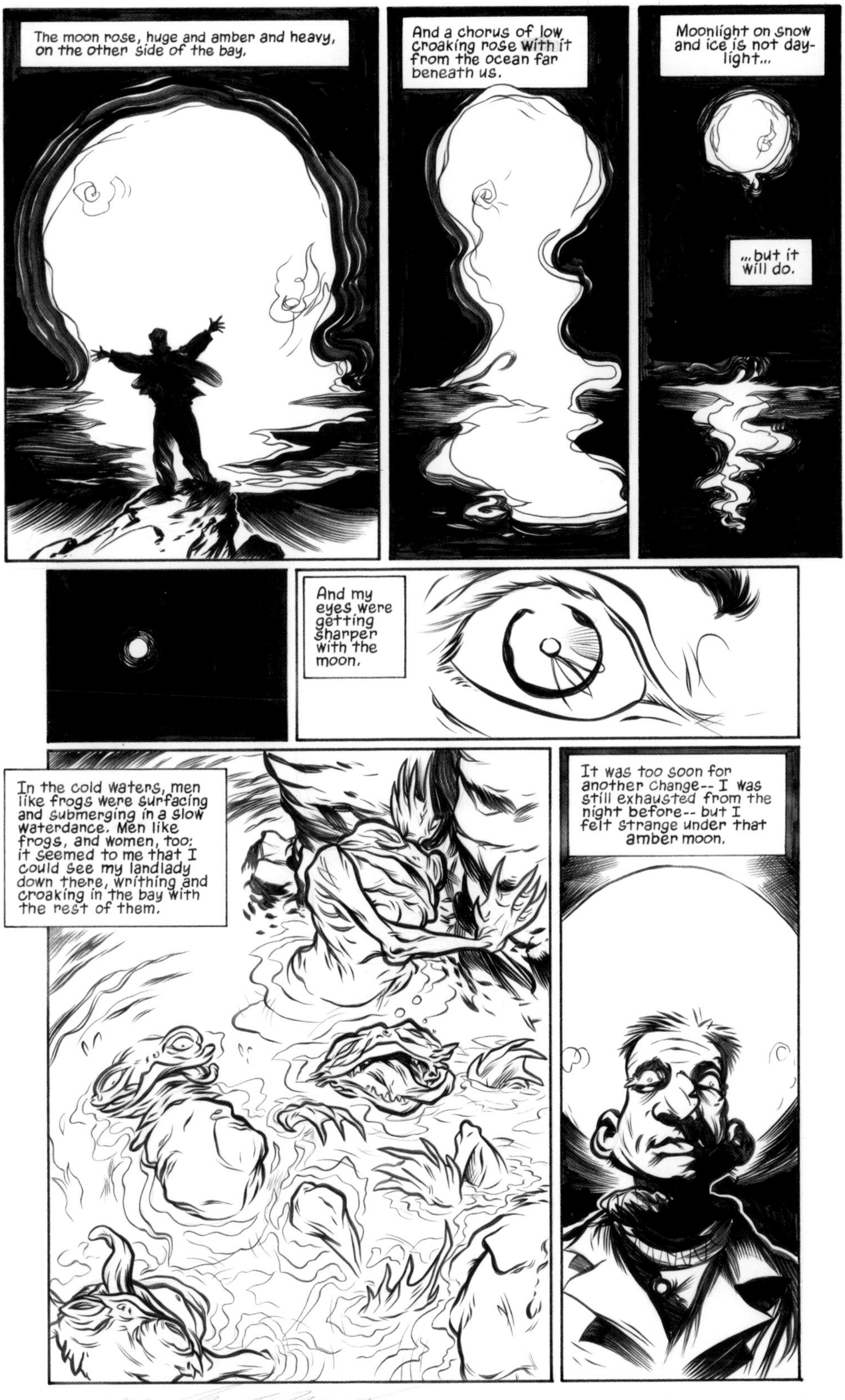
The moon rose, huge and amber and heavy, on the other side of the bay,
And a chorus of low croaking rose with it from the ocean far beneath us.
Moonlight on snow and ice is not daylight...
...but it will do.
And my eyes were getting sharper with the moon.
In the cold waters, men like frogs were surfacing and submerging in a slow waterdance. Men like frogs, and women, too; it seemed to me that I could see my landlady down there, writhing and croaking in the bay with the rest of them.
It was too soon for another Change-- I was still exhausted from the night before-- but I felt strange under that amber moon.

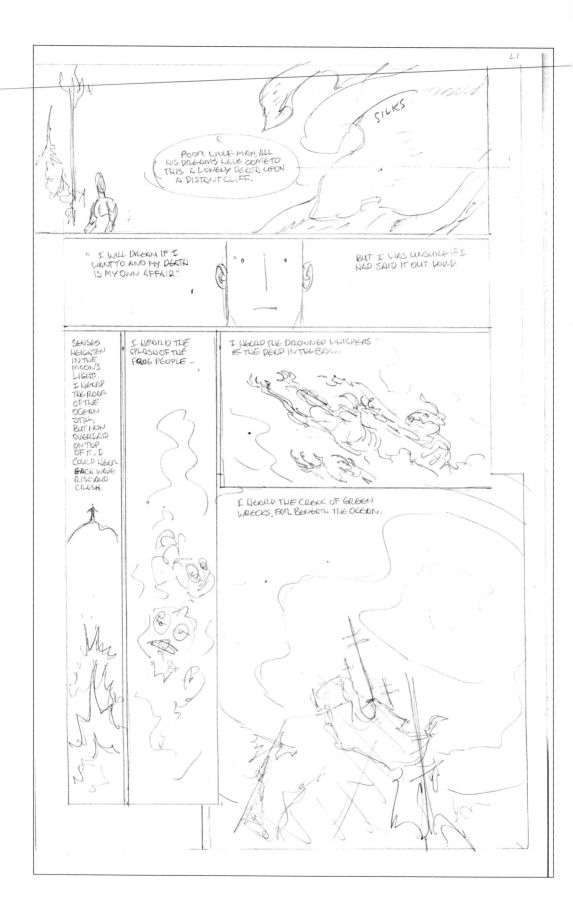

SILKS

POOR WOLF-MAN, ALL HIS DREAMS HAVE COME TO THIS. A LONELY DEATH UPON A DISTANT CLIFF.

" I WILL DREAM IF I WANT TO AND MY DEATH IS MY OWN AFFAIR"

BUT I WAS UNSURE IF I HAD SAID IT OUT LOUD

SENSES HEIGHTEN IN THE MOON'S LIGHT. I HEARD THE ROAR OF THE OCEAN STILL, BUT NOW OVERLAID ON TOP OF IT, I COULD HEAR EACH WAVE RISE AND CRASH.

I HEARD THE SPLASH OF THE FROG PEOPLE ..

I HEARD THE DROWNED WHISPERS OF THE DEAD IN THE BAY....

I HEARD THE CREAK OF GREEN WRECKS, FAR BENEATH THE OCEAN.

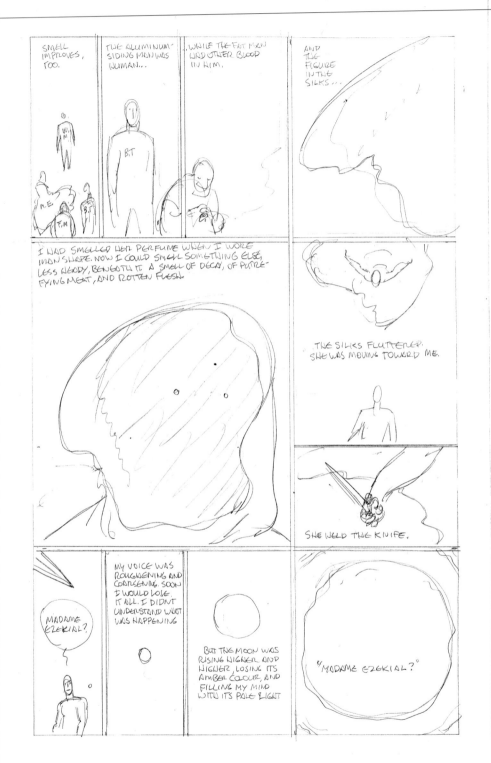

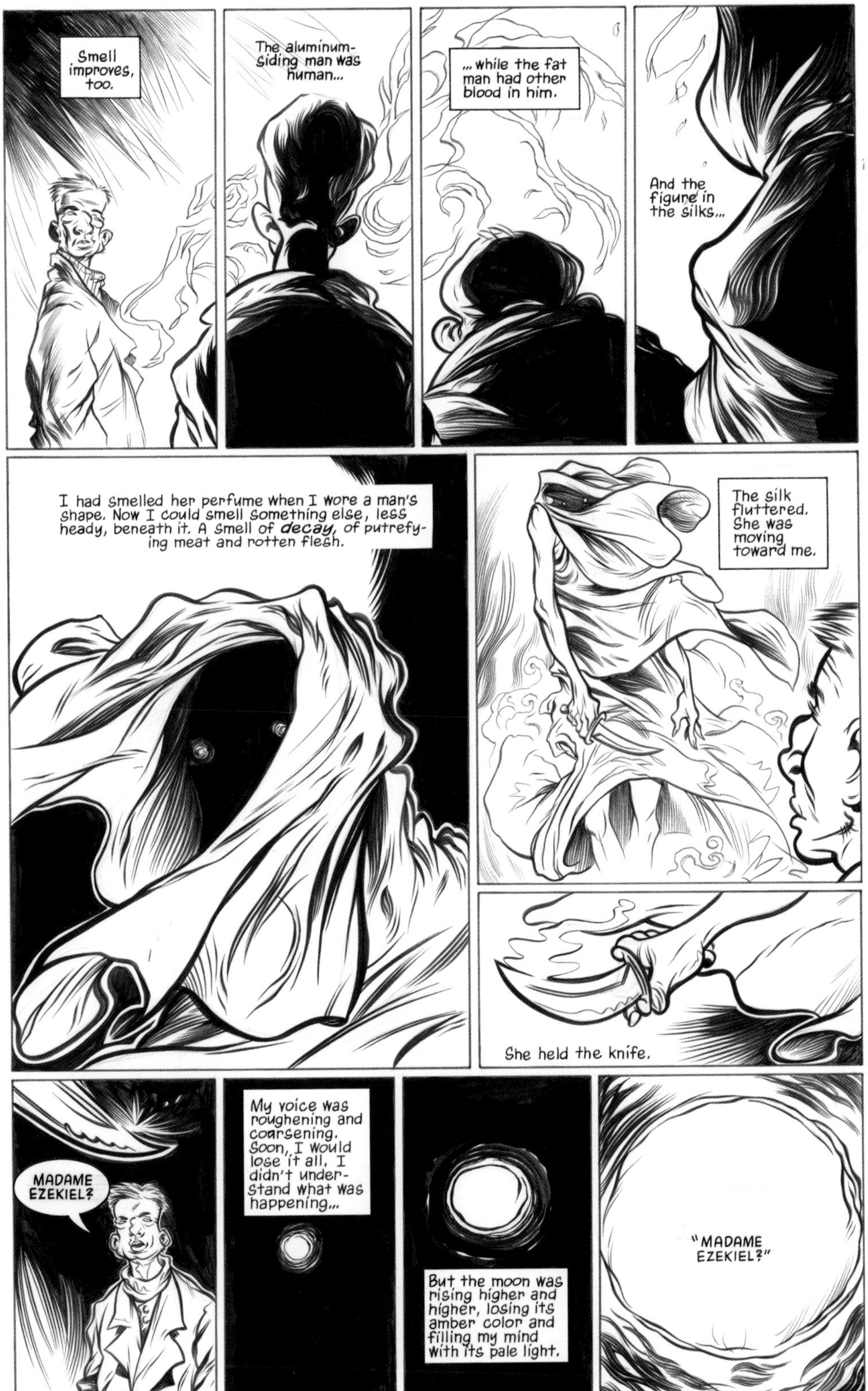
Smell improves, too.
The aluminum-siding man was human...
...while the fat man had other blood in him.
And the figure in the silks...
I had smelled her perfume when I wore a man's shape. Now I could smell something else, less heady, beneath it. A smell of decay, of putrefying meat and rotten flesh.
The silk fluttered. She was moving toward me.
She held the knife.
MADAME EZEKIEL?
My voice was roughening and coarsening. Soon, I would lose it all. I didn't understand what was happening...
But the moon was rising higher and higher, losing its amber color and filling my mind with its pale light.
"MADAME EZEKIEL?"

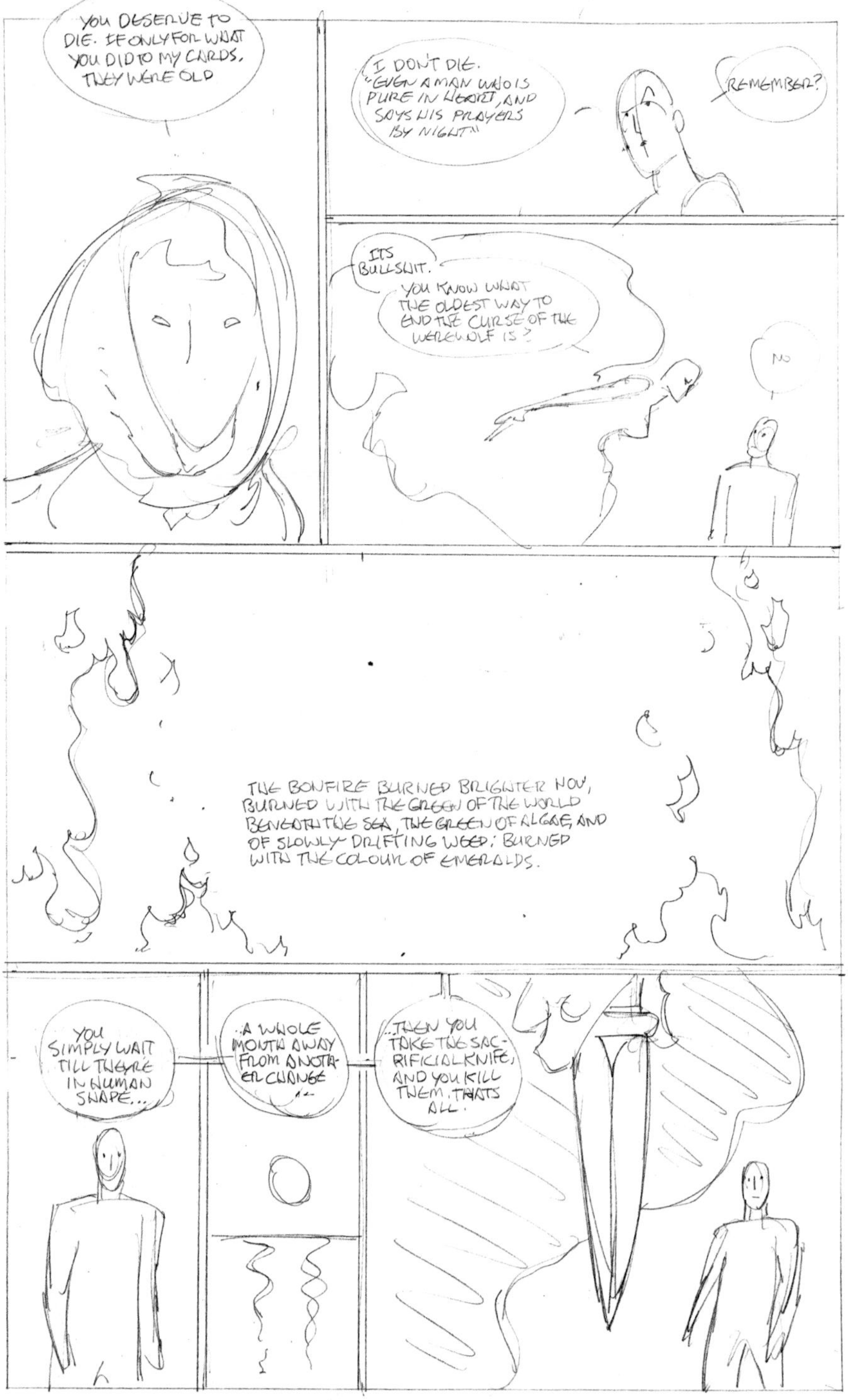
YOU DESERVE TO DIE. IF ONLY FOR WHAT YOU DID TO MY CARDS. THEY WERE OLD
I DON'T DIE. "EVEN A MAN WHO IS PURE IN HEART, AND SAYS HIS PRAYERS BY NIGHT"
REMEMBER?
ITS BULLSHIT.
YOU KNOW WHAT THE OLDEST WAY TO END THE CURSE OF THE WEREWOLF IS?
NO
THE BONFIRE BURNED BRIGHTER NOW, BURNED WITH THE GREEN OF THE WORLD BENEATH THE SEA, THE GREEN OF ALGAE, AND OF SLOWLY DRIFTING WEED; BURNED WITH THE COLOUR OF EMERALDS.
YOU SIMPLY WAIT TILL THEY'RE IN HUMAN SHAPE...
...A WHOLE MONTH AWAY FROM ANOTHER CHANGE
...THEN YOU TAKE THE SACRIFICIAL KNIFE, AND YOU KILL THEM. THATS ALL.

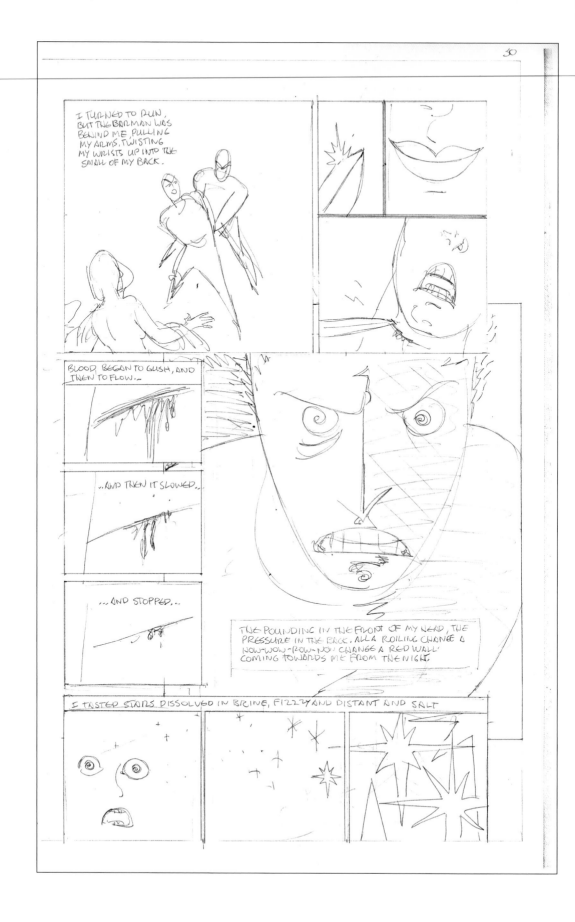

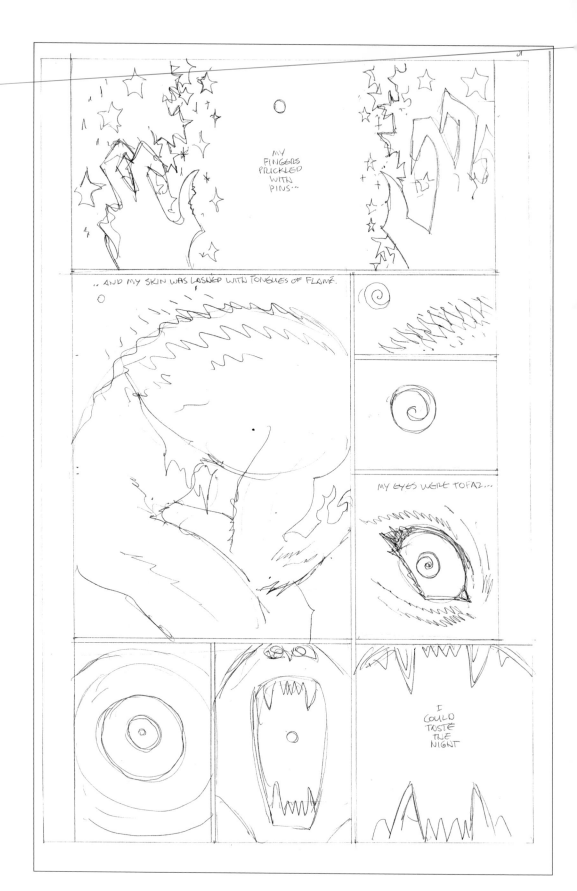

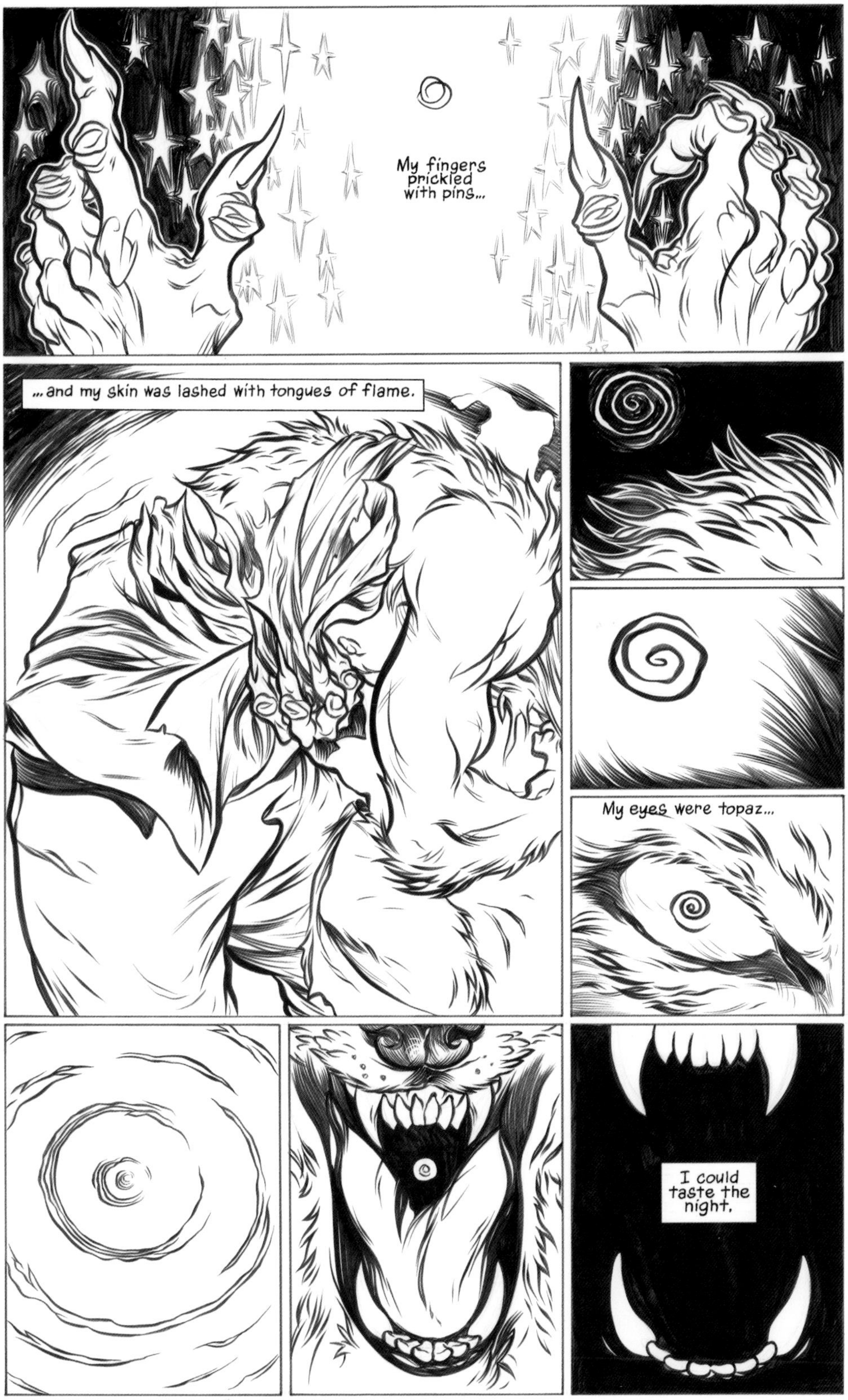
My fingers prickled with pins...
...and my skin was lashed with tongues of flame.
My eyes were topaz...
I could taste the night,

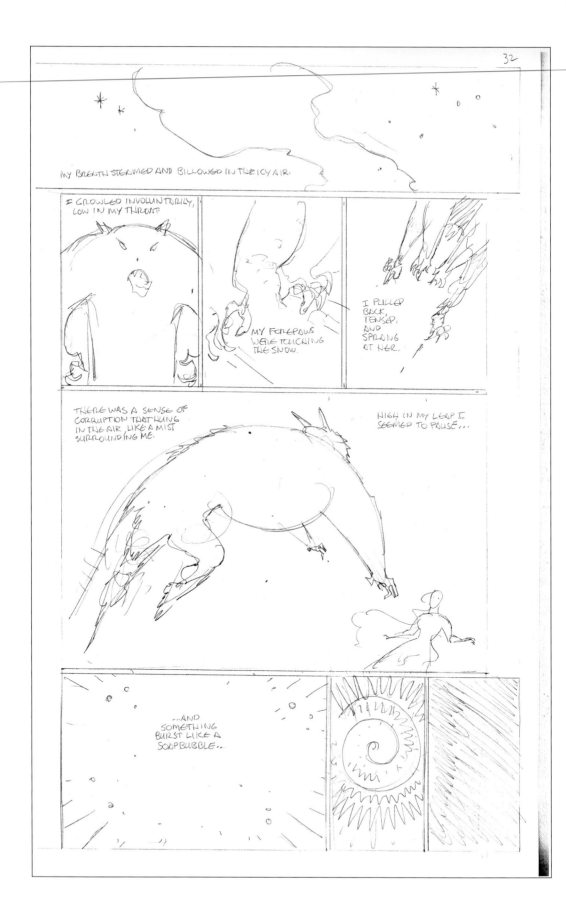

MY BREATH STEAMED AND BILLOWED IN THE ICY AIR.

I GROWLED INVOLUNTARILY, LOW IN MY THROAT.

MY FOREPAWS WERE TOUCHING THE SNOW.

I PULLED BACK, TENSED, AND SPRANG AT HER.

THERE WAS A SENSE OF CORRUPTION THAT HUNG IN THE AIR, LIKE A MIST SURROUNDING ME.

HIGH IN MY LEAP I SEEMED TO PAUSE...

...AND SOMETHING BURST LIKE A SOAPBUBBLE...

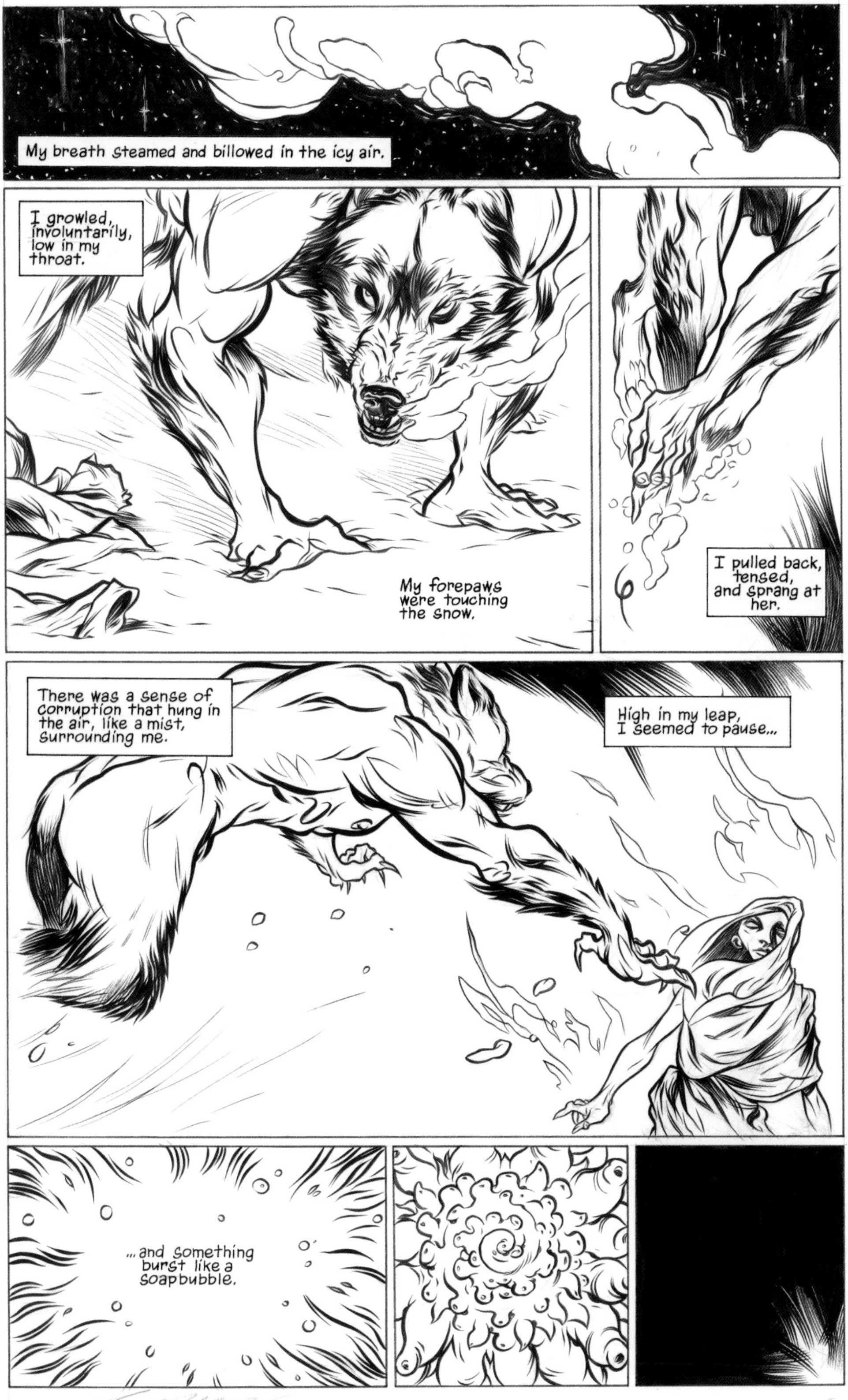
My breath steamed and billowed in the icy air.
I growled, involuntarily, low in my throat.
My forepaws were touching the snow.
I pulled back, tensed, and sprang at her.
There was a sense of corruption that hung in the air, like a mist, surrounding me.
High in my leap, I seemed to pause...
...and something burst like a soapbubble.

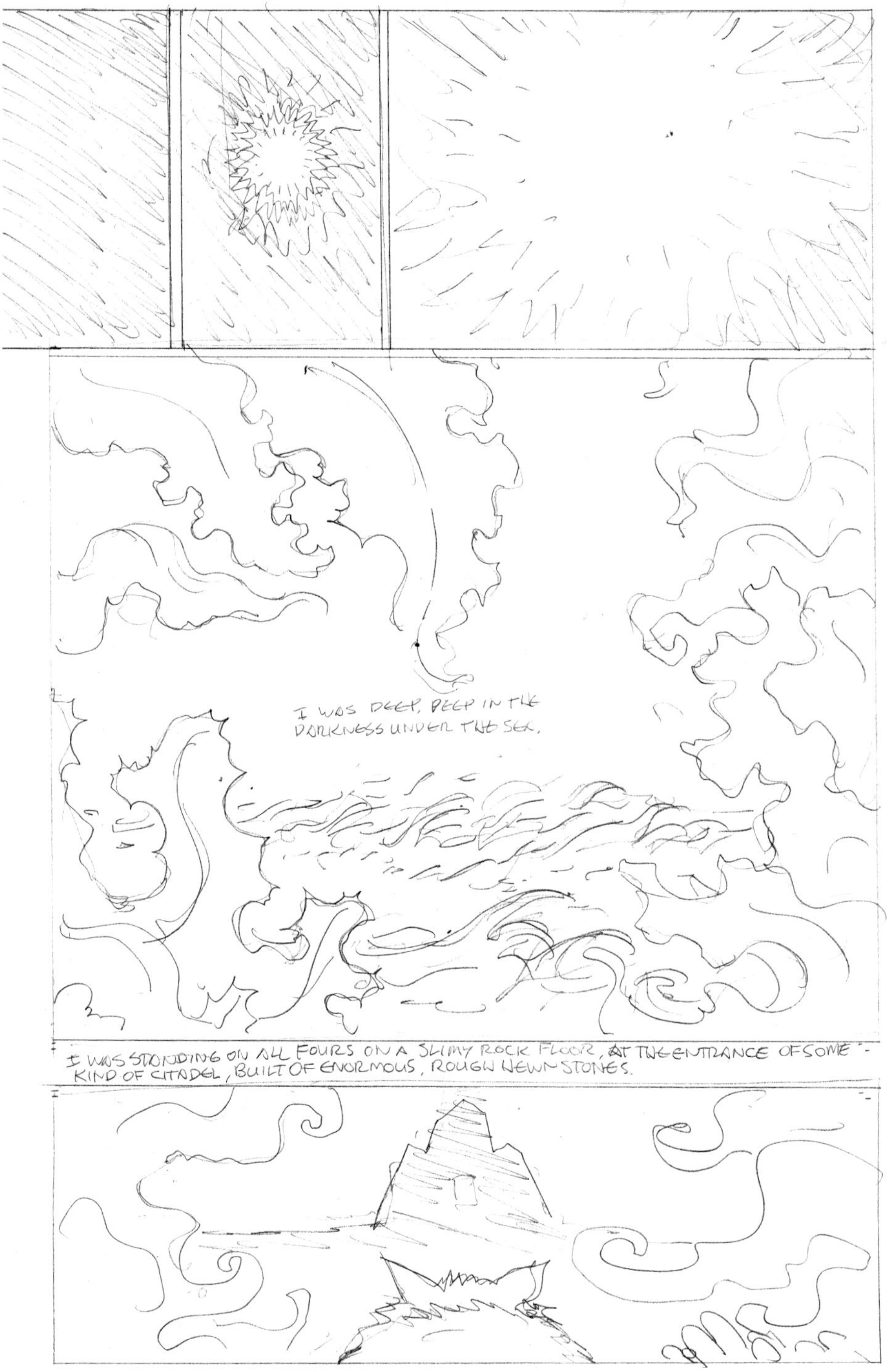
I WAS DEEP, DEEP IN THE DARKNESS UNDER THE SEA.
I WAS STANDING ON ALL FOURS ON A SLIMY ROCK FLOOR, AT THE ENTRANCE OF SOME KIND OF CITADEL, BUILT OF ENORMOUS, ROUGH HEWN STONES.

I was deep, deep in the darkness under the sea.

I was standing on all fours on a slimy rock floor, at the entrance of some kind of citadel, built of enormous, rough-hewn stones.

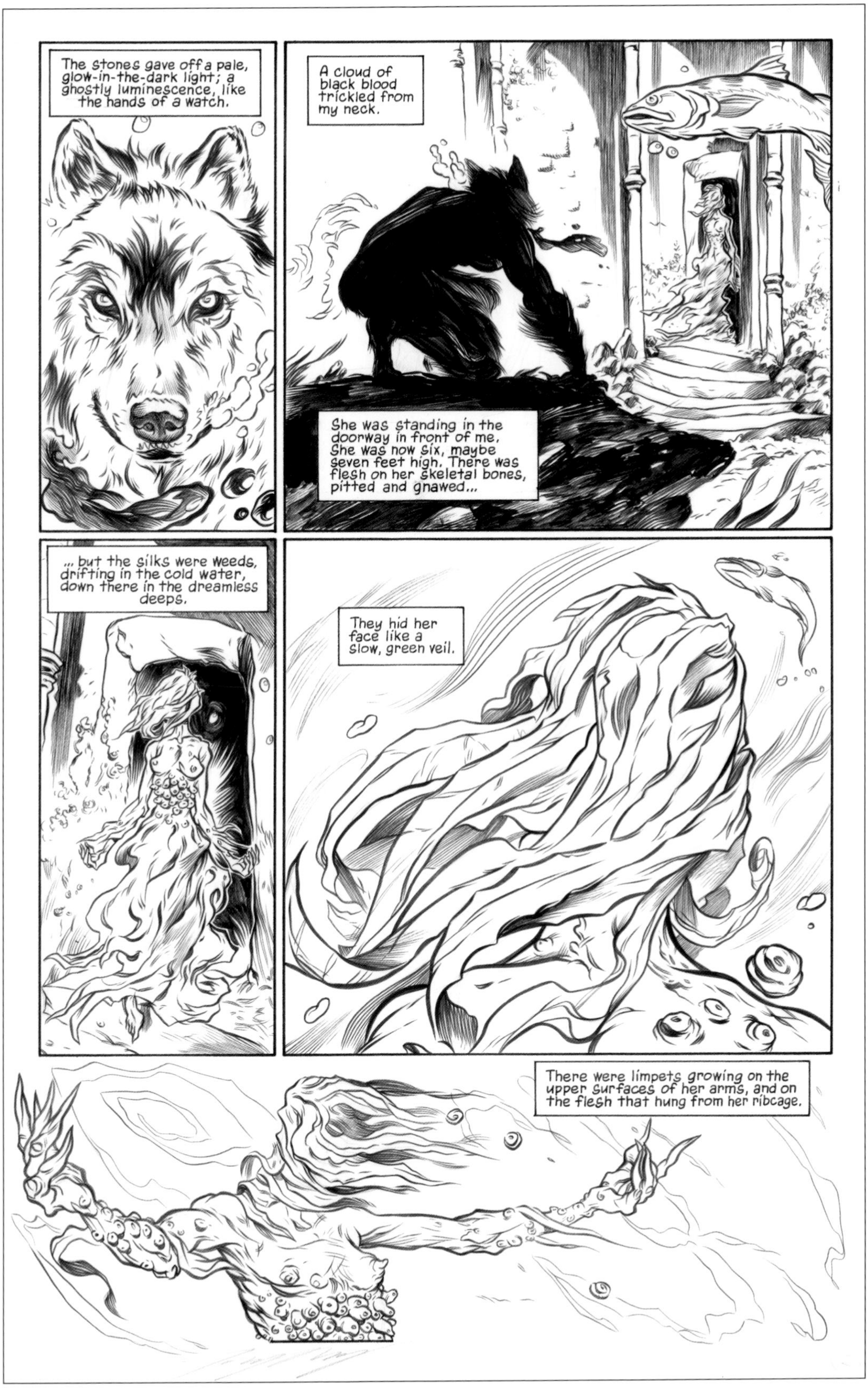
The stones gave off a pale, glow-in-the-dark light; a ghostly luminescence, like the hands of a watch.
A cloud of black blood trickled from my neck.
She was standing in the doorway in front of me. She was now six, maybe seven feet high. There was flesh on her skeletal bones, pitted and gnawed...
... but the silks were weeds, drifting in the cold water, down there in the dreamless deeps.
They hid her face like a slow, green veil.
There were limpets growing on the upper surfaces of her arms, and on the flesh that hung from her ribcage.

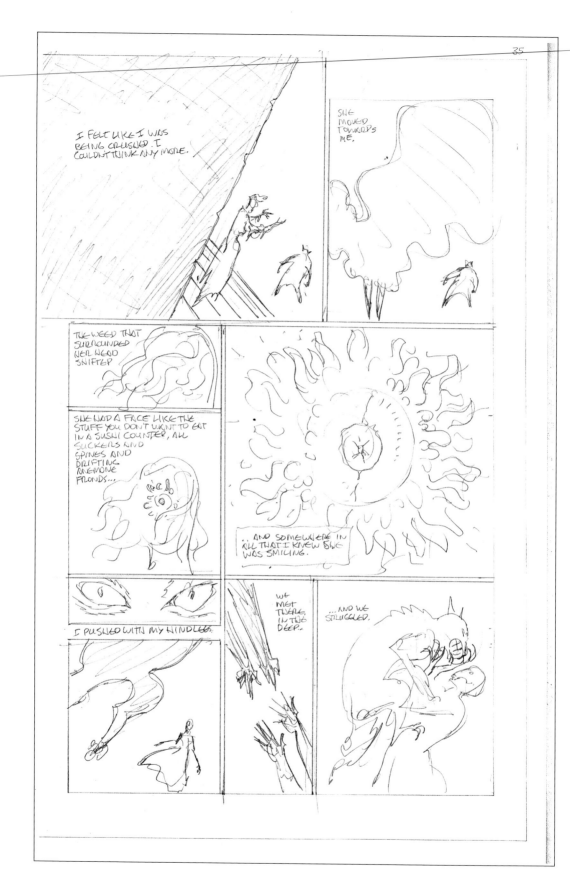

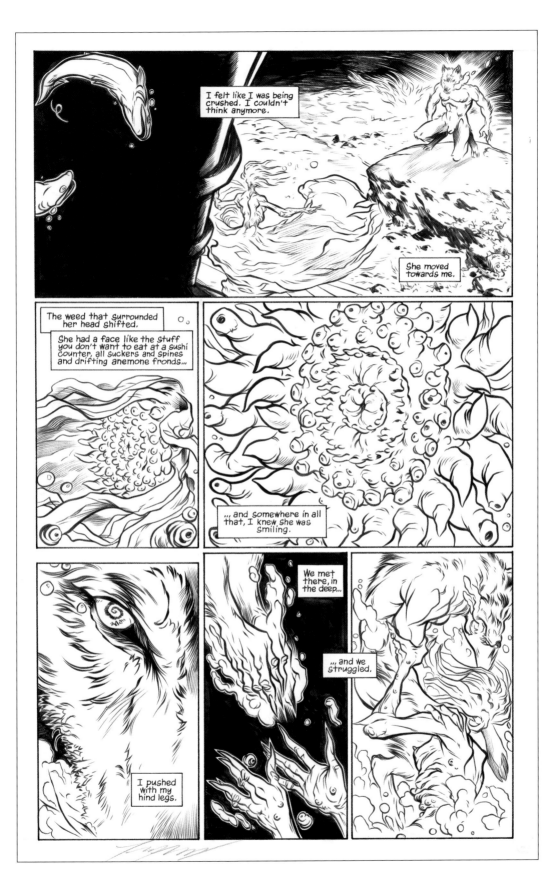

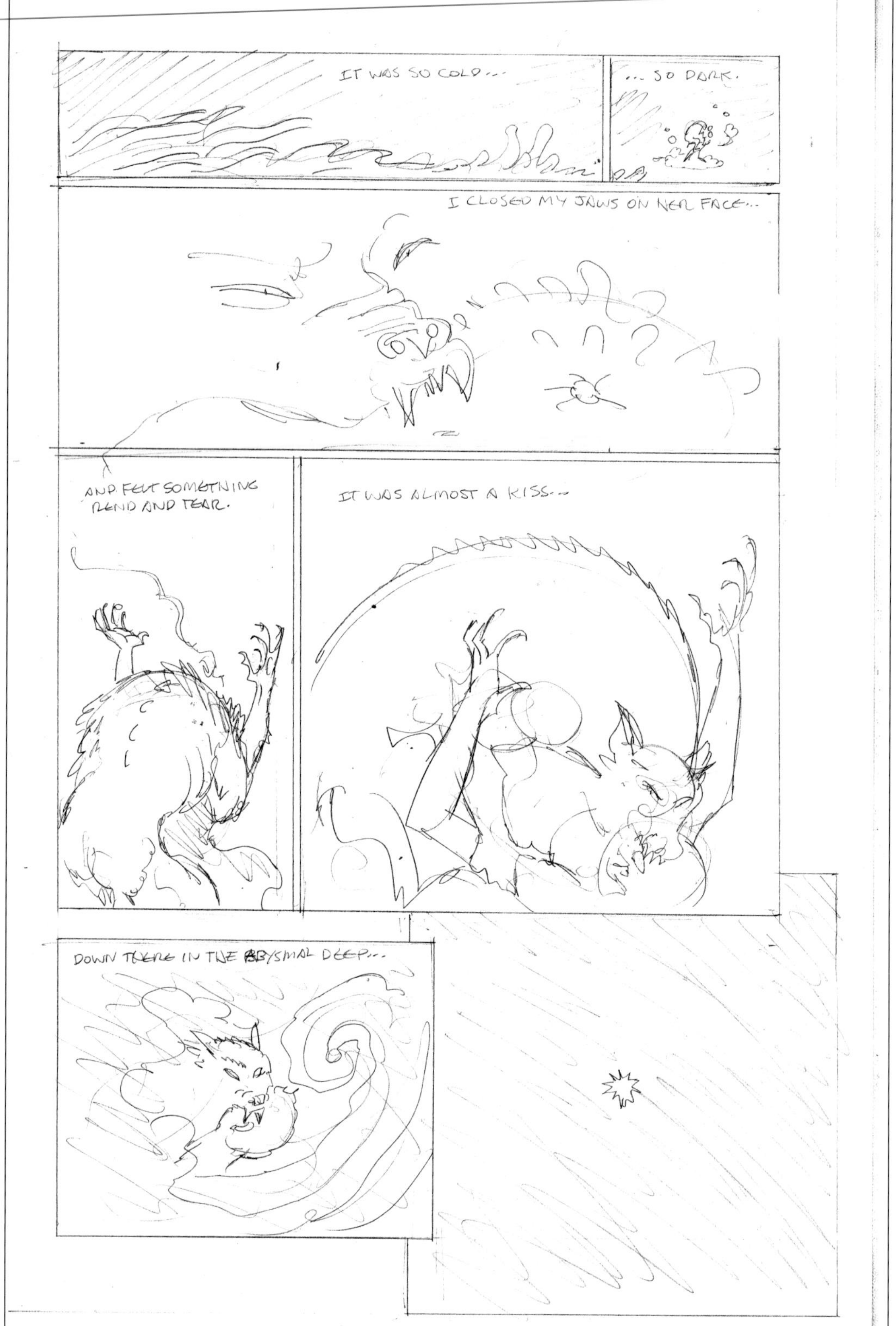
IT WAS SO COLD...
...SO DARK.
I CLOSED MY JAWS ON HER FACE...
AND FELT SOMETHING REND AND TEAR.
IT WAS ALMOST A KISS...
DOWN THERE IN THE ABYSMAL DEEP...

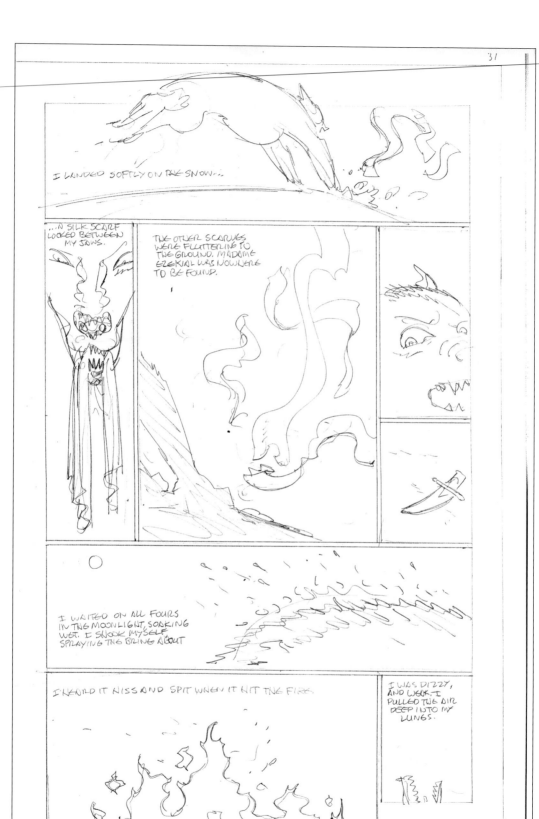

I LANDED SOFTLY ON THE SNOW...

...A SILK SCARF LOCKED BETWEEN MY JAWS.

THE OTHER SCARVES WERE FLUTTERING TO THE GROUND. MADAME EZEKIAL WAS NOWHERE TO BE FOUND.

I WAITED ON ALL FOURS IN THE MOONLIGHT, SOAKING WET. I SHOOK MYSELF SPRAYING THE BRINE ABOUT

I HEARD IT HISS AND SPIT WHEN IT HIT THE FIRE.

I WAS DIZZY, AND WEAK. I PULLED THE AIR DEEP INTO MY LUNGS.

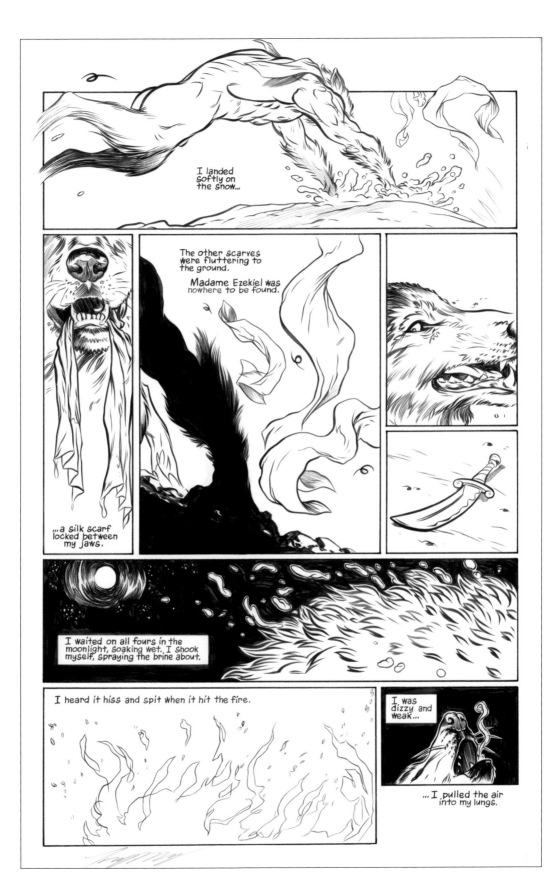

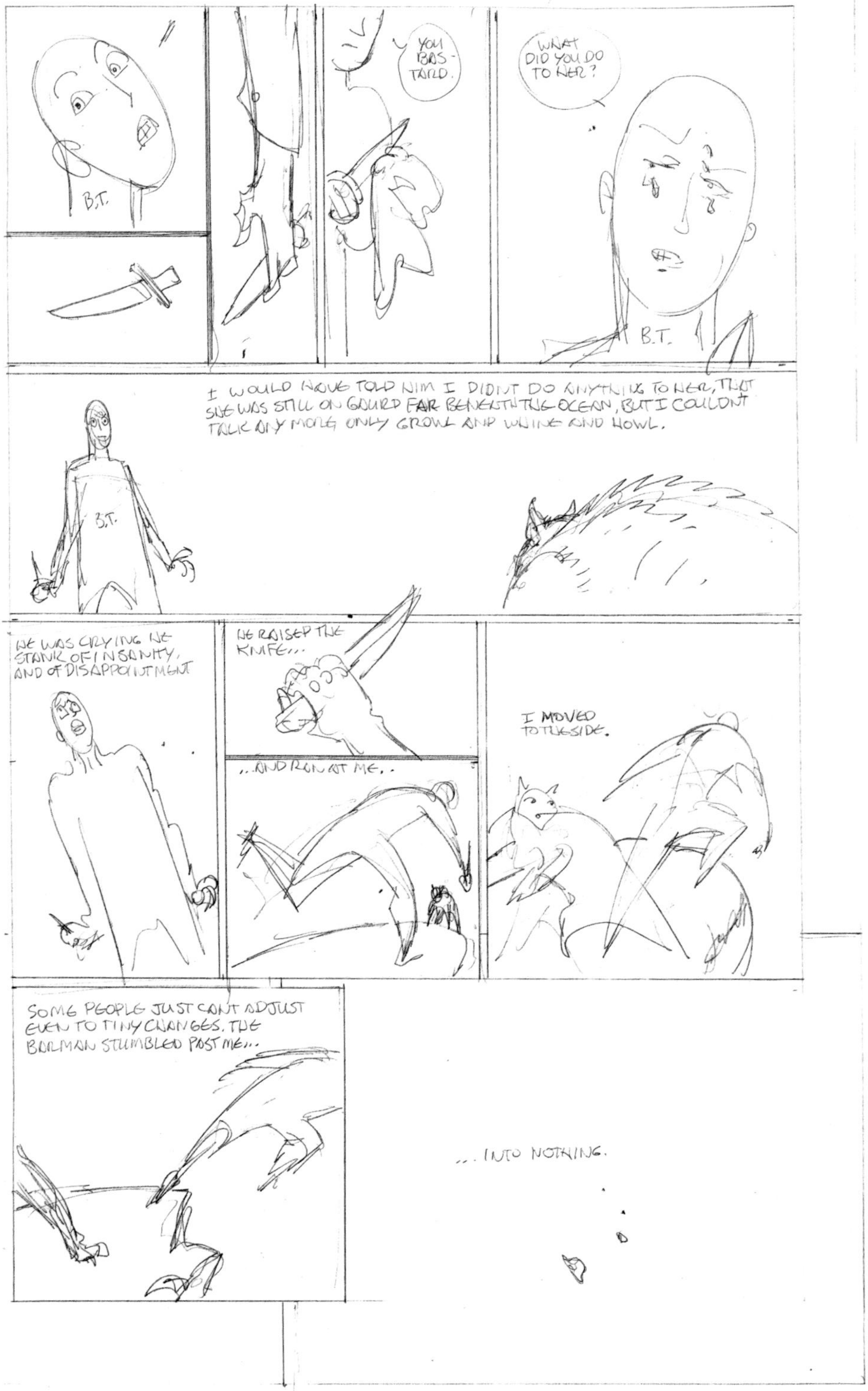
YOU BASTARD.
WHAT DID YOU DO TO HER?
I WOULD HAVE TOLD HIM I DIDNT DO ANYTHING TO HER, THAT SHE WAS STILL ON BOARD FAR BENEATH THE OCEAN, BUT I COULDNT TALK ANY MORE ONLY GROWL AND WHINE AND HOWL.
HE WAS CRYING HE STANK OF INSANITY, AND OF DISAPPOINTMENT
HE RAISED THE KNIFE...
...AND RAN AT ME..
I MOVED TO THE SIDE.
SOME PEOPLE JUST CANT ADJUST EVEN TO TINY CHANGES. THE BARMAN STUMBLED PAST ME...
...INTO NOTHING.

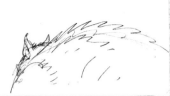

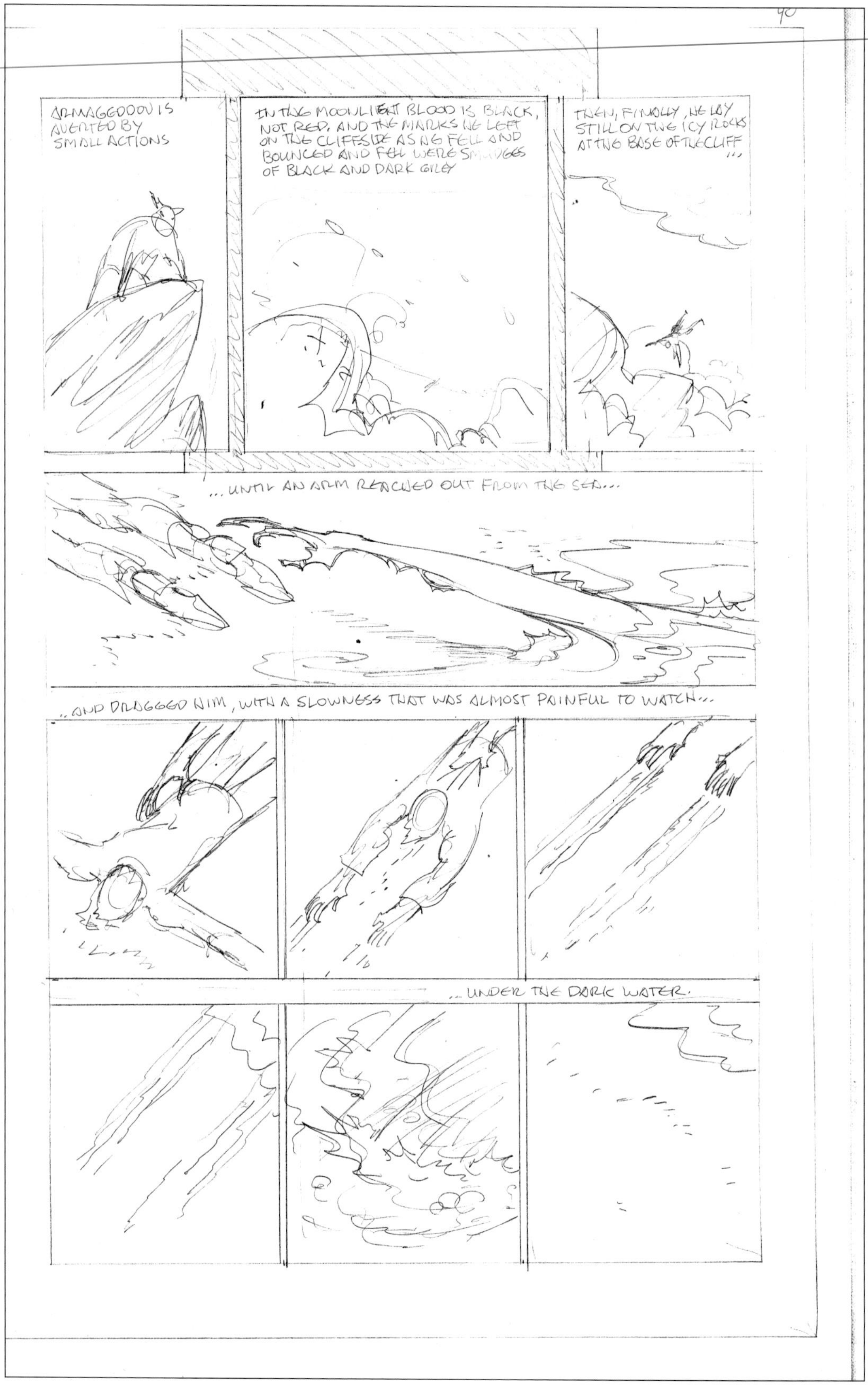
40
ARMAGEDDON IS AVERTED BY SMALL ACTIONS
IN THE MOONLIGHT BLOOD IS BLACK, NOT RED. AND THE MARKS HE LEFT ON THE CLIFFSIDE AS HE FELL AND BOUNCED AND FELL WERE SMUDGES OF BLACK AND DARK GREY
THEN, FINALLY, HE LAY STILL ON THE ICY ROCKS AT THE BASE OF THE CLIFF...
...UNTIL AN ARM REACHED OUT FROM THE SEA...
...AND DRAGGED HIM, WITH A SLOWNESS THAT WAS ALMOST PAINFUL TO WATCH...
...UNDER THE DARK WATER.

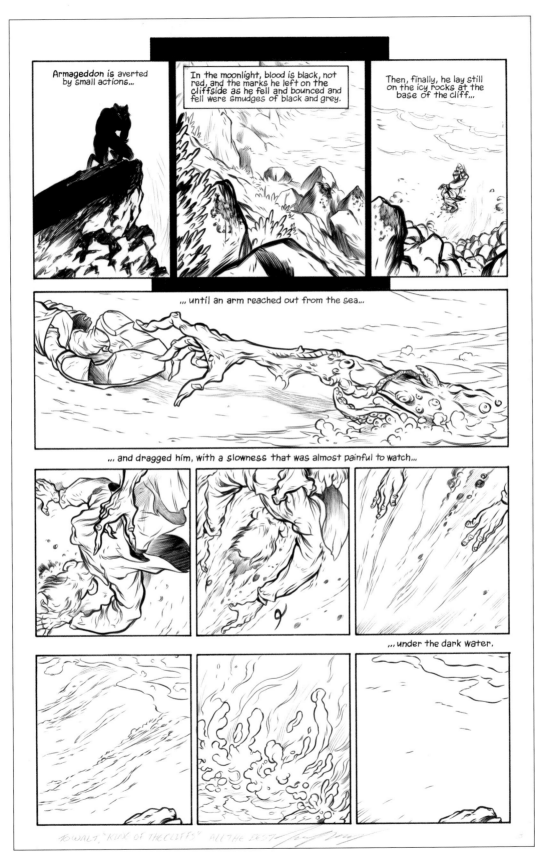

Armageddon is averted by small actions...

In the moonlight, blood is black, not red, and the marks he left on the cliffside as he fell and bounced and fell were smudges of black and grey.

Then, finally, he lay still on the icy rocks at the base of the cliff...

... until an arm reached out from the sea...

... and dragged him, with a slowness that was almost painful to watch...

... under the dark water.

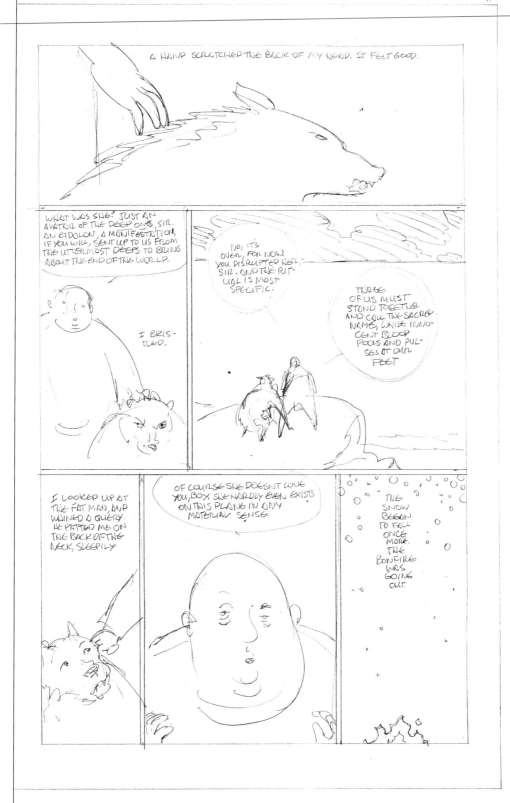

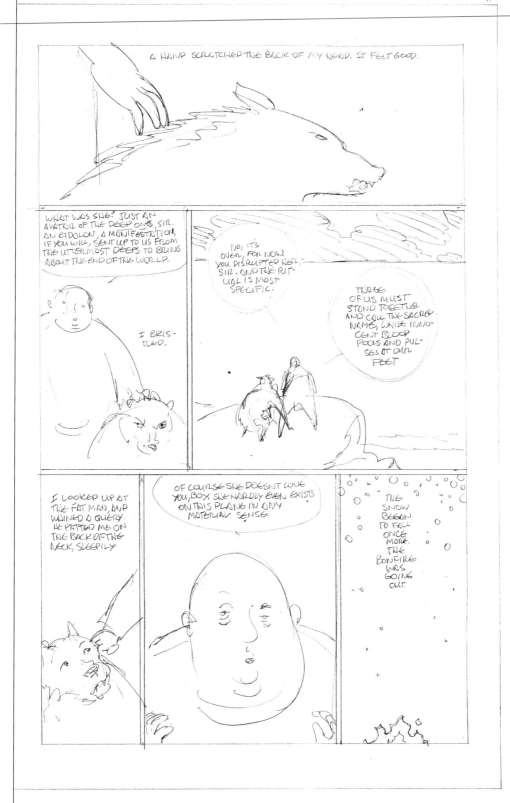

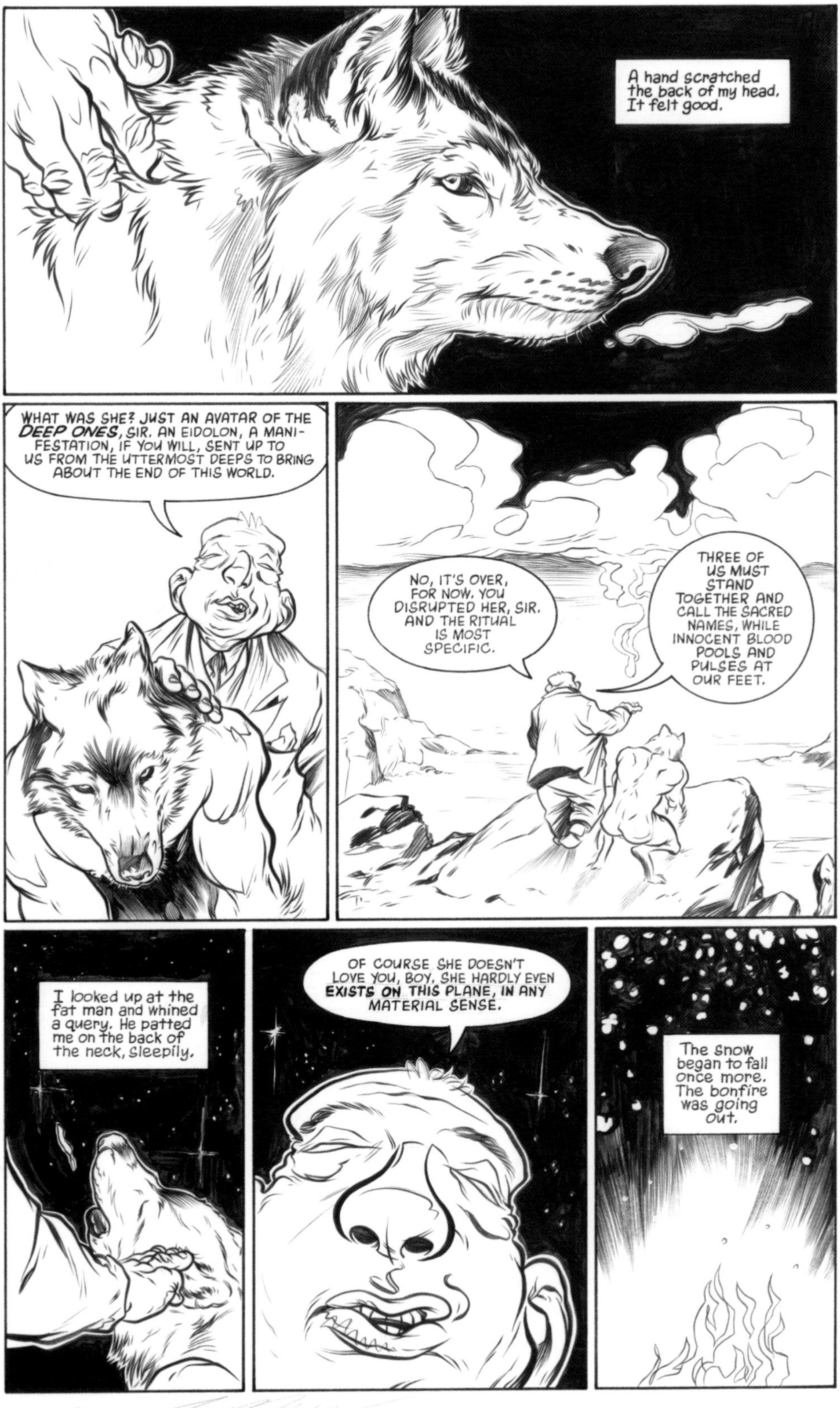
A hand scratched the back of my head. It felt good.
WHAT WAS SHE? JUST AN AVATAR OF THE DEEP ONES, SIR. AN EIDOLON, A MANIFESTATION, IF YOU WILL, SENT UP TO US FROM THE UTTERMOST DEEPS TO BRING ABOUT THE END OF THIS WORLD.
NO, IT'S OVER, FOR NOW. YOU DISRUPTED HER, SIR. AND THE RITUAL IS MOST SPECIFIC.
THREE OF US MUST STAND TOGETHER AND CALL THE SACRED NAMES, WHILE INNOCENT BLOOD POOLS AND PULSES AT OUR FEET.
I looked up at the fat man and whined a query. He patted me on the back of the neck, sleepily.
OF COURSE SHE DOESN'T LOVE YOU, BOY. SHE HARDLY EVEN EXISTS ON THIS PLANE, IN ANY MATERIAL SENSE.
The snow began to fall once more. The bonfire was going out.

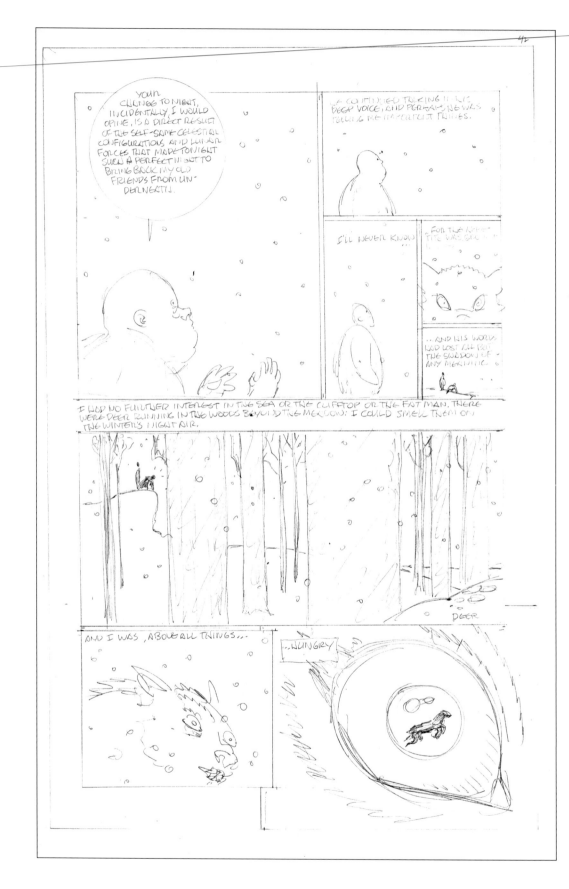

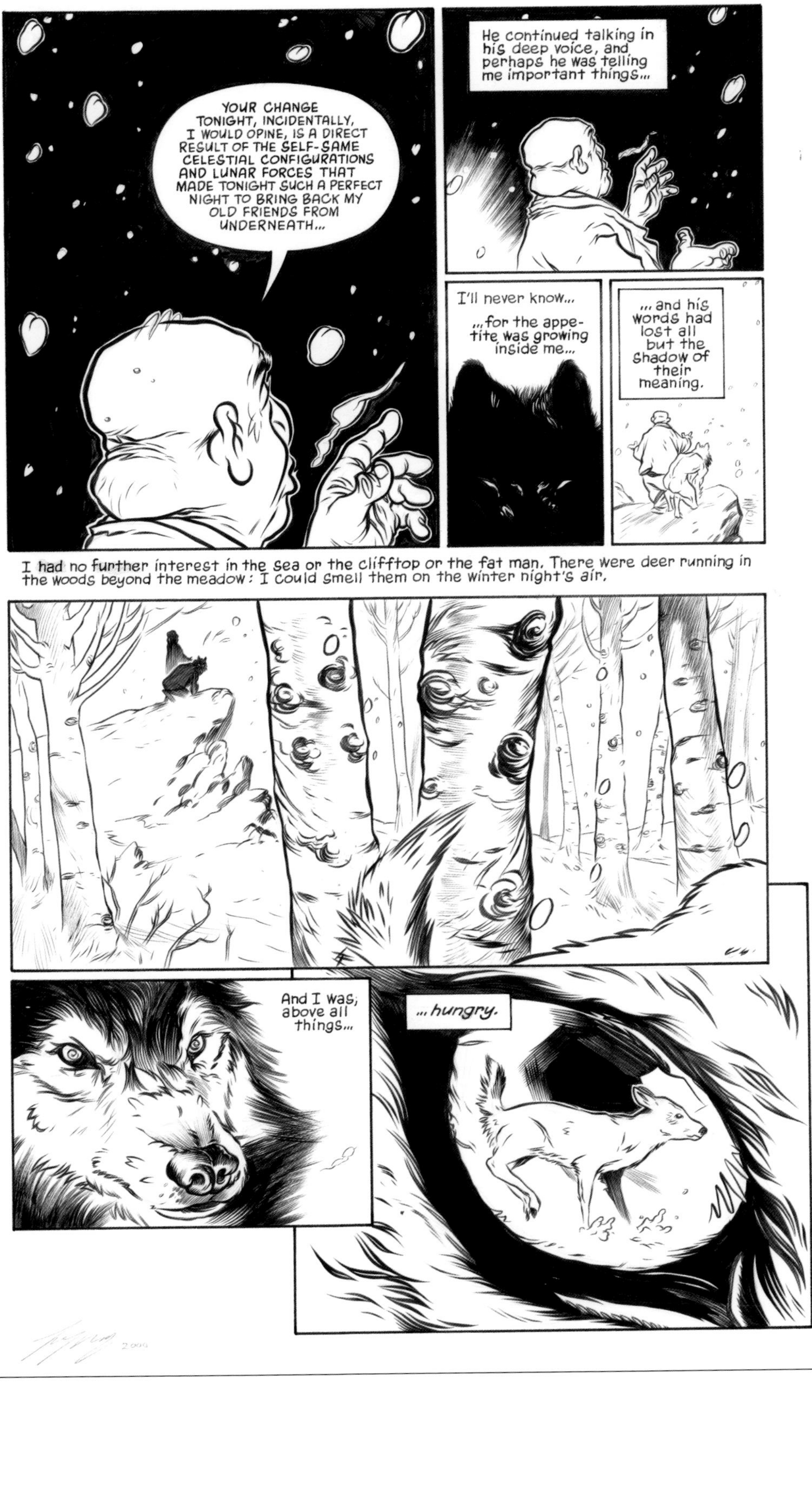
YOUR CHANGE TONIGHT, INCIDENTALLY, I WOULD OPINE, IS A DIRECT RESULT OF THE SELF-SAME CELESTIAL CONFIGURATIONS AND LUNAR FORCES THAT MADE TONIGHT SUCH A PERFECT NIGHT TO BRING BACK MY OLD FRIENDS FROM UNDERNEATH...
He continued talking in his deep voice, and perhaps he was telling me important things...
I'll never know...
...for the appetite was growing inside me...
...and his words had lost all but the shadow of their meaning.
I had no further interest in the sea or the clifftop or the fat man. There were deer running in the woods beyond the meadow: I could smell them on the winter night's air.
And I was, above all things...
...hungry.

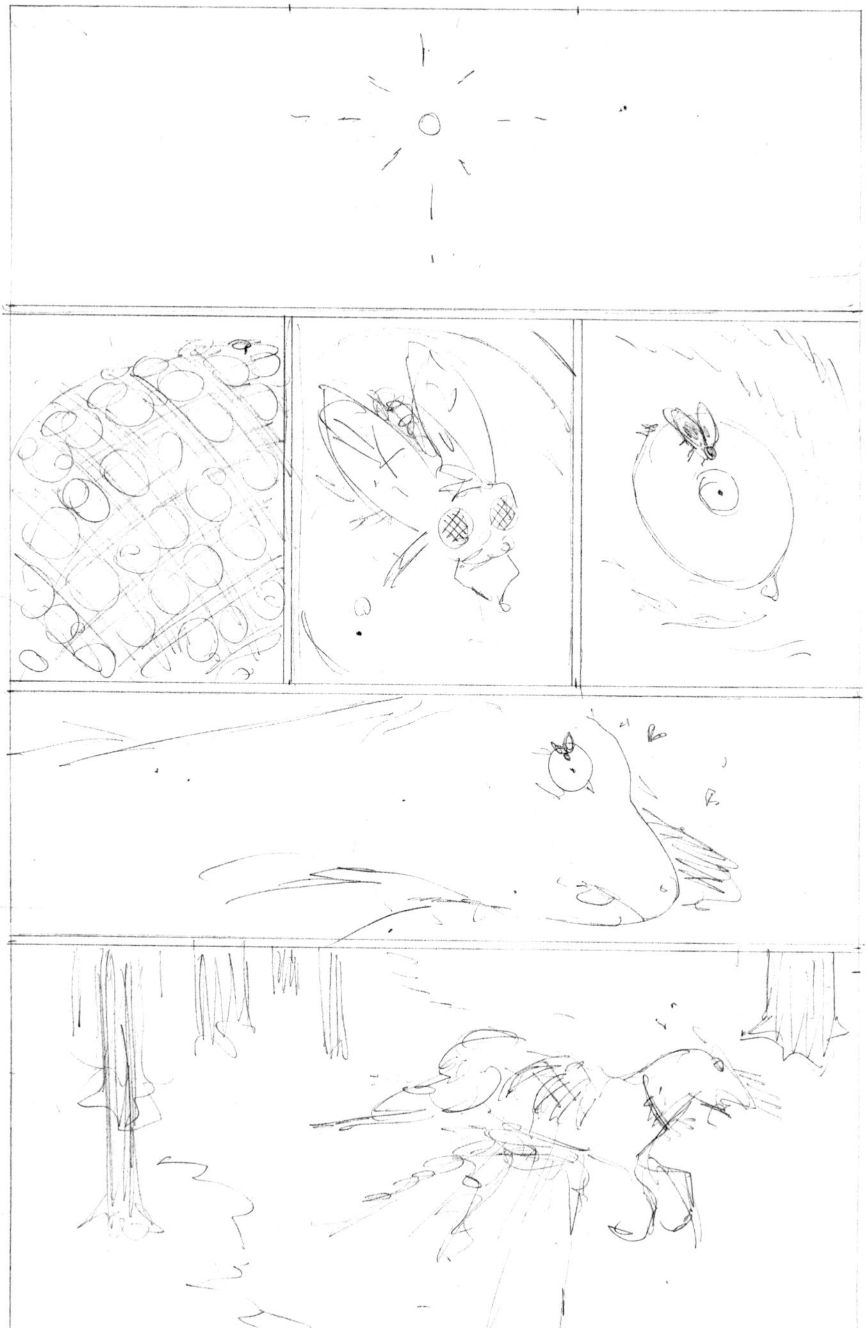

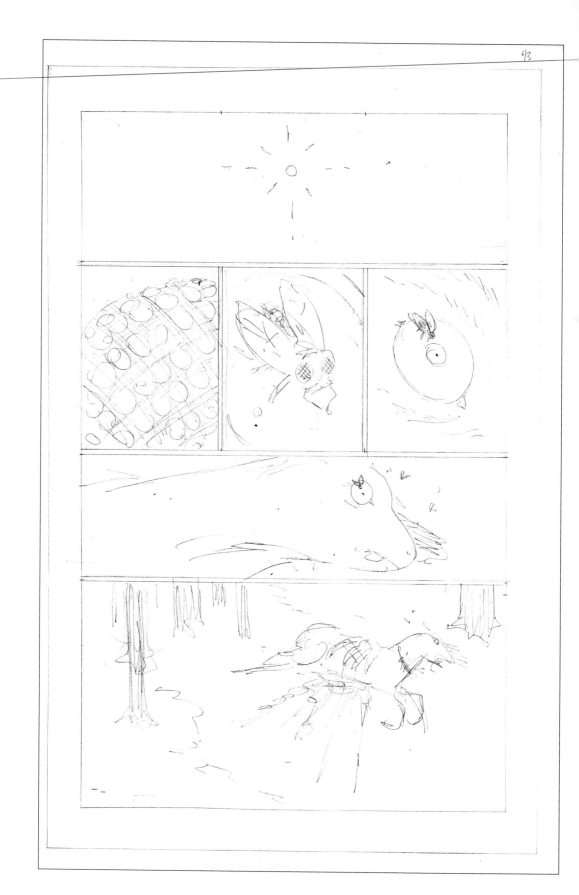

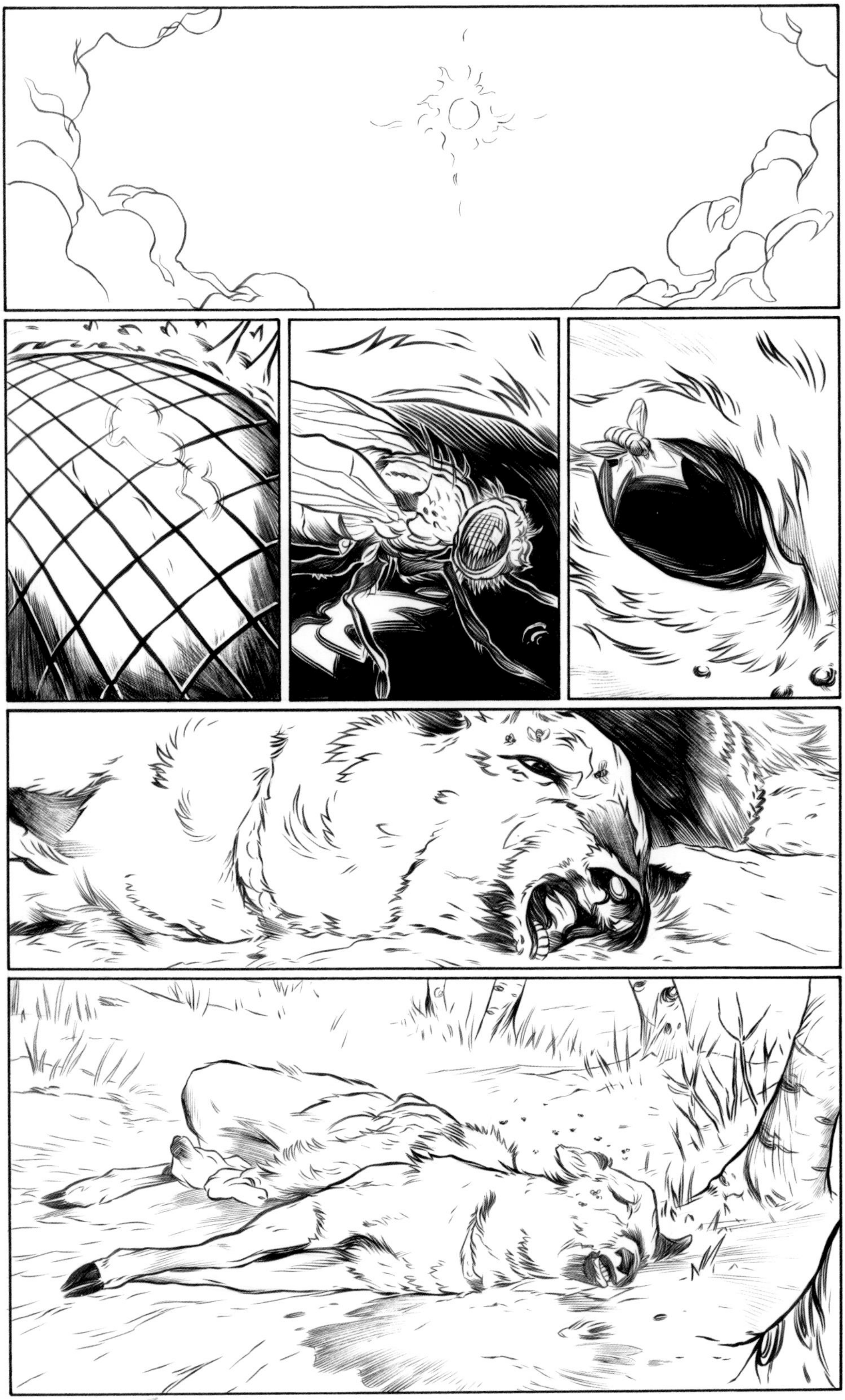

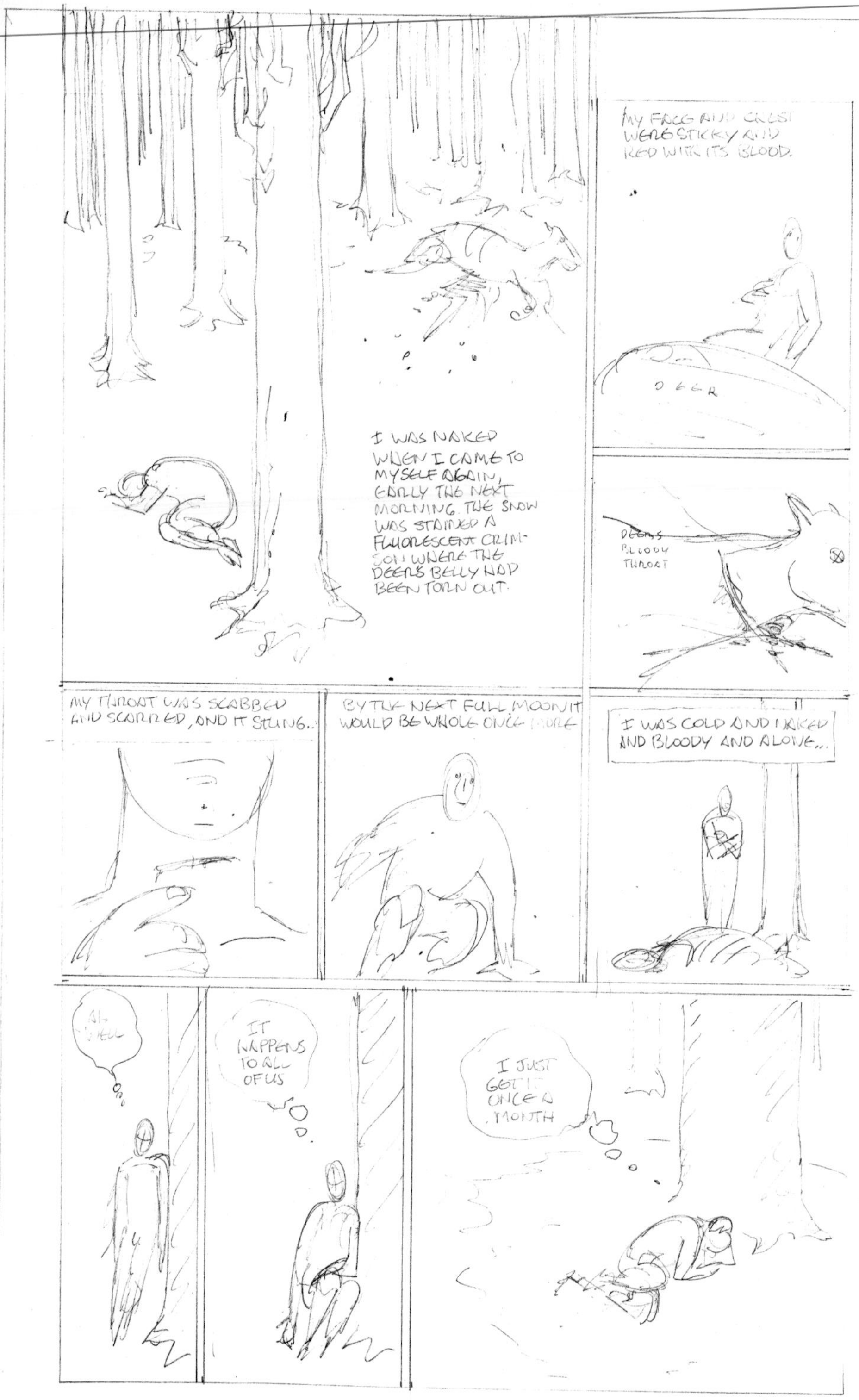
I WAS NAKED WHEN I CAME TO MYSELF AGAIN, EARLY THE NEXT MORNING. THE SNOW WAS STAINED A FLUORESCENT CRIMSON WHERE THE DEER'S BELLY HAD BEEN TORN OUT.
MY FACE AND CHEST WERE STICKY AND RED WITH ITS BLOOD.
DEER
DEER'S BLOODY THROAT
MY THROAT WAS SCABBED AND SCARRED, AND IT STUNG..
BY THE NEXT FULL MOON IT WOULD BE WHOLE ONCE MORE
I WAS COLD AND NAKED AND BLOODY AND ALONE...
AH WELL
IT HAPPENS TO ALL OF US
I JUST GET IT ONCE A MONTH

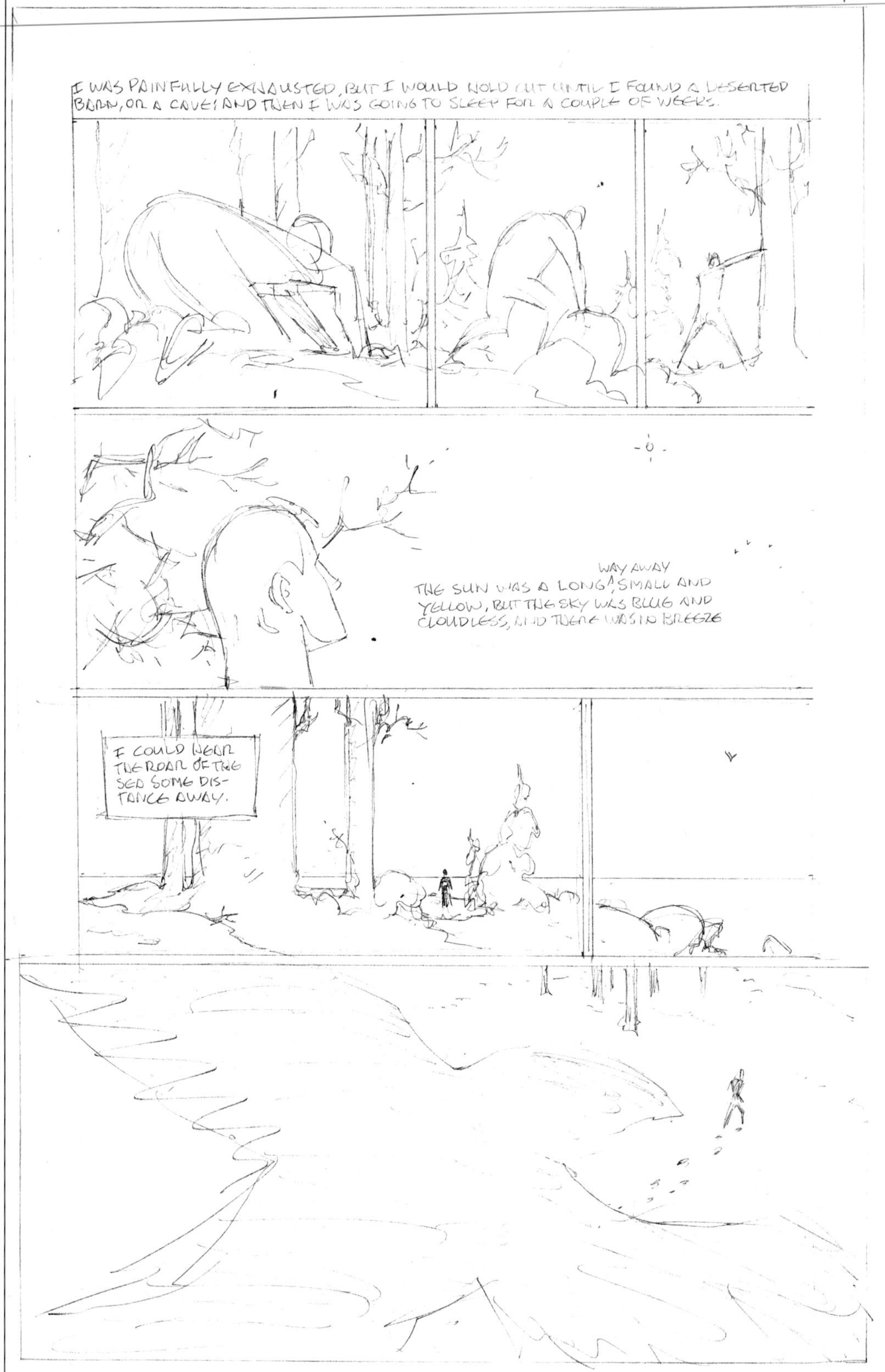
I WAS PAINFULLY EXHAUSTED, BUT I WOULD HOLD OUT UNTIL I FOUND A DESERTED BARN, OR A CAVE; AND THEN I WAS GOING TO SLEEP FOR A COUPLE OF WEEKS.
THE SUN WAS A LONG WAY AWAY, SMALL AND YELLOW, BUT THE SKY WAS BLUE AND CLOUDLESS, AND THERE WAS NO BREEZE
I COULD HEAR THE ROAR OF THE SEA SOME DISTANCE AWAY.

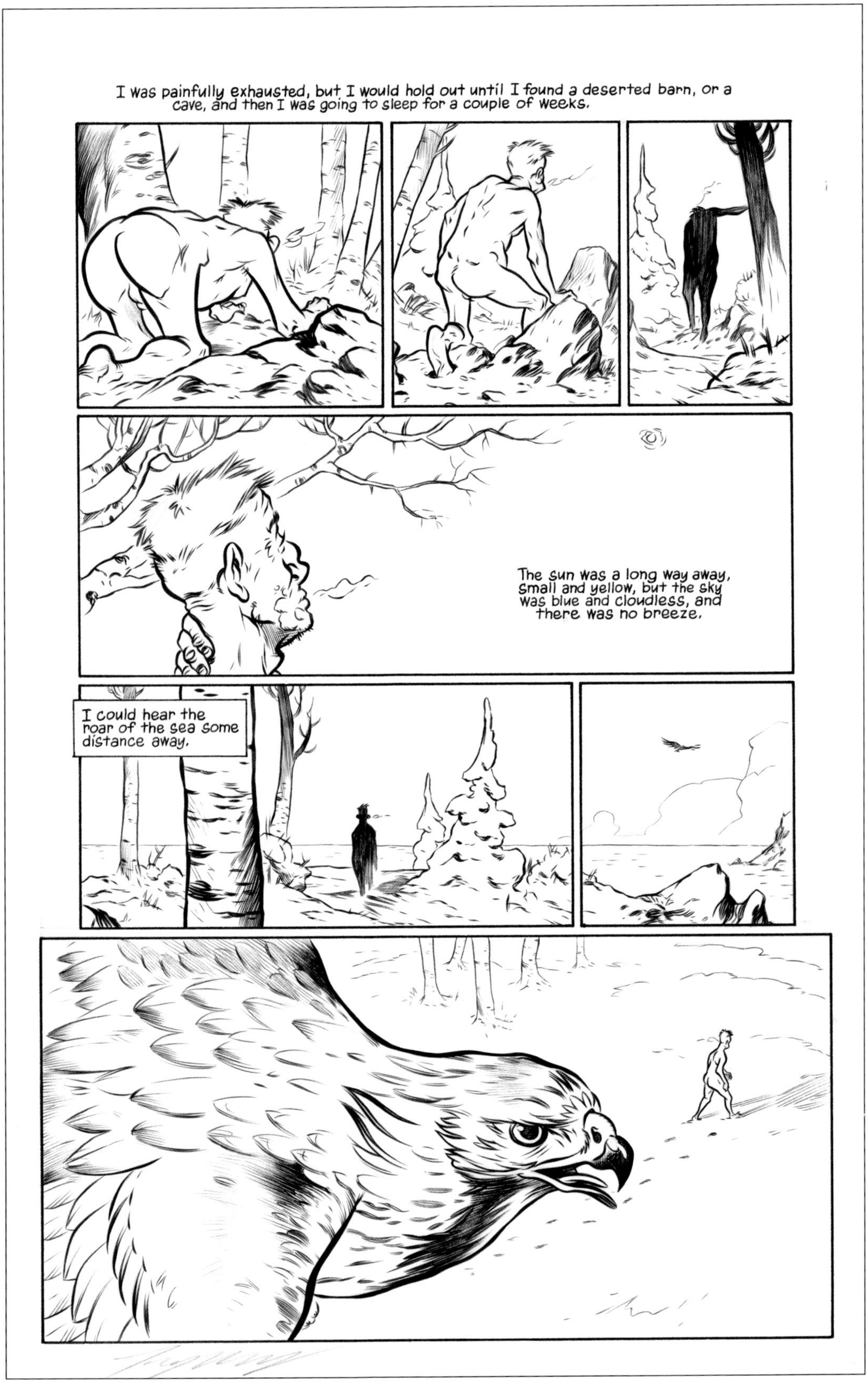
I was painfully exhausted, but I would hold out until I found a deserted barn, or a cave, and then I was going to sleep for a couple of weeks.
The sun was a long way away, small and yellow, but the sky was blue and cloudless, and there was no breeze.
I could hear the roar of the sea some distance away.

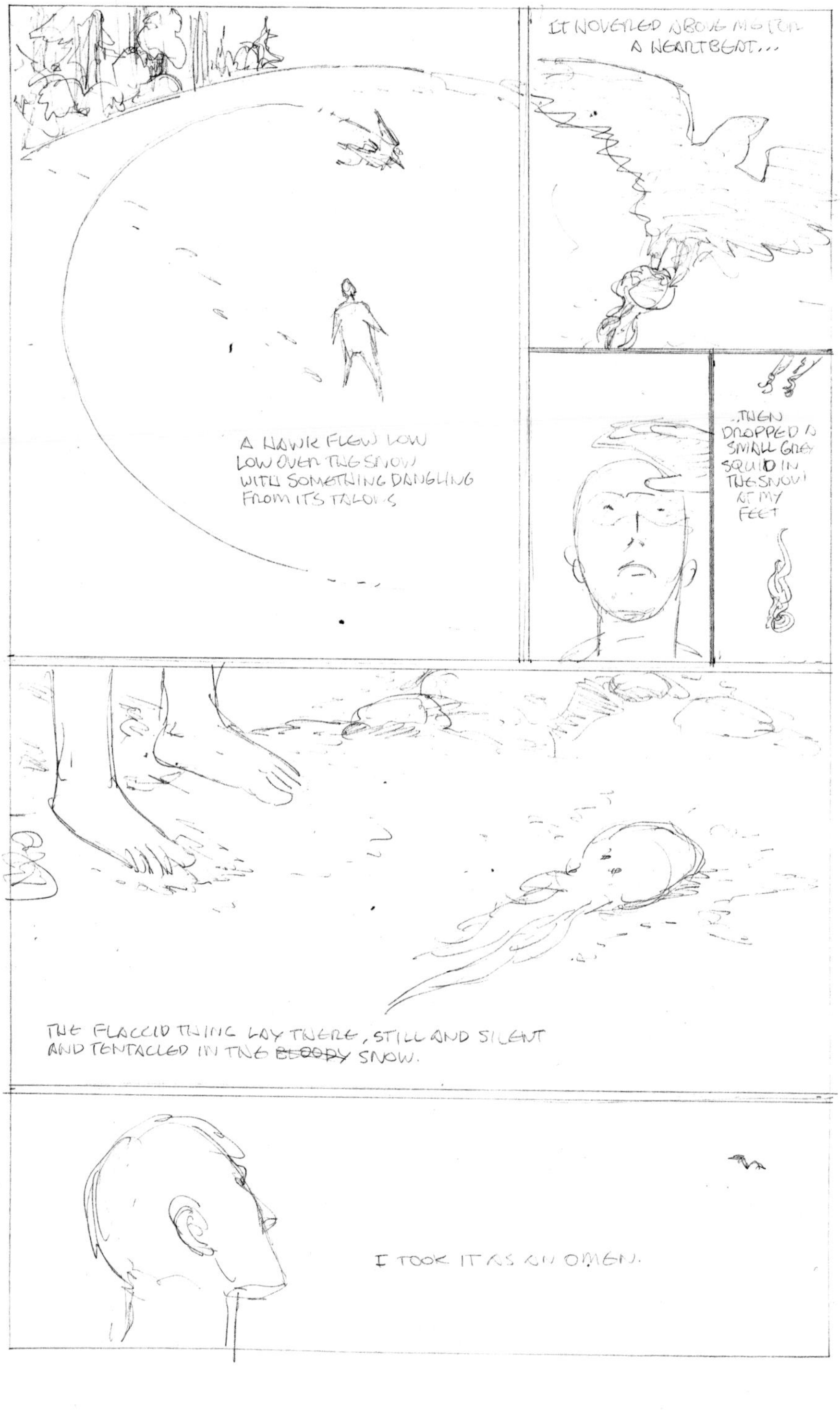
A HAWK FLEW LOW
LOW OVER THE SNOW
WITH SOMETHING DANGLING
FROM ITS TALONS
IT HOVERED ABOVE ME FOR
A HEARTBEAT...
..THEN
DROPPED A
SMALL GREY
SQUID IN
THE SNOW
AT MY
FEET
THE FLACCID THING LAY THERE, STILL AND SILENT
AND TENTACLED IN THE ~~BLOODY~~ SNOW.
I TOOK IT AS AN OMEN.

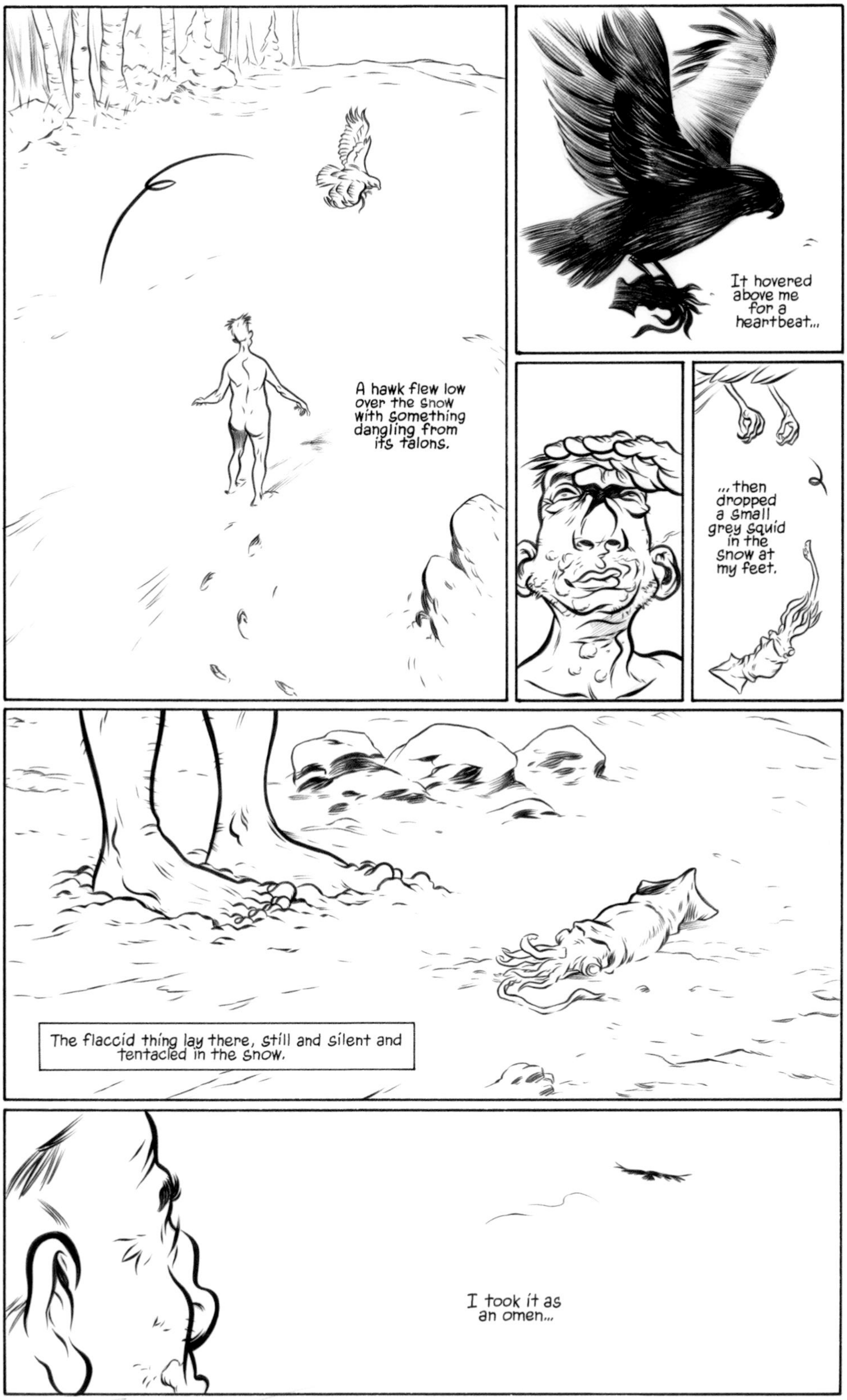
A hawk flew low over the snow with something dangling from its talons.
It hovered above me for a heartbeat...
...then dropped a small grey squid in the snow at my feet.
The flaccid thing lay there, still and silent and tentacled in the snow.
I took it as an omen...

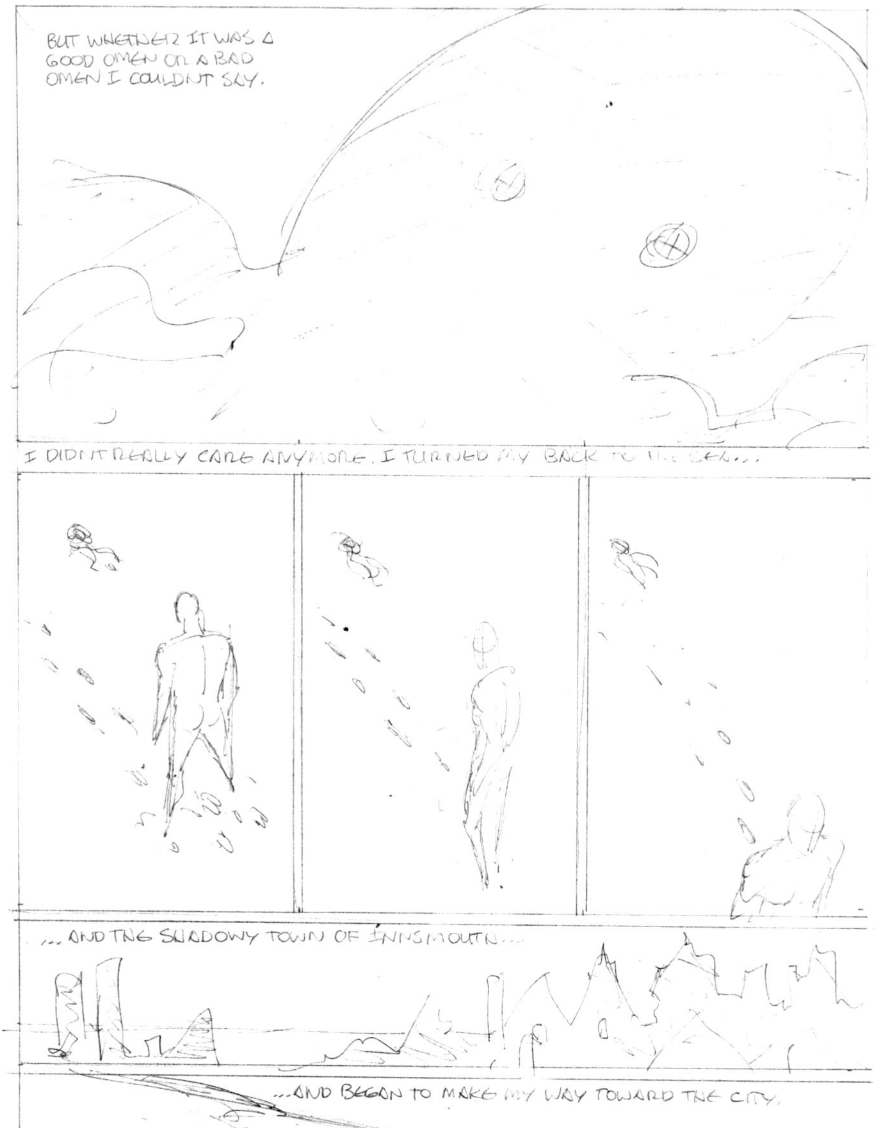
BUT WHETHER IT WAS A GOOD OMEN OR A BAD OMEN I COULDNT SAY.
I DIDNT REALLY CARE ANYMORE. I TURNED MY BACK TO THE SEA...
...AND THE SHADOWY TOWN OF INNSMOUTH...
...AND BEGAN TO MAKE MY WAY TOWARD THE CITY.

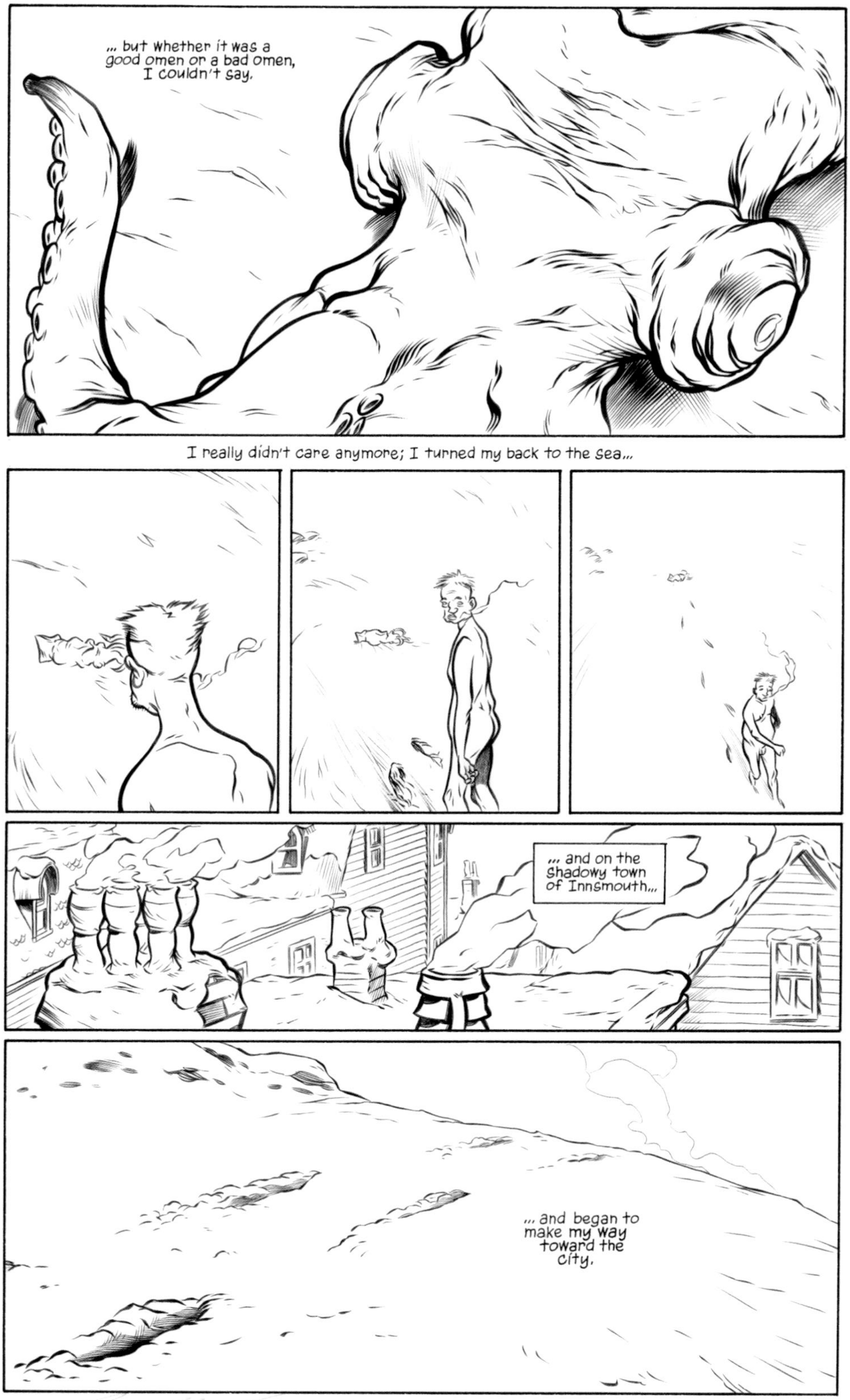
... but whether it was a good omen or a bad omen, I couldn't say.
I really didn't care anymore; I turned my back to the sea...
... and on the shadowy town of Innsmouth...
... and began to make my way toward the city.

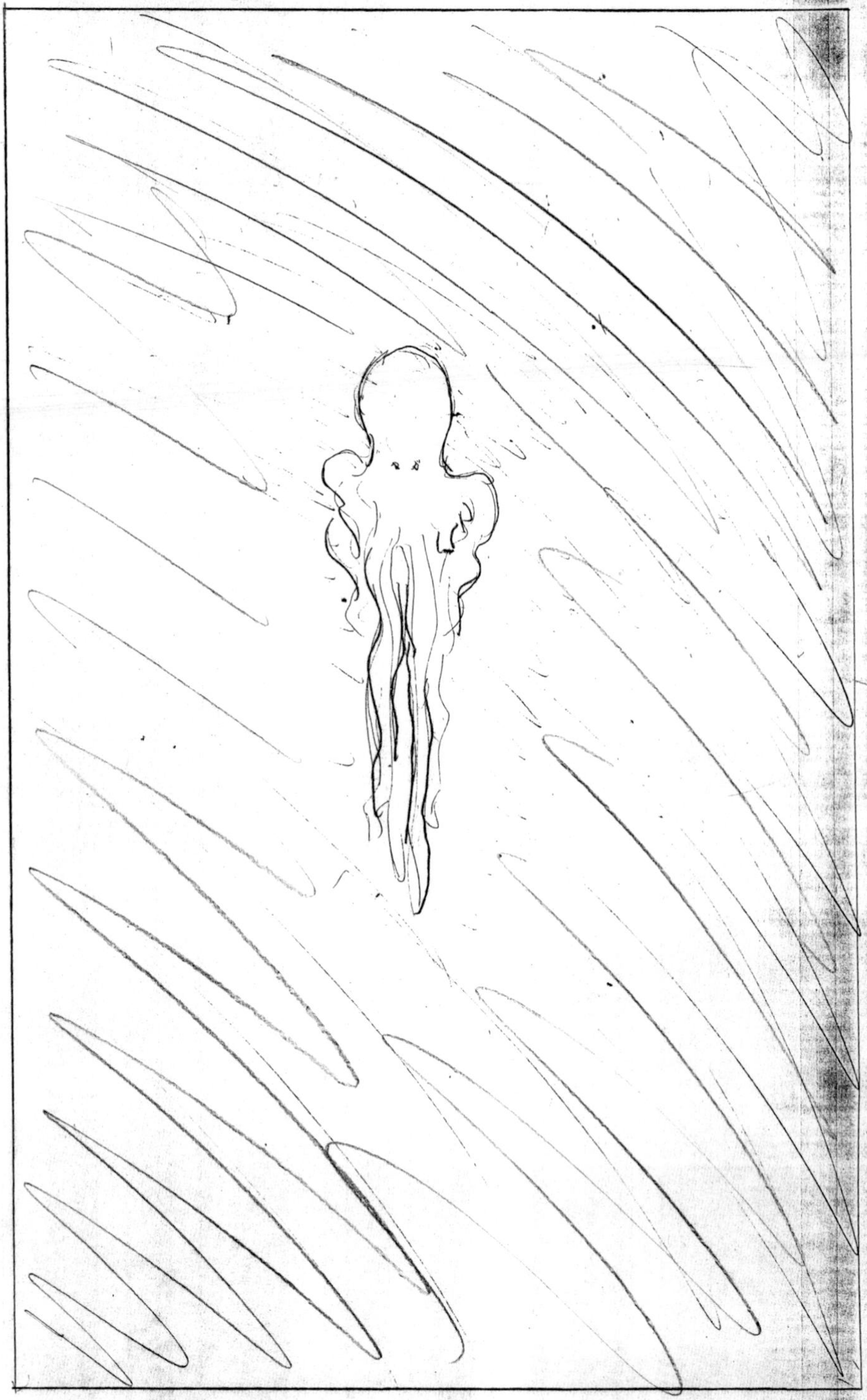

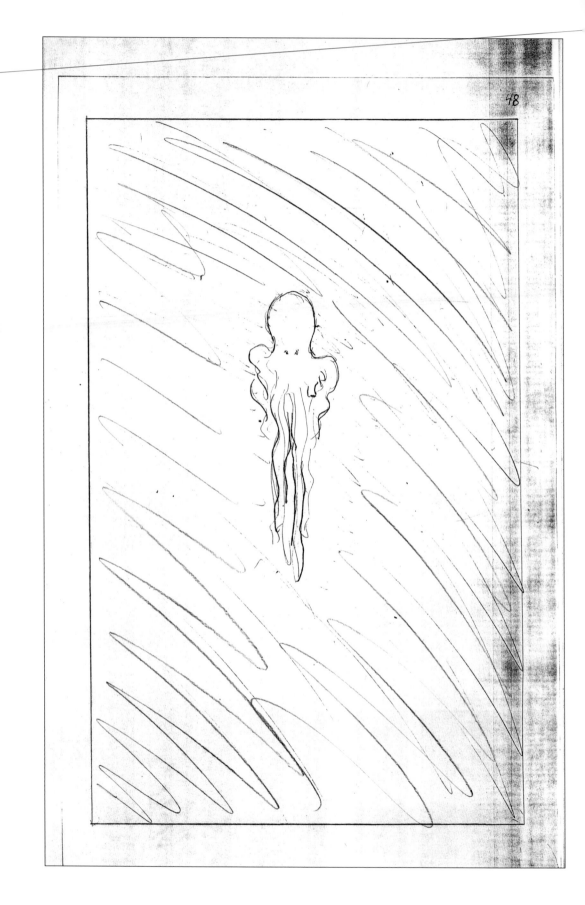

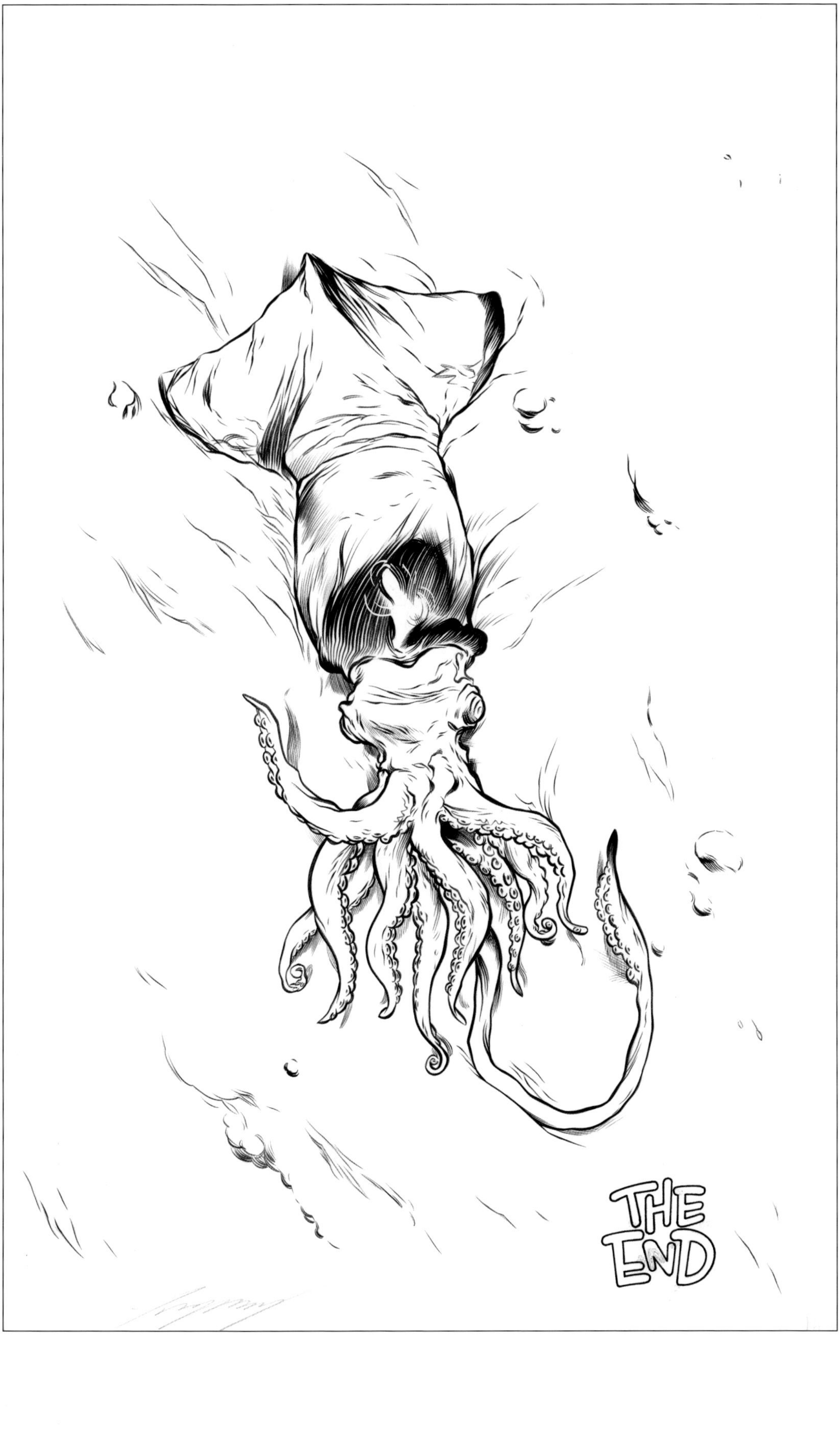
THE END

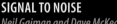